PEGGY & BALMER

TWO JOURNALISTS AT
THE EDGE OF HISTORY

Peggy & Balmer

TOM RADFORD

With a Foreword by William Thorsell

NeWest Press

NeWest Press wishes to acknowledge that the land on which we operate is Treaty 6 territory and Métis Nation of Alberta Region 4, a traditional meeting ground and home for many Indigenous Peoples, including Cree, Saulteaux, Niitsitapi (Blackfoot), Métis, Dene, and Nakota Sioux, since time immemorial.

NeWest Press prohibits the use of *Peggy & Balmer* in connection with the development of any software program, including, without limitation, training a machine learning or generative artificial intelligence (AI) system.

Library and Archives Canada Cataloguing in Publication
Title: Peggy & Balmer : two journalists at the edge of history / Tom Radford ; with a foreword by William Thorsell.
Other titles: Peggy and Balmer
Names: Radford, Tom, 1946– author. | Thorsell, William, writer of foreword.
Description: Includes bibliographical references.
Identifiers: Canadiana (print) 20240355792 | Canadiana (ebook) 20240355822 |
ISBN 9781774391068 (softcover) | ISBN 9781774391075 (EPUB)
Subjects: LCSH: Watt, Arthur Balmer. | LCSH: Watt, Gertrude Balmer. | LCSH: Journalists—Alberta—Biography. | LCSH: Women journalists—Alberta—Biography. | LCSH: Journalism—Alberta—History—20th century. | CSH: Alberta—History—1905–1945. | LCGFT: Biographies.
Classification: LCC PN4912 .R33 2024 | DDC 070.92/27123—dc23

Editor for the Press: Leslie Vermeer
Cover and interior design: Natalie Olsen, Kisscut Design
Cover painting: Fort Edmonton 1856 by Paul Kane © ARTGEN / Alamy Stock Photo

NeWest Press acknowledges the support of the Canada Council for the Arts, the Government of Alberta through the Ministry of Arts, Culture and Status of Women, and the Edmonton Arts Council for support of our publishing program. We acknowledge the financial support of the Government of Canada through the Canada Book Fund for our publishing activities.

NeWest Press
NeWest Press
#201, 8540-109 Street
Edmonton, Alberta T6G 1E6
www.newestpress.com

No bison were harmed in the making of this book.
Printed and bound in Canada.

To Peggy, Becky, Eva, Sheila, Emma, and Lucia —
five generations of Watt women who have
been the inspiration for this book.

CONTENTS

Book Two

1912–1935

The Precision of Place

Book Three

1936–1964

The Darkling Plain

ACKNOWLEDGEMENTS

Kirsten Christopherson, Steve Glassman, Myrna Kostash, Francois Paulette, Larry Pratt, Sheila Pratt, Eva Radford, Peter Raymont, Glenn Rollans, Jerome Slavik, Fred Stenson, William Thorsell, Leslie Vermeer, Jan Walter, Rudy Wiebe

FOREWORD

Alberta is a puzzle, born in hope and anger, blessed with valuable assets, and still an odd man out in Canada for its insistence on victimhood in even the best of circumstances.

Created with Saskatchewan in 1905, by division of the North-West Territory, Alberta quickly showed its distinct personality, restless on the mountain prairies and shaded in the country as a whole. Within six years of Alberta's birth, a Liberal member of the provincial legislature, Alwyn Bramley-Moore, published *Canada and Her Colonies; Or Home Rule for Alberta*, a furious denunciation of the constitution's discrimination against Alberta in the ownership of natural resources — Canada's Original Sin in the birth of this province. Soon Alberta was rife with hostile memes about greedy Eastern banks, rakish continental railways, punishing tariffs, and wormy national governments. Hard times in subsequent decades cemented these attitudes to the point that good times in later ones could not abate them.

Late to Confederation, judging itself born in injustice and perpetually overridden by exploitive majorities at distance, Alberta would carry its sense of persecution like a birthmark on its face, visible in the mirror daily — all this while harbouring a deeply romantic attachment to its fabulous landscapes and a robust sense of individuality forged of geographic isolation and endurance against the elements. Alberta's obsessions and myths made for a compelling story through the twentieth century, a story worthy of a serious aficionado of history and teller of tales.

Tom Radford finds the perfect vector for this story in Balmer and Peggy Watt, his grandparents, journalists both, who came from Ontario to Alberta to witness its proclamation by Sir Wilfrid Laurier on September 1, 1905, and stayed until their deaths more than fifty years later. Peggy had an eye for social conditions and physical landscapes that shaped a crusading journalism, rich in colour and detail. Balmer matched this talent with a political sensibility capturing Alberta's vigorous partisan dynamics to the point of winning a Pulitzer Citation at the *Edmonton Journal* for his defence of press freedom against fascistic attacks in the 1930s. The filaments of their lives, entwined with others influential in Alberta's development, provide a personal context for the social story that is Alberta's alone. And Tom Radford continues the tradition in his own life as filmmaker and author, woven into these historical events.

How do we seek to understand this precocious Alberta, the long-wealthiest in Canada in 2024, so enraged about its most recent experience with climate concerns and declines in global petroleum price that it flirts again with separation from Canada? How do we understand the impulse in Alberta to build a "firewall" against Canada in recent decades, despite Alberta's economic preeminence? Despite the sometimes-extravagant efforts of Brian Mulroney between 1984 and 1993 to placate Alberta's sense of grievance? Despite the dominance of a Calgary MP as prime minister of Canada for two recent terms? Can it be reduced to the arithmetic of dollars, the number of seats in Parliament, the hours-delayed disability of Mountain Time?

There is more than the facts of history in a story which opens with Alberta's first separatist, Alwyn Bramley-Moore, and includes

William Aberhart, Marshall McLuhan, Peter Lougheed, and, recently, Jason Kenney and Danielle Smith. There is a collective unconscious at work in the province, a psychological imperative rooted in circumstances not easily divined.

This is where an apparently episodic recounting of perceptions, aspirations, and reversals — aside from events — offers insight into the mysteries and eccentricities of Alberta.

And this is where, in bringing his own passionate relationship to Alberta to the present, Tom Radford weaves ineluctably and unintentionally something of an "analysis" of Alberta's condition — not didactic, but rather intuitive and more telling. Much of this history has the flavour of a novel in its unbundling of character, the scent of fiction providing perhaps the only key to the real mystery of the place. The accumulation of stories, from trains groaning through winter nights chock with immigrants, to schoolhouse meetings organizing women and farmers against the fates, to chimerical throws of the dice to change those fates through unconventional politics, fervent religion, and recurrent rejection reveal, by dollops, a deeper personality. It is an essentially narcissistic personality, and thus insatiable in its insecurity.

This kind of storytelling, as history, is rare in its eclecticism and frank association with a fundamental theme. The stories themselves fascinate and transport. And like personal anecdotes told over time to a friend, unveil something much more about the teller, something that speaks to roots without artifice or design. Accounts that summon up Alberta's angels and demons in the life and times of Peggy and Balmer Watt. Bred in the bone and shape of the spirit.

William Thorsell
Toronto, February 2024

PROLOGUE

A Far Country

And then suddenly, all the old anchors of
experience were lifted or broken and the train
bore me ever westward and northward, on and
on to a point whither the insatiable adventure-
lust of man had pushed the frontier of civilization.
And there the train stopped and I got out. There
was nothing else to do. It was the end of the line.

EDMUND KEMPER BROADUS

First train arrives
in Edmonton, 1902

Peggy and Balmer presents a love affair with the Alberta frontier at the turn of the twentieth century, a passion for place that consumed the lives of two extraordinary journalists, Gertrude Hogg and Arthur Balmer Watt. An irreverent investigative reporter and an ambitious publisher, they established a weekly newspaper in Edmonton in the winter of 1905, the *Saturday News*. Peggy, as she became known, became the city's first domestic correspondent, catholic in her tastes and outrageous in her opinions. Her column, "The Mirror," spared no one, man or beast, reflecting the helter-skelter community in which she found herself. Her acid portrayal of the city's leading citizens soon made the paper a precarious business proposition. Within weeks of its first issue, Balmer found himself smoothing the ruffled feathers of advertisers and readers alike. It was a sign of things to come — a voice of reason doing its best to limit the damage his wife had so willfully inflicted. Like the paper, the marriage would fall on hard times as the Alberta saga unfolded. Yet the greater canvas of Canada, to their youthful eyes the beautiful, impossible country they had crossed on the journey west, would never fail to bring them back together.

From the beginning their journalism posed a serious question: what was to become of the frontier, the "next year country" that carried the hopes of so many? With Big Oil on the march, settlers were displacing First Nations, and the delusion of sovereignty was transforming politics. The two journalists could never have imagined how the stories they unearthed foreshadowed the century that lay ahead. The rise of fascism, the corporate state, disinformation, the death of the independent newspaper — each in turn would threaten the democracy that was struggling to take root on the Prairies. Yet Peggy and Balmer continued to defend the idea of a Last Best West, the vision of the future that had changed their lives. In the years ahead, their crusade to protect the freedom of the press would lead to the first Pulitzer Prize awarded outside the United States.

As their train wound its way across a boundless landscape, the young couple expressed profound disillusionment with the world they were leaving behind. In Alberta they could re-imagine Canada — from a hidebound colonial society to a country founded on dreams. Surely there was room for an independent voice in the nation's affairs, a new kind of newspaper beyond the control of the stick-in-the-mud Ontario establishment.

They were the first to admit the decision to found "A Journal of Arts and Criticism" in Edmonton was a long shot. In a community of fewer than ten thousand people it would be difficult to sell enough papers to survive. Friends and family who helped get the paper off the ground worried from the start that their investment might be doomed. Yet the stubborn young woman whose eyes travelled across the snow-covered plains was bound and determined to make a go of it. "The far country," as locals called it, had already won a place in her heart.

Peggy and Balmer were my grandparents. When they died in the 1960s, it was that geography of the mind, the belief in a level playing field in Alberta, that they passed on to future generations of the family. My own career as a filmmaker, which began ten years after their deaths, would carry on that legacy as I made documentaries that explored what had become of the region they loved. The story of a "lost Alberta" would run through those films: the province's radical beginnings as recorded in the cameras of Ernest Brown and Gladys Reeves; Irene Parlby's vision of Alberta's first populist government, the United Farmers; the fight against the privatization of public health care with Bill Phipps; the environmental impact of the oil sands with David Schindler. In the tradition of Peggy and Balmer, independent journalism speaking truth to power.

On September 1, 1905, on the hardscrabble shore of the North Saskatchewan River, Wilfrid Laurier declared Alberta the country's eighth province. The name was chosen to honour the fourth daughter of Queen Victoria, Princess Louise Caroline Alberta, a young woman who had no connection to either the remote region or the people who lived there. The name had been chosen by distant governments who regarded the North-West Territories, a blank space on the map of the Dominion, as a final extension of empire, a frontier to which responsible government could now be either conferred or withheld. As Peggy met the federal officials, especially the minister of the interior, Frank Oliver, she had her doubts about just how much autonomy the new province would be granted.

Nevertheless, at the extravagant outdoor ceremony that followed, the prime minister announced Alberta would be integral to the century that lay ahead, described as "Canada's Century" in his rousing speech. Unfortunately, his grand vision had to compete with a mob of unruly chickens that ran loose across the fairground. Balmer also noted that a hanging had been postponed so the festivities could proceed. Not that the distractions really mattered. The more worldly wise of the settlers told Balmer that the next morning the officials would get back on their train to Ottawa, two thousand miles to the east, never to give Alberta another thought. At least not until oil was discovered at Turner Valley in 1914, when the curtain would rise on the boom-and-bust spectacle of the province's history.

Standing by the makeshift stage, notebook in hand, Peggy reported Laurier's speech in the hope the Eastern papers would pick up the story. She and Balmer had come west on a delayed honeymoon, and she hoped she could pay some of their expenses by documenting the day's events. She had two strikes against her: first, she was a woman, whose sex was not regarded as having reliable political opinions since women couldn't vote; second, a contingent of men, representing the Eastern establishment press, had travelled west with the prime minister and would defend the status quo in their stories. But inspired by the homesteaders she met that day, Peggy wrote about a new Canada built "from the ground up." Maybe she sang the praises of the Quebec prime minister too earnestly for hard-bitten Toronto editors? In any event, none of her dispatches were picked up.

But the effort was not wasted. In the greater scheme of things Peggy was beginning to consider a major change in her and Balmer's life — to jettison their routine careers in Ontario and answer the prime minister's call to come west, to document the frontier firsthand in a newspaper of their own. For whatever reason, Edmonton, no more than a one-horse town built around a fur trade post, had captured her imagination. Standing at the shore of the fast-flowing North Saskatchewan, she sensed the sweep of western history that lay ahead. What if they were to record that history?

To her astonishment, Balmer, exhausted by the responsibility for a failing paper in Woodstock, Ontario, agreed. In fact, he had a name in mind for the venture: the *Saturday News*, inspired by Edmund Sheppard's weekly *Saturday Night* in Toronto, the most controversial publication of its day.

Within hours of their decision, Peggy set about postponing their return trip. Instead of travelling with the prime minister to the Saskatchewan inauguration in Regina three days later, Peggy convinced Balmer to stay another week in Edmonton to look into the financial feasibility of her wild scheme. She was convinced that if they were willing to borrow the money, buy a secondhand press, and write all the copy themselves, they could make a go of it. Peggy promised to take photographs for the front page with the small roll-film Kodak camera she had bought especially for the trip. Balmer would set the type, using the small metal characters he had found in a pawnshop across the street from their hotel. It was a craft he had learned as a teenager when he had worked as an apprentice on his uncle's paper, the *Woodstock Sentinel Review*.

The next day the young couple, inveterate walkers, set out on the trails along the river valley's edge that led to the open country from which the river flowed on the western horizon. Away from the noise of the settlement's chaotic streets, they could discuss the first issue of the paper, planned for Christmas, only four months away. As they lay among the swaths of golden wheat, Peggy swore she had never seen a sky so blue, a landscape that seemed to promise so much.

Gertrude Balmer Watt was not the nineteenth-century Ontario woman you might expect. Until she was eighteen, she had grown up in Loretto Abbey, a convent school in Toronto, placed there by her father, Jock Hogg, the sheriff in Guelph County, an hour to the west. With the exception of visits to her grandparents, she had known little of family life, counting the nuns as her closest friends. Her mother had run off with a cavalry officer when Peggy was five, driving "Wild Jock," as he became known, to the bottle. You might have expected Peggy, a virtual orphan, to retreat into herself, but instead she grew so outspoken the nuns at the Abbey despaired for her future. A young woman would have to know her place in the world of men that lay ahead, especially the cutthroat profession of journalism she had chosen to pursue.

That must have been the attraction of Balmer — a quiet, gentle man dedicated to making his uncle's small-town paper a force for good. When Peggy met him, Balmer was working to save the business from bankruptcy while at the same time looking after the dying mother after whom he was named. The young journalist's devotion to family was a good sign for the marriage that lay ahead, but his round-the-clock commitment to the paper left the care of their first child completely in Peggy's hands — just as she was beginning her own career as a reporter and columnist. Little wonder it was Peggy who made the final decision to pull up stakes and travel west. Leaving their four-year-old son Frederick in the care of Balmer's aunt, they would make the Alberta journey the honeymoon they'd never had.

Publishing the Edmonton paper would present a unique opportunity for Peggy to establish herself as a journalist. She was fed up with the limited jobs available to women in the Ontario papers, where she felt she had been little more than a token. Here at last was the possibility of stepping out on her own, and in the process throwing down the gauntlet to the Canadian newspaper establishment. And she knew that Balmer, ever the gambler, could not resist the temptation of a new enterprise. If he sold his share in the Woodstock paper, they would have the start-up capital for the *Saturday News*.

After their retirement as journalists in 1948, Peggy and Balmer set about sorting through a lifetime of photographs and clippings that chronicled the saga of the newspapers they had edited or published: the *Saturday News,* the *Independent Mirror,* the

Daily Capital, the *Alberta Homestead,* and the *Edmonton Journal.*
Incurable "pack rats," they had stashed the faded newsprint in the
attic of their home overlooking the North Saskatchewan River in
downtown Edmonton.

Oil had been discovered at Leduc the year before, bringing
with it the biggest boom in the province's history. Not long before,
Alberta had been the poorest province in Canada; now it seemed
as if money grew on trees. Overnight both my parents were out
on the streets looking for work in the newfound fossil fuel economy. Every morning they would drop me off at "the Big House," as
I called it, my grandparents' red-brick residence, while they visited the oil fields and the businesses that had sprung up on every
street corner. Even though I was only four, I found myself staring
up at the stack of old newspapers Peggy and Balmer were sorting
through. By the time I was six, I had made myself indispensable
by pasting the articles, if not myself, into a growing collection of
scrapbooks. By the time I was ten, Peggy and Balmer had begun to
tell me stories about the women and men whose lives the clippings
documented — and why they mattered. The "Lost Alberta" they
had spent a lifetime documenting began to take shape.

Each scrapbook entry had to be carefully annotated as to place
of origin, author, and, when there was still room in the margin,
Peggy's personal recollections of the event. Over the years she
had discovered an extraordinary cast of characters to chronicle: Marie-Anne Gaboury, the first white woman in Alberta and
the grandmother of Louis Riel; Crowfoot, Chief of the Blackfoot
Confederacy, forced to stand by helpless as his people's way of life
was destroyed; Donald Smith, Lord Strathcona, driver of the Last
Spike and founder of Anglo-Persian Oil; James "Peace River Jim"
Cornwall, scoundrel and steamboat tycoon; Joseph Burr Tyrell,
dinosaur hunter and discoverer of the untapped wealth of the
tar sands; Irene Parlby, radical rancher and champion of women's

suffrage; and surprisingly "Bible Bill" Aberhart, Peggy's favourite, who had called down eternal damnation on the banks.

To Peggy's mind each of these larger-than-life personalities had laid the foundation for the new social order the early-twentieth-century immigration posters promised. But she also realized what lay in the way — the old-world establishment of Toronto and Montreal lawyers who had formed Alberta's first government.

Nonetheless, there was still reason for optimism. That ruling class, white and male, had not taken into account the groundswell of prairie populism taking form in the province: the arrival of radical non-partisan farmers from the Dakotas; the protests that demanded women be treated as equals; the wheat pools designed to end the monopoly control of the Winnipeg Grain Exchange; the credit unions that offered an alternative to the usurious banks; and eventually the medicare system that would become a birth-right for all Canadians.

Likening these social movements to the billowing thunder-heads that rose each day on the western horizon, Peggy delighted in describing the distinct society she felt lay ahead. At heart she was a storyteller as much as a journalist, expanding or contracting events to suit whatever future she had in mind. As entertaining as her exaggeration or editing of events might be, they present a problem for *this* book, which aims to be as much a history as a personal account. What to do when the two diverge? How to give subjective memory its due when it seems to stray from accepted facts? As we assembled the scrapbooks I could often feel that tension in the air: Balmer, the veteran newspaper editor, refusing to accept Peggy's "creative" description of events. Yet what he saw as outlandish in her accounts, she maintained was simply an intuitive reading of history. Yes, he had been there, but so had she.

For the purposes of this book, when such an impasse presents itself, I have chosen to record both versions, to give as much weight to Peggy's sense of drama as to Balmer's careful consideration. It means there are times, when Balmer isn't in the room, when the story must depend on a highly unreliable narrator. So be it. Peggy would insist on the validity of her storytelling, reminding me that fact, as we think we know it, can just as easily be a fiction.

As the years passed, despite the arguments, the scope of the scrapbooks steadily grew, and I began to realize a highly idiosyncratic history of Alberta was taking shape. Enlivened by the dialectic that moved back and forth between the two old warriors, the disputes ended where both parties recognized they should: identifying what really mattered in the life of the province. Only much later did I realize how much had been at stake. The albums we assembled were in fact recycled ledger books, the columns of which recorded the dwindling cash flow that had spelt disaster for their original small newspapers. Peggy and Balmer must have sensed that irony, pasting stories and characters they had saved from extinction over the rows of unforgiving figures that had spelled their own doom.

For me the scrapbooks turned out to be an epiphany of sorts. The photographs and clippings spoke for a time when the province had documented its own story, considered its own destiny. The media centres of Toronto and New York were still distant enough that a distinct regional identity could flourish in Alberta. Newspapers like the *Saturday News* and the *Alberta Homestead* provided a clear and resonant voice in which prairie culture could be heard. Whatever false steps Peggy and Balmer may have taken as business people, and there were many, they treasured the experience of documenting the new world the immigration posters had promised. As my grandmother would say with a sparkle in her eye: *we were in at the making of things.*

Since Peggy's death, Alberta history has followed a very different trajectory. The western frontier, which once seemed an opportunity to redeem Canada's past, has instead become a dire warning for the country's future. From the object of Peggy and Balmer's fondest hopes, the province has turned into a "sacrifice zone," as scientist David Schindler described it, a dark kingdom of strip mines and offshore corporations. Warning of the power of industry to alter climate, landscape, ecology, and ultimately community itself, Schindler challenged the powers that be who had sold out the province.

In the years ahead, there is every chance Alberta's story will turn to tragedy. What was once a place of renewal — a chance to build a simpler, fairer society — has been transformed into the leading edge of catastrophe as the province pumps more emissions into the atmosphere than any other jurisdiction in Canada. As global warming takes its toll, the fossil fuel industry will only double down, championing its role as the necessary engine for growth — and much more of Alberta may be lost.

For fifty years two journalists recorded both the inspiration and the betrayal of the Alberta dream. This is their story.

Give to me the life I love,

Let the lave go by me;

Give the jolly heaven above

And the by-way nigh me.

Bed in the bush with the stars to see,

Bread I dip in the river —

There's the life for a man like me,

There's the life forever.

ROBERT LOUIS STEVENSON, "THE VAGABOND"

Book One

1905–1912
THE LAST BEST WEST

1

Wolverine

When I consider that the nobler animals
have been exterminated here — the cougar,
the panther, lynx, wolverine, wolf, bear,
moose, the beaver, the turkey ... I cannot
but feel as if I lived in a tamed and, as it
were, emasculated country. I wish to know
an entire heaven and an entire earth.

HENRY DAVID THOREAU

Prime Minister
Wilfrid Laurier,
amidst a sea of
homesteaders
in Edmonton,
declares Alberta
a province,
September 1, 1905

A river of flame engulfs the land. Where the wind catches it, the fire leaps and tumbles, a wave incinerating everything in its path. At its leading edge, two deer stand frozen, unsure whether to remain or flee. A hydrocarbon haze obscures the massive bitumen upgraders on the horizon. The sky is a livid red.

We're shooting aerials over the oil sands, documenting a wildfire that threatens the suburbs of Fort McMurray in 2016. In the intervening years the scene has repeated itself across Canada, from Kelowna to Yellowknife to northern Quebec, the never-ceasing advance of climate change; within seven years we'll see the worst year for forest fires in Canada's recorded history.

The helicopter loses altitude once we clear the fire zone, hugs the shore of the Athabasca River, skimming the tops of the poplars and tamaracks that have been spared. The pilot spots a wolverine climbing out of a den below, doing its best to escape the billowing smoke. Within moments the animal's powerful gait takes it to the top of a ridge, where it swings its head back, as if to warn off the helicopter. Carcajou, in my grandfather's stories, defender of the northern wilds.

I try to imagine the animal, eyes fierce as the illustrations in books I loved as a boy, spread out on the floor of Balmer's library. Well-worn volumes of the work of the naturalist Ernest Thompson

Seton, author of *Lives of the Hunted* — a portrait of the animal kingdom that once made this wilderness its home. When Seton travelled down the Athabasca River in 1907, his Métis guide Bellalise was treed near Fort Chipewyan by a wolverine protecting her cubs. Seton described the creature:

> The greatest plague the hunter knows, solitary, tireless, the wolverine often covers a territory of up to 400 square miles, scavenging the kills of predators like the wolf and the grizzly, springing traps, robbing the caches carefully set aside by man.

Today Carcajou, once native to most of the continent, is being pushed further and further into the remoteness of the north. The United States Fish and Wildlife Service has proposed "endangered species" protection for the animal as it is extirpated in its original range. A lone wolverine, tagged in Montana, travelled 1,287 kilometres looking for a home territory before being shot by a rancher in North Dakota in 2016. As it is for all manner of species, the advance of the energy frontier is catastrophic.

The helicopter is climbing again to avoid the fire. Below, the river stretches to the horizon of its arctic journey. The roar of the engine startles the wolverine, which with a final burst of speed disappears into the sweep of the great boreal forest. This is the country my journalist uncle, Ted Watt, Peggy and Balmer's son, flew with Wop May in the 1920s, a time when an ocean of trees stretched to the horizon — the longest unbroken tract of forest in the world. Watt's assignment was to document the mercy missions bush pilots were flying to remote northern communities in need of medicine. Crossing uncharted territory, May usually carried extra barrels of fuel, not passengers, but Watt was an old friend from the First World War. At night the bush pilot would land his small plane in the middle of a frozen lake and lay on the ice in his sleeping bag, his body wrapped around the plane's oil pan for warmth. It was a reciprocal arrangement, his body heat keeping the oil viscous enough for the engine to start in the morning.

The tar sands, as yet undeveloped, lay beneath the hundreds of square miles of muskeg May's plane traversed. It was flat country with few discernible landmarks except for the rivers that traced a pattern across the landscape like the arteries of a hand. Their course provided a map the newcomer could follow — Alexander Mackenzie, Peter Pond, and John Franklin had all passed this way in search of a northwest passage to Asia — unlocking the resource rich interior of the continent to commerce as they went. But it was the bush pilot who had opened a new chapter. As Ted Watt wrote,

> They were young men in a hurry. Charged with the dynamism of wartime air battles, they were breaking open a million square miles of harsh new terrain. They ranged over distant reaches of tundra and mountain in a fraction of the time it had taken earlier explorers. A moment's poor judgement or bad luck, a lost gamble, could put a flier down in the forest or tundra ... Survival depended on wisdom and experience borrowed from the native people, plus a wide streak of courage and stubbornness.

Wilfrid Reid "Wop" May personified the breed. Dressed in his black leather bomber jacket, he had taken Edmonton by storm on his return from the Great War. My mother Becky, Peggy and Balmer's daughter, remembered watching him fly beneath the High Level Bridge that day, barely skimming the waters of the North Saskatchewan. Such bravado earned him a stiff fine from city council when he landed. Peggy's column maintained that it was no way to treat the hero who had shot down Baron von Richthofen, the most feared German flier of the war. Now, ten years later, when May's plane arrived at each lonely outpost, Ted Watt would telegraph dispatches to Balmer in Edmonton. The next day the whole city would marvel at front page news of this dangerous northern odyssey.

Balmer's fascination with the North never left him. His library contained not only all the Seton wildlife books but a scrapbook he and Peggy had assembled to honour the bush pilots. That album included photos of the first airmail flight to Aklavik, beyond the Arctic Circle. Ted Watt's articles, carefully preserved, documented a mercy flight to Little Red River with medicines to combat a feared outbreak of diphtheria. At the time there were no through roads in northern Alberta and the nearest telegraph station was often a day's journey away.

One corner of Balmer's library was stacked with boxes of artifacts I was conscripted to sort through. At the bottom of one I found the stocks Balmer had purchased in defunct tar sands companies going back to the 1920s. To Peggy's dismay he had never lost hope in what he was convinced would be Alberta's Eldorado. Year after year he had invested in the most unlikely local initiatives to refine the heavy oil. But the promised technology — a cost-effective way to separate the bitumen from the sand — never materialized. As every scheme failed and each newfangled company went bankrupt, Balmer would pass on the worthless share certificates to his grandchildren to use as play money. *Bitumount, The Clark Hot Water Separation Process, Great Canadian Oil Sands* — the names, promising so much, echo through my childhood.

Balmer never lived to see that Eldorado. The tar sands were still touch and go when he died in 1964, as conventional oil flooded the world market. But the environmental and social cost of large-scale northern development was already becoming evident. The boreal forest and the rivers Wop May and Ted Watt had followed in the 1920s were being torn apart by the strip mines necessary to extract the bitumen. The refining process that followed was fraught with danger. Huge tailings ponds were being built on the shore of the Athabasca River to contain the chemical byproducts contained in the heavy oil. Yet the walls would turn out to be so porous that toxins escaping into the river would be detected all the way to the Arctic Ocean, contaminating the water supply of the twenty-three Indigenous communities on its route.

For the old journalist there was an irony in the massive development, financed by an American corporation in Philadelphia, Sun Oil. What had started as an Edmonton bush pilot flying mercy missions to isolated northern communities became part of an expansion of industry that began to consume the communities themselves.

In 1905, near Alberta's eastern border, a steam engine, a mere speck on the landscape, pulls a string of colonist cars across the prairie. Ahead lies "the great lone land," as described by William Francis Butler, an early explorer in the region. The train carries Prime Minister Wilfred Laurier and a host of reporters en route to inaugurate Alberta as Canada's newest province. One imagines Peggy writing in the diary open on her lap:

> For days now there has been nothing to break the solitude
> of the endless prairie. Next to me, Balmer is asleep, oblivi-
> ous to the hard bench and cold wind rattling the window.
> This is the fourth day of our journey from Toronto's
> Union Station to the end of the line in Edmonton. It feels
> like an eternity.

To make matters worse, she has discovered that press access to the government party has been restricted to the big Toronto and Montreal papers. Peggy hasn't had as much as a glimpse of Laurier, riding at the rear of the train in his own private car. As she shifts her weight on the wooden bench she and Balmer share, she can only imagine the softness of the sofa on which the prime minister reclines.

> But there is something about this country which stirs my heart ... six in the morning, passing through the little towns, we see on every hand signs of life; for the fresh hours of dawning are very precious in this new land, where every moment counts. Oh, but it's good to see a people so early astir, so thoroughly in earnest to make good, that the day is too short for the work planned out ... Leaving the ambitious hamlets in the rear, one comes upon solitary wagoneers driving their heavily-laden carts out onto the broad, empty prairie. I never see them but I immediately start to frame a story regarding the young fellow and his probable destiny ...

The question of what form that destiny will take perplexes Peggy — the contrast between Laurier's vision of "Canada's Century" and the bone-chilling cold of these northern prairies. As the journey progresses she finds little evidence of the abundance promised in the immigration posters, pasted as an act of faith on the wall of every railway station they stop at. Noticeable by their absence are the First Nations, removed from their traditional lands. The ghostly sight of residential schools, set far back from the tracks, haunts the empty landscape. How can a new society be built on such poisoned ground?

Yet when the train stops to refuel, Peggy never fails to marvel at the crowds of settlers who gather around the engine. She loves the sense of occasion — sometimes sombre, sometimes celebratory — they bring to the stations. Even when the brooding Laurier fails to come out to greet them, the choruses of "O Canada" follow the train as it continues its journey.

How many settlers looking out and seeing the steady, unflinching light, and hearing the roar of an advancing train have felt comforted and been made stout of heart, knowing that through its medium they are made once more a part of the great busy world they have left, and that in the belching steam from the huge engine lies their hope of future prosperity.

Two months later, with their five-year-old son Frederick squeezed between them, Peggy and Balmer repeat the lonely journey, but this time with the first snows of winter covering the land. Their affairs in Woodstock successfully concluded, they now engage in an endless tug-of-war about the content and design of the *Saturday News*. The presentation of her column, "The Mirror," is a major bone of contention. Balmer wants to see it incorporated into the main body of the paper. Already suspicious of his affiliation with the government, Peggy wants to see it published as a separate section of the paper. As a journalist, at least the perception of independence is important to her.

She has already filled two of the three notebooks she brought with her, pencil drawings interspersed with the text. West of the Saskatchewan border, a bend in the track finally allows her to sketch the train as it crosses the prairie ahead, the line of carriages weaving a serpentine pattern across the land. She wakes Frederick so he can see the engine climb the banks of a coulee onto higher ground. Two men, black with soot, shovel extra coal into the firebox for the ascent. Peggy can hear the steam explode in the boilers and the wheels strain under the weight of the line of cars. The boy is transfixed.

That afternoon, Peggy wanders the carriages, making acquaintances in the pidgin English spoken on the train. Most of the families have their household goods piled beside them in the aisle, which at mealtimes doubles as a makeshift kitchen. The heavy scent of garlic and sheepskin coats fills the air, joined by the rhapsody of a violin from the next carriage. Young women dance on the benches, their dresses an explosion of colour.

Bargaining for one of the shawls the women wear, Peggy discovers that the families in her car come from the Austro-Hungarian Empire, farmers from Galicia in western Ukraine. The conversation is interrupted by the conductor, a superior, Rule Britannia–type, who has come to put an end to the dancers' "defacement of railway property." Peggy is not impressed when he refers to her new friends as "bohunks."

> Stolid Galicians in ill-fitting togs, accompanied by their great strapping wives stand in the aisle … a man's coat about the women's shoulders. Over all is a hush of expectancy, broken only by short, subdued conversations, held in an undertone. It reminds you of the dramatic moment before the curtain raises on some great play.

As the conductor tells them to move on, Peggy remarks on his tone. It's not the kind of question he is used to being asked, especially from a woman. It is becoming clearer in her mind the kind of journalist she wants to become, free of the prejudice of a class for whom this frontier is clearly little more than an extension of empire.

Writing again in her diary, she considers what awaits these people in the winter ahead. Railway officials have told her there is no longer accommodation available for the immigrants in Edmonton. According to the conductor, the city is already overrun with "these people"; they will have to live in the tent city that has been thrown up along the river. As Peggy's gaze takes in the frozen landscape that stretches outside the window, she wonders how they will survive the cold. She looks up to see a young girl staring at her. So beautiful, so vulnerable. Yet when Peggy makes the motion of a greeting, the girl runs back to her parents.

Only when they pass a homestead is there a point of reference that allows her to measure the extent of the Great Plains as the maps describe it. She realizes she had no idea of this epic geography when Laurier announced the creation of the new provinces. In her head she's already writing a book about the immigrant experience: *A Woman in the West*. She's sure she can interest a publisher in Brantford or Woodstock, maybe even Toronto.

When Balmer wakes up she tells him about the arrogance of the conductor. Balmer thinks she's overreacting. Her description of the incident soon prompts a familiar argument — who's in charge in what is still essentially a colony and whose interests do they represent? From the politicians to the most minor official, she detects the superiority of attitudes of Britishness, the ruling class she hoped to leave behind in Ontario. Balmer is quick to defend the new administration, made up in part of his classmates from the University of Toronto. The influence of his ex-fraternity brother Charles Cross, soon to be the first attorney general of the province, will be crucial in getting the *Saturday News* off the ground. For the first time he tells her that Cross has already agreed to invest in the paper. They had best be careful not to bite the hand that feeds them.

In the freight car immediately behind the engine is the only article of furniture she and Balmer have brought with them, a writing desk for their new office, as mystical to Peggy's mind as it is practical. The desk is made of New England oak, with brass handles and an inset green baize top, the desk of small-town newspaper people forever struggling to make ends meet. Compact, efficient in design, meant to encourage the economy of thought preached by their Puritan forefathers, the desk breaks down into three pieces, not beyond their strength to lift. The polished wood shows the scratches and scrapes of being taken from one Ontario town to another in the closing years of the nineteenth century. Two journalists learning the writer's and editor's craft, in anticipation of their great leap into the unknown.

But Peggy is beginning to have her doubts. Her friends in the Women's Press Club have written copious letters, urging her not to turn her back on the years it has taken to establish a career in Ontario. More jobs for women are opening up in the Toronto papers — with her experience she would certainly qualify. Each letter confirms what she has already realized: how much she has to lose.

Peggy knows there will be no changing Balmer's mind. The more unrealistic the idea, the more stubborn he can be, simply smiling when she lists all the things that can go wrong, reminding her that this was all her idea in the first place. This is the chance they've been waiting for — to get out on their own, be their own publishers, beholden to no one for the content of the paper. "The Mirror," the women's section of the paper, will be unique in the country, political and cultural in its viewpoint, not the usual social claptrap.

Peggy doesn't appreciate the patronizing tone. She makes a decision. She will help him get the paper off the ground, write her columns for the rest of the winter, then announce her decision to return to Ontario in the spring. There will be the inevitable fight, but with any luck she'll be home in time for Easter.

When the engine stops to take on coal and water at Blackfoot Crossing in southern Alberta, Peggy walks to the edge of a nearby ridge. A chinook has been blowing and the snow has disappeared from the prairie. Hitching up her skirt, she climbs on a boulder the size of a small house, an erratic left over from the last ice age. Beyond the rock lies a sweep of land and sky unlike any she has ever seen. On the horizon stands a range of snow-capped mountains, her first view of the Rockies, from whose base a river, silver in the midday sun, makes its way across the prairie. Rising on the air are chevrons of ducks and geese setting out on their annual migration south. The fragrance of wolf willow travels on the wind.

In the distance, a Blackfoot family makes their way across the Bow River to trade in the nearby town of Gleichen. The scene reminds her of the narratives of David Thompson, described to her in an interview she had conducted before leaving Toronto with the geologist Joseph Tyrrell, who had discovered the explorer's handwritten maps in an abandoned fur trade post. In 1787, at the age of fifteen, Thompson had been sent west by the Hudson's Bay Company with a party of voyageurs to document the region. Heavy snows that winter provided him with the opportunity to spend a winter with Saukamappee, a Peigan Elder, and do his best to learn the Blackfoot language. The relationship between the two men was an uneasy one, Saukamappee fearing what the coming of the young white man would mean for his people. Were the detailed maps Thompson worked on every night part of a larger plan for the occupation of Blackfoot land? Already to the north at a place on the Great River called amiskwaciy-wâskahikan, later Edmonton, forts had been built by three different companies of traders.

Based on what she has seen in the course of the train journey, Peggy knows Saukamappee's fears have come to pass. The massive terminals of the Grain Exchange in Winnipeg; spur lines bringing coal from the Estevan mines in Saskatchewan; gas plants in Medicine Hat with what Rudyard Kipling would later call "all hell for a basement." On the station platform in Calgary Balmer hears rumours that the same Joseph Tyrrell, working for the Royal Geological Survey, has tabled his report on the mineral deposits of the Fort McMurray region. First results indicate what may be the world's largest single deposit of oil. The phrase "tar sand" is suddenly on everyone's lips.

Along the shore of the Athabasca River, the helicopter circles back to see whether we can catch a final glimpse of the wolverine. But soon the forest gives way to the massive Syncrude upgrader and the highway leading to Fort McMurray jammed with cars and trucks fleeing the wildfire.

Suddenly the ground falls away as a jagged pit opens below, a strip mine as dark as a black hole in some distant galaxy. The bitumen deposits are so dense it feels as if they will pull us down from the sky. Headlights pierce the gloom as massive trucks haul hundred-ton loads out of the mine. Here there is no horizon, no reference point in nature, only swirling clouds of smoke and dust spewed from the vast cavity. Even with fire raging in the vicinity, production has not slowed down. Three 8-hour shifts, 24 hours a day, 365 days a year.

It's hard to imagine that this is the same province that captured Peggy's heart a century before.

2

Canadian Born

… rivers have life and sound and movement and infinity of variation, rivers are veins of the earth through which the lifeblood returns to the heart.

RODERICK HAIG-BROWN

Galicians in a
colonist car
heading west

All her life Peggy dreamed of a river. Cold and clear, teepees and a stockade on the shore, a forest wilderness on every side. She'd first imagined the scene after seeing a Paul Kane painting of Fort Edmonton as a girl, part of an exhibition at a small gallery on Wellington Street in Toronto. She was a regular at the gallery, just down the street from the grey convent where she spent her youth, exiled from family and friends.

As she stood before the painting she'd been carried away by the current in the river, kisiskâciwanisîpiy, "swiftly flowing" in Cree, according to Kane's notes. It was as if the rippling water provided a spirit guide for a journey yet to come. Peggy had already determined to travel to the land from which the river flowed, one day when her life was her own.

She was in her eighties and I was only fourteen on the fall day she first described the painting to me. As winter approached, the waters of the North Saskatchewan below us had become the glacial blue of the painting, free of the silt of the river's many tributaries. Sitting in her sun porch overlooking the valley, Peggy marvelled at the "line of beauty" the s-shape the river traced through the city. Called an ogee in architecture, nature's design carried great meaning for her — the hope that such a double curve could be found in time as well as space.

The North Saskatchewan valley had been a human gathering place for thousands of years. Would its river connect her to the spirit of the Indigenous Peoples who had been coming here since the last ice age, migrating from Asia over the Bering land bridge to settle this beautiful valley, abundant in game, edible plants, and medicines?

As a girl at the convent, Peggy had first encountered the idea of an ogee in William Hogarth's book *Analysis of Beauty,* written in 1753. Hogarth maintained that s-shaped curves signified life, as opposed to straight lines, which signified stasis or death. Seventy years later, Peggy laughed at the thought, admitting that her life had contained very few straight anythings. The exception was the track of the maddening CPR railway as it made its way across Saskatchewan. She swore that on her journey west, noting the distance posts beside the track, she counted fifty consecutive miles during which the engine's course didn't diverge a foot to the right or the left. At least when it reached the Alberta border it followed the curves of the rolling hills and valleys that wound their way onto the prairie, a relief in the landscape that reminded her of the southern Ontario she grew up in.

The two towns Peggy and Balmer left behind in 1905, Woodstock and Brantford, were small but prosperous communities where industry was replacing agriculture, factories supplying the continent with pump organs, shotguns, and Massey Ferguson farm machinery. To this day, handsome brick buildings speak to the ingenuity of the towns' builders. Woodstock's Francis Hincks, the member of parliament for Oxford County, was John A. Macdonald's minister of finance, responsible for the Bank Act of 1871, facilitating the construction of the Canadian Pacific Railway. Brantford's claim to fame was Alexander Graham Bell, who invented the first successful telephone. And not to forget, a century later, the birth-place of Wayne Gretzky.

Peggy had been born in 1879 to a family that ran the hard-ware store in nearby Guelph. Her eccentric grandfather had built a statue of himself at its front door with a golden plaque announ-cing the owner as "John Hogg, the Wonderful Man." His way with commerce allowed him to provide generously for his sons, one of whom, Peggy's father Wild Jock was a hopeless reprobate. Jock had two daughters before his wife left him, one of the earliest divor-ces on record in Ontario. The younger, Gertrude Hogg, who soon became known as "Peggy," was brought up by her grandparents until the age of five. But with the sudden death of the Wonderful Man in 1888, Wild Jock returned to collect his inheritance and promptly placed his daughter in the Loretto Abbey convent, a vir-tual orphan. As strong a woman as Peggy was to become, there was always the pain of those years, preventing her from completely trusting anyone, including Balmer.

Loretto Abbey was a school of established reputation, and the precocious child took every advantage of the opportunities it provided. Greek, Latin, literature, the piano, Peggy tackled them all, much to the astonishment of the nuns. "I grew to love the sis-ters," she later told my mother, "so they must have loved me as well." At eighteen, she graduated to the Brantford Ladies College where William Watt was chairman of the board. One Sunday she was invited to visit the Watt home for tea, and by chance William's son came home from Toronto for the afternoon. Peggy met Balmer, and the course of her life changed once again. Here was a serious young journalist who, like herself, longed to experience the outside world. What's more, his family respected her ambitions as a journal-ist, rare for a woman of the time. Balmer's aunt Eliza had been the first woman to attend classes at the University of Toronto in 1883, conducting a sit-in outside the classroom until she was admitted.

In 1904, at Balmer's urging, Peggy would convince the *Brantford Expositor* to assign her to cover the St. Louis World Fair, celebrating the hundredth anniversary of the Louisiana Purchase. The fair would be remembered for its Greco-Roman architecture and popularizing of the ice cream cone, but manifest destiny, the expansion of American interests around the world, was its real message. A major exhibition paid tribute to the recent occupation of the Philippines and Cuba by U.S. Marines, imperial adventures in which hundreds of thousands of Indigenous people had died.

Those invasions, hard upon the seizure of Texas and California from Mexico, had many Canadians, including Peggy, worried their country might be next. The new president, the sabre-rattling Theodore Roosevelt, had advanced the idea that the U.S. border should be redrawn to include the drainage system of rivers like the Missouri, the Red, and the Columbia. The annexation necessary to make that possible would include portions of southern Manitoba, Saskatchewan, Alberta, and British Columbia.

On the long train journey to Missouri, Peggy and fifteen other reporters formed the Canadian Women's Press Club. The organization meant to advance the careers of female journalists in the established press, but just as importantly to articulate a worldview unique to Canada. Faced with Roosevelt's provocations, Peggy was convinced newspapers should challenge the complacency of Canada's citizens — to dissuade them from passively accepting the colonization of their own country.

One of the women on the train was a journalist from Edmonton, Katherine Hughes, in the midst of writing a biography of Albert Lacombe, a pioneer priest on the prairies. Hughes had travelled to the frontier from Ireland, anxious to escape the centuries-old English occupation of her country. It was in Hughes's descriptions of the North-West Territories that Peggy first encountered the empowerment of next year country, the ability of the frontier to change lives, especially those of women. But Hughes neglected to tell her of an abiding British imperial presence. By the time Peggy reached Edmonton, Hughes was gone, having returned to Dublin to join the IRA in its armed struggle for Irish independence. As Peggy would tell her grandchildren fifty years later, she had met her first terrorist.

En route to St. Louise, Peggy's eyes were opened by an article she read written by Ida Tarbell, a young reporter working for *McClure's* magazine in New York. New to the trade, Tarbell had published an exposé of the business dealings of the richest man in America, John D. Rockefeller, considered off-limits by most journalists. Tarbell was immediately blackballed by her profession. Rockefeller called her "Miss Tarbarrel."

The trust Rockefeller managed under the cover of Standard Oil of New Jersey was the focus of Tarbell's investigations, the concentration of power that presented a grave danger to the business world. For the rest of her life Peggy would watch as her own country's economy was overwhelmed by massive American corporations like Standard Oil. The octopus-like creature that Tarbell described in such detail had tentacles that reached far beyond the border of the United States. One of them would be Imperial Oil in Alberta, which in time would determine the development of the province's vast energy reserves.

Tarbell had become a prime target for the guardians of corporate America, the opponents of anti-trust legislation. The scandal her reporting provoked not only revolutionized American journalism but empowered women working in the trade, including the Canadian reporters covering the World's Fair. Peggy quickly became an advocate for her fellow journalist's cause, writing letters to the editors of the New York papers, speaking out against Rockefeller and Roosevelt in St Louis. Already at the vanguard of the fight for women's suffrage, she expressed her rage at the misogynist and racist mindset of what she considered a foreign culture. Her first day in St. Louis would confirm those misgivings. The Apache chief Geronimo had been brought to the Fair by the U.S. Army and was on display on the grounds as a prisoner of war. When Peggy visited the teepee that had been set up for the Chief's benefit, surrounded by the Fair's security service, she wrote,

> It was hard to imagine that this dignified old man had been the leader of the historic resistance that fought the expansion of America to a standstill. Visiting the enclosure was like watching a lion confined to a circus cage.

Geronimo's eyes registered what had been done to his people, the genocide taking place at the western edge of the continent. In the years ahead Peggy would write at length about two different approaches to nation building. Canada, she believed, had tried to retain the "Honour of the Crown," the British parliamentary tradition that viewed Indigenous Peoples as sovereign entities. Treaties with Indigenous Peoples would be signed to reflect an agreement between sovereign nations, a negotiated peace both sides would do their utmost to preserve. In the United States there would be no peace until one side had destroyed the other. Claiming the spoils of war, treaties were charades the government in Washington had no intent of honouring.

When Peggy returned to Brantford from St. Louis, she attended a poetry reading by a Mohawk woman, Emily Pauline Johnson. *Canadian Born*, a collection of writing that celebrated the poet's mixed-blood ancestry, had created a stir in anglophone Ontario. Also known as Tekahionwake, "between two worlds," as a child Johnson had been the recipient of a traditional Mohawk upbringing from her father, a hereditary Chief, and an education in literature from her English mother. But government regulations required that she attend an Anglican College in Brantford, established to educate the "heathen." Even though the government had signed treaties with Indigenous Peoples, it was determined to "civilize" future generations.

A poem that night moved Peggy to tears — the description of an old Mohawk woman, forced by poverty and the loss of her land to harvest corn on a white man's farm:

Hard by the Indian lodges, where the bush
    Breaks in a clearing, through ill-fashioned fields,
She comes to labour, when the first still hush
    Of autumn follows large and recent yields.

Age in her fingers, hunger in her face,
    Her shoulders stooped with weight of work and years,
But rich in tawny colouring of her race,
    She comes a-field to strip the purple ears.

And all her thoughts are with the days gone by,
    Ere might's injustice banished from their lands
Her people, that to-day unheeded lie,
    Like the dead husks that rustle through her hands.

Pauline's ancestors had been allies of England in the Revolutionary War, fighting to prevent the Americans seizing their land in upstate New York. At the war's conclusion the Mohawks had become exiles, following their own "trail of tears" north into the bush. The last 450 members of the band, led by Joseph Brant, found a new home on the Grand River in Upper Canada, where they settled in what became Brantford. Their neighbours were United Empire Loyalists who also had fled the war, English and Scottish settlers loyal to the Crown. From an early age Pauline's mother, Emily Susanna

Howells, had encouraged her daughter to explore her Indigenous ancestry in poetry.

> Women are fonder of me than men are. I have had none fail
> me, and I hope I have failed none. It is a keen pleasure for
> me to meet a congenial woman, one that I feel will under-
> stand me, and will in turn let me peep into her own life —
> having confidence in me, that is one of the dearest things
> between friends, strangers, acquaintances, or kindred.

Peggy had found a comrade for the struggles that lay ahead, besides Balmer her first true friend in the world outside the convent.

Peggy had recently been sued for libel by the prestigious Toronto *Globe and Empire* for defaming a reporter much more senior than herself. The scandal forced Balmer to publish an abject apology to avoid the court case that would have bankrupted the paper. However, the infamy of the case served to cement Peggy's friendship with the outspoken Mohawk poet.

Canada in 1904 was by no means free of racism, the terms of which were set out in agonizing detail in the country's Indian Act, which abolished customs native to the country's original inhabit-ants. Integrating Indigenous Peoples into white society became the goal of the Act, no matter what the means. Peggy had heard stories emerging from the Mohawk Institute, known as "the Mush Hole," in Brantford. Children speaking their parents' language was pro-hibited, and rumours of unmarked graves haunted the institution. The boiler room in the basement was said to be the site of sexual abuse of both boys and girls, the furnace drowning out the cries of the victims. Pauline knew the rumours were true:

> There are those who think they pay me a compliment in
> saying that I am just like a white woman. My aim, my joy,
> my pride is to sing the glories of my own people. Ours

was the race that gave the world its measure of heroism, its standard of physical prowess. Ours was the race that taught the world that avarice veiled by any name is crime. Ours were the people of the blue air and the green woods, and ours the faith that taught men to live without greed and to die without fear.

Johnson had recently returned from a poetry tour of what was still the North-West Territories. She had much to tell Peggy about Edmonton and nearby Fort Saskatchewan, where she had been a guest of the Royal Canadian Mounted Police and the premier of the Territories, Frederick Haultain. An ardent regionalist dedicated to an independent path for the West, Haultain had recruited Pauline to the cause, especially his bold proposals to protect the rights of First Nations in the new province.

But in Edmonton, Frank Oliver, federal member of parliament and soon to be minister of the interior in the Laurier government, stood firmly in the way. Oliver was publisher of the *Bulletin*, the city's first newspaper, that for decades had campaigned against equal rights for Indigenous Peoples, dehumanizing the native population in the public eye. Working in collusion with the local chamber of commerce, Oliver set out to rob Edmonton's original inhabitants of both their treaty rights and their land.

Listening to Pauline's account, Peggy begins to understand the importance of the independent newspaper Balmer proposes to publish, free of government control. Oliver's corruption of power had gone unreported in the mainstream press. She remembers as a girl of six hearing the news that Louis Riel had been hanged in Regina. How for weeks the Ontario newspapers had vilified the Métis leader, clamouring for his execution. The fate of Indigenous Peoples and the life of a man many believed to be innocent were the price the country had to pay for a press owned by a small number of men.

3

Strange Empire

I will perhaps be one day acknowledged as more
than a leader of the half-breeds, and if I am,
I will have an opportunity of being acknowledged
as a leader of good in this great country.

LOUIS RIEL

Balmer outside
the trapper's cabin
that served as the
first home of the
Saturday News,
Edmonton, 1905

Ice begins to form on the train window as night falls. Peggy must wrap Frederick in the thick blanket she has packed. He struggles to stay awake, not wanting to miss the towns, few and far between. His mother writes in her notebook:

> We catch the twinkling from the lights in the cottages ... a will o' the wisp view of the gaily illuminated main streets. Out from the vast stretches of country there comes a dreamy charm ... then the hills close in about us and the great Night comes on.

At dawn she is awakened by the sun tracing patterns on the glass, now fully encrusted with frost. Over Balmer's protest she opens the window to peer out. The frigid air bites at her lungs and the smoke from the locomotive stings her eyes. Again the engine swings into view ahead, its pistons driving the huge steel wheels forward. They are crossing the lonely plateau that forms an extension of the Missouri Coteau south of the American border. While Peggy sleeps, Balmer makes note of a band of Métis, dressed in rags, struggling to pull a travois through the snow. Behind them is a gravel road running parallel to the railroad tracks with a shantytown in the ditch beside it. These are Road Allowance People, as the settlers call them, forced to abandon their Métis communities in the aftermath of the 1885 Resistance. The survivors now live on the margins of the subdivisions the Queen's surveyors are laying out on the prairie, anticipating the waves of immigration the railway will bring — the land theft the rebellion vainly attempted to prevent. Living alongside the tracks, displaced buffalo hunters who once enjoyed the freedom of the plains have been forced to make the ditches their home. Balmer asks the conductor about the train's present location: maybe he can convince Peggy to write an article describing the tragedy he had witnessed.

At the time of Peggy's birth, Louis Riel was an exile in the United States, chopping wood for steamboats along the Missouri River, a warrant out for his arrest in Canada for leading the 1870 Métis uprising in what would become Manitoba. But each summer he would join his people on the Great Plains as they followed the buffalo, irrespective of the white man's border. The great herds had declined in Canada, forcing the summer-long hunting expeditions to travel as far south as the escarpments along the Missouri river. It was in this epic landscape that Riel met and married Marguerite Monet, *dit* Bellehumeur, the daughter of one of the captains of the hunt. Each day, as they followed the great migrations, Riel and Marguerite could feel the earth move as the vast herds were stampeded by the Métis riders. Thirty-five years later, as Peggy watches the snow drift across the empty plains, she can see the patterns in the grass the buffalo have left behind. Like brass rubbings taken from a great cathedral, each trail speaks of a time when the land and its inhabitants lived as one.

Each year when the hunting season came to a close, Riel would look for work in Montana, eventually finding a job as a schoolteacher in Sun River, a remote community along the eastern slope of the Rocky Mountains. Bringing up a young family, he hoped to escape the long arm of history. But across the border, the Canadians still had a warrant for his arrest.

One morning the silhouettes of two horsemen appear on the ridge line to the east. Exhausted from eight hundred miles of riding, Gabriel Dumont and Charles Isbister approach the school and ask for Riel. They have come to bring him and Marguerite home, not to Canada but to the independent Métis Republic they are about to declare on the northern prairies.

In the fall of 1884, the young couple and their three children pack their belongings in a wagon and accompany the two riders across the plains to join the Northwest Resistance. Canadian government surveyors and police have invaded land the Métis regard as theirs. Cree, French, and Scottish fur traders and farmers have banded together to establish an independent nation centred in the village of Batoche on the South Saskatchewan River, challenging Ottawa's claim to the surrounding territory.

The insurrection grows when Cree chiefs Poundmaker and Big Bear, disillusioned with federal Indian policy, join the alliance. Prime Minister John A. Macdonald responds by sending heavily armed battalions led by a veteran of Great Britain's imperial wars, Sir Frederick Dobson Middleton, who has previously crushed a Māori uprising in New Zealand and the Sepoy mutiny in India, killing thousands.

Upon his arrival in Batoche, Riel is named the leader of the new nation, but with Crowfoot's change of heart, the greater Indigenous alliance falters, and the Métis and Cree are left to fight alone. When battle is joined with the Canadians, the single-shot Métis hunting rifles run out of ammunition, forcing the fighters to fire nuts and bolts, no match for Middleton's repeater rifles and Gatling gun. Dumont's cavalry soon have their horses shot from under them, reducing the Resistance to old men and boys, trapped in the rifle pits they have dug to defend the town.

Macdonald's troops win an easy victory. While Riel is led away to Regina to be tried, Dumont manages to escape, travelling by night to avoid the patrols of mounted police who now seek him for treason. Moving among what remained of the great buffalo herds — some said he was capable of becoming a buffalo himself — Dumont reaches the amnesty of the border with the United States. But there is little sanctuary to be found among the Americans. For the next fifteen years he will be put on display as a defeated Resistance leader in Buffalo Bill's Wild West Show, much as Geronimo would be at the St. Louis Fair. Still a crack shot, Dumont is reduced to shooting silver dollars out of the air in cramped arenas crowded with hecklers. A far cry from the silence of the Great Plains he had shared with Riel on their trek from Montana to Batoche, now a universe away.

At the conclusion of the Resistance, Peggy is taken on a day trip by her uncle to the town of Millbrook, north and east of Toronto, to watch the victorious return of the Canadian troops. Among the spoils of war on display is the church bell from the village of Batoche, its capture celebrated as the triumph of Protestant Ontario over French "papists." The image of the bell being roughly passed from soldier to soldier will be an uncomfortable memory for the girl, anticipating as it does the news that Louis Riel has been hanged. Peering out the window of the westbound train, Peggy is only now beginning to understand the bigotry of orange Ontario.

To Peggy's mind, Riel's presence can be felt everywhere on the windswept prairie that day. Balmer maintains the Métis leader was not the traitor to Canada for which he was hanged. Yet the press had discounted him as a dangerous religious fanatic who spoke in tongues. Such a penchant for exaggeration and disinformation characterized the major papers, anti-Catholic in their bias. The fact that the Canadian parliament officially thanked Middleton for the slaughter and awarded him a twenty-thousand-dollar bonus was front page news, while the question of what was to become of the Métis people, and for that matter the West itself, was ignored.

In Ottawa John A. Macdonald had turned to constructing the Dominion his corporate backers had envisaged from the beginning. His Conservative government legislated what became known as the National Policy, a combination of bold financial legislation, the construction of a transcontinental railway, immigration incentives, and protective tariffs — measures that would consolidate Eastern control of Canada's expansion westward. Meanwhile, in Battleford eight Cree warriors, including the War Chief Wandering Spirit, were hanged on November 27, 1885, the largest mass execution in Canadian history. Little Bear, Round the Sky, Bad Arrow, Miserable Man, Iron Body, Crooked Leg, and Man Without Blood. Macdonald explained the order: "We must vindicate the position of the white man; we must teach the Indians what law is."

Balmer maintained that the dream of an autonomous Indigenous nation in the West died with Riel and Wandering Spirit. So in many respects did the possibility of a peaceful Canada in the century ahead. Quebec would never forgive the outrage of Riel's execution. At a rally in the Champ de Mars in Montreal the following Sunday, a young Member of Parliament, Wilfrid Laurier, pledged his allegiance to the doomed Métis cause: "Had I been born on the banks of the Saskatchewan, I would myself have shouldered a musket to fight against the neglect of governments and the shameless greed of speculators."

When Laurier becomes prime minister eleven years later, Dumont is finally allowed to return to Canada. He operates the ferry at Gabriel's Crossing on the South Saskatchewan upstream from Batoche until his death in 1906. It takes weeks for the river to carry the news of his passing to his people, now scattered across the north, the diaspora of the defeated.

Now in its fourth day, the train journey is beginning to wear on the family. Peggy is relieved when the conductor tells Frederick that the engine will stop for coal at Blackfoot Crossing on the Bow River. The boy will have an hour to get down from the train and stretch his legs. Peggy remembers her first view of the Rockies from this same spot in the fall. As the steel wheels grind to a halt, Frederick is the first out of the carriage, racing ahead to chase a herd of Blackfoot ponies grazing by the track. Peggy lets him go, once again enchanted by the vista that opens to the west, a horizon so vast she swears she can see the curve of the earth. As the light leaves the evening sky, a passenger tells her this is the place where Crowfoot, Chief of the Blackfoot, signed Treaty 7 in 1877.

Peggy knows the story from an interview she conducted in Toronto with Richard Barrington Nevitt, once the doctor for the North West Mounted Police in nearby Fort McLeod. Nevitt showed Peggy a sketchbook of his years in the west, portraying the First Nations peoples and the landscape that had been their home. During the treaty negotiations he painted a watercolour he called "The Gloaming," a sunset from the spot where the train now stands, capturing the light as it faded over the river to the west. Peggy knows the painting well. The year they decided to come west, it had been given to Balmer as a farewell gift from Goldwin Smith, the editor of *Canadian Monthly*. A sentimental historian of the British Empire, Smith felt the painting should return to the land that had inspired it.

The day Peggy met Nevitt in Toronto, he had shown her a series of pencil sketches that recorded the signing of Treaty 7 with the Blackfoot. The doctor had understood the significance of the event, the fact that its provisions would prevent Crowfoot from being part of the Resistance. Nevitt's depiction of the day had a sombre tone, as the Blackfoot faced the inevitability of living out their days on a reserve.

Today the drawings are part of the Glenbow Museum collection in Calgary; they also formed the basis of *The Great Lone Land*, a documentary I made for History Television. In the film, historian Hugh Dempsey describes how the Crowfoot's people saw the end coming:

> They saw the steel ribbon of railway tracks which had brought such changes to their lives; they saw the homesteads and ranches which dotted the old buffalo plains; they saw the towns and villages which had sprung up during the past few years. "The Real People" had become strangers in their own land and their only haven was in the sheltered valley at Blackfoot Crossing. There Crowfoot went to die.

John Peter Turner, successor to Nevitt as doctor to the North West Mounted Police, recorded the dying Crowfoot's last words:

> A little while and I will be gone from among you, whither I cannot tell. From nowhere we came, into nowhere we go. What is life? It is the flash of a firefly in the night. It is a breath of a buffalo in the winter time. It is as the little shadow that runs across the grass and loses itself in the sunset.

In "The Gloaming" a coyote howls at the rising moon from the ridge above the Blackfoot camp. On its crest stands a single teepee, smoke curling from its top, about to be engulfed by night. Balmer would point out all these details as he recounted Crowfoot's death to me as a child. On this high ground the old chief could look out over the prairie he'd walked "in beauty" all his life, experiencing a freedom on these plains none of us will ever know.

Today the painting hangs in the front hallway of my house, a memory not only of my grandparents but of the Alberta they carried in their hearts. As the sun sets over the Rockies to the west, Nevitt's watercolour sky fades to the oblivion of night.

4

Next Year Country

And only where the forest fires have sped,
Scorching relentlessly the cool north lands,
A sweet wild flower lifts its purple head,
And, like some gentle spirit sorrow-fed.

PAULINE JOHNSON

Edmonton's
Market Square
with Mrs. English's
boarding house
to the rear,
Frederick Watt in
the foreground

The next morning, a cold wind is beginning to blow as the train turns north into the full force of winter. The homesteads it passes seem to cling to the prairie like barnacles. Peggy's doubts are already returning:

> Sitting day after day gazing at the dead level prairie; snow covered, desolate. Next to me sits a wee boy, intensely, oh so intensely, enjoying the situation. For him there is no looking back — all life lies before him — but half of mine I have left behind … I won't, oh I won't be buried in this God-forsaken country.

As the icicle-encrusted train approaches Edmonton, now hours behind schedule, the conductor announces the end of the line. Everyone will have to vacate their seats. It is well after midnight, and Frederick fights to keep his eyes open. Peggy wraps the boy in his warmest clothes to protect him from the ice fog that hangs over the settlement. She wishes she had bought more than a shawl from the Ukrainians.

The engine pulls into Strathcona, across the river from the old Hudson's Bay Company fort around which Edmonton has been built. It's twenty below, a cold front having descended from the Arctic the day before. Balmer is hardly recognizable in an old muskrat coat he has borrowed from his father in Woodstock. Peggy and Frederick set off to collect Boozer, the family dog who has travelled in the unheated baggage car at the rear of the train. Boozer is a beat-up pit bull rescued the year before when his owner, the Brantford town drunk, was found dead in his shack at the edge of town. Balmer is less than pleased Peggy has brought the dog, given the lack of accommodation in the town. He has already rented a room overlooking Market Square from a Mrs. English, with no mention of a dog. Now he fears the animal will become an issue.

As the sled approaches the valley of the North Saskatchewan River, Peggy is transfixed by the torch-lit tableau that unfolds before them.

> Cutting down the slope to the river, we came upon such a lively panorama as would astonish anyone … Teams everywhere — horses' heads touching the carts in front, apparently an unending stream of them … loads of coal and loads of gravel … and where there weren't carts there were men; men with picks chopping gravel, thawed by the aid of little fires, others loading the waiting teams … here it comes to you that existence is after all a solemn thing.

Winding down the steep banks, they cross the North Saskatchewan on the ferry run by an old-timer, Donald Ross. The floes of ice that bump and scrape the bottom are a concern as he explains the river is close to freeze-up. Peggy is both too cold and too tired to recognize this as the river of her dreams in the Paul Kane painting. By chance the ferry docks at the very spot from which the river was painted.

Finally the sled pulls up to a clapboard rooming house with a group of immigrants milling around the front door looking for a room. Balmer was right to worry. Mrs. English is a dour widow and does not take kindly to the dog. The walls and floor are bare and covered with grime, but Peggy is too tired to register her disappointment. Once Balmer has hauled her bags up the stairs, she digs out her notebooks and shows him her handwritten accounts of the trip, divided into a series of articles, enough to make up a two-page insert in the first *Saturday News*. She will name the insert "The Mirror," in effect the first women's paper to be published in western Canada. Peggy has written the entire issue on the train.

After the wonder of sleeping in a bed once again, Peggy is woken by a band playing out-of-tune below her window. Edmonton has just been named the provincial capital, no small accomplishment with the larger, more prosperous Calgary as a rival. A day of celebration has already begun. Thinking ahead to the first issue of the *Saturday News* she unpacks her camera and loads it with film. As she's still learning the ins and outs of the contraption, her photographs of the festivities are over-exposed or out of focus, but taken together they have their own charm. Society women carefully lifting their long white dresses as they tiptoe though the snow; mounted police riding in formation down Jasper Avenue; ladies of the night hurling flowers from the balcony of the Pendennis Hotel; arches of spruce bows erected over a painted banner, "Canada — Trusted, Tried, and True." The city seems to have been built overnight — riverboats, lumber mills, corrals, saloons, coal mines dug deep into the valley of the North Saskatchewan. On the high ground, livery stables, hardware stores, immigration offices, clapboard churches, and a red brick bank. Cree families look on from the edge of town, camped near the Hudson's Bay Company fort where they have come to trade furs. The makeshift community reminds Peggy of her favourite Robert Service poems describing the Klondike gold rush.

One thing Balmer quickly comes to realize is that the political calculations that made the city the capital were anything but makeshift. Centre stage at the celebrations is Frank Oliver, now minister of the interior in the federal government, the "fixer" of the legislation that created the new province. Calgary had been the obvious choice, but backroom politics in Ottawa had tilted the playing field toward the northern city. Despite the good fortune the decision represents for the *Saturday News,* Peggy has taken an instant dislike to Oliver, sensing from their first meeting that he has little time for reporters not in his hire, especially women. What's worse, he owns the rival newspaper in town, the *Bulletin*, a well-established frontier weekly that has recently become a daily. She finds it hard to believe he is a colleague of the free-thinking Laurier in Ottawa. Maybe she's been wrong about the prime minister all along?

Winter comes early that year, and it comes to stay. Peggy has never been so cold in her life as she continues to search out stories for *A Woman in the West*. Locals warn her that the temperature will drop to thirty below. One afternoon, as she listens to Oliver's promises of prosperity at an outdoor rally at the fairgrounds, she can't take her eyes off the children in the shadow of the stage, huddled from the cold. Many appear as if they haven't had a bath in weeks and their clothes, inadequate to protect them from the cold, are in tatters. Oliver repeats Laurier's promise in his speech: "the twentieth century belongs to Canada." You'd never know it by the squalor of the immigrant camps. Peggy can no longer feel her feet and walks in circles just to keep her circulation going, but nothing can protect her from the wind. As the speeches drone on, she decides to follow the children back to their parents' ragged tents along the river.

To her surprise she discovers the Galician families she met on the train, gathered around a campfire. But as they greet her there is none of the exuberance she remembers, their faces showing the desperate circumstances in which they're living. Balmer will not be pleased, but Peggy has already decided to write a very different article than the one he asked for on Oliver's speech.

Along the shore a crew of men bundled in buffalo coats is cutting ice for the hotels in town. The river is now completely frozen, and the blue blocks they hoist from its bed onto their horse-drawn wagon make her feel that much colder. From one block a frozen sturgeon, disturbed from its winter hibernation, stares back at her.

That night an exhausted Peggy returns to the overcrowded boarding house on Market Square where Balmer has convinced Mrs. English to take in Boozer as a paid customer. He can keep the dog tied up in a shed at the back. The lobby is packed with newcomers sleeping on the floor, happy just to have a roof over their heads to protect them from the cold. As Peggy squeezes into the tiny room under the eaves, she is assaulted by the shouts of the revellers who seem to have taken up permanent residence in the street below. She wonders whether these celebrations will ever end as she gathers her thoughts to write the article Balmer is waiting for:

> Over the brow of the hill in Edmonton, down the banks of the river and along the flats, I discovered where the coal camps pitch their tents, where the men who haul the sand and gravel erect their homes ... The first thing that attracted my attention was the little group of stores, quaint country-like places of trade where there were any number of farmers' wagons hitched out front, and inside you could purchase anything from a violin to a roast of beef. The families are very poor. In the window of one shack I saw a tin can with a little sprig of green. [Given the freezing cold] ... such a thing takes captive of all my curiosity ...

Peggy's first impression of the frontier had come in much more benign circumstances — the warm October night she heard Frederick Haultain describe the West's future in a by-election debate in Oxford Country, Ontario. It was the fall of 1904 when, on Pauline Johnson's recommendation, she and Balmer had come to the Woodstock Town Hall to interview Haultain about the new province he proposed to create in the west, to be called Buffalo. The proposed jurisdiction would include all of what is now Alberta and Saskatchewan, making it nearly as large as Ontario. As much as the expansiveness of his ideas impressed Peggy, she doubted such a powerful new province would be acceptable in the minds of the Ottawa mandarins who would make the decision.

Haultain's opponent that night was the ubiquitous Frank Oliver, now an advisor to the prime minister. Oliver, who tended to treat the West as a personal fiefdom, favoured two provinces: easier to control, and their administration would provide twice as many patronage appointments to hand out to his friends. Those men — and they were nearly all men — would in turn become officials in high places who could help him disenfranchise the Indigenous Peoples whose land grants had recently become of great interest to developers.

By contrast, the radical Haultain still believed in the honour of the Crown. Ever wary of the Liberals, he favoured an electoral system where political parties wouldn't even be allowed in the legis-lature — to his mind a more representative form of democracy. As premier he had instituted "non-partisan" government in the North-West Territories, eliminating the control of corrupt party managers like Oliver. Each member of the house simply represented his constituency, free of the established power centres in the East.

Haultain had grown up under the heel of the Family Compact in Ontario, the old boys' club that had crushed the Métis resist-ance. Now he was an outspoken prairie lawyer in Fort McLeod, a small town along the foothills of the Rockies, cutting a dashing figure in Peggy's eyes — the kind of rugged individual she associated with the West. Oliver, by contrast was the ultimate backroom politician, more at home in the smoke-filled rooms of Ottawa than in the Edmonton constituency he represented.

At one time or another Haultain, ever the populist, had defended every citizen in Fort McLeod, from local whiskey traders and prostitutes to wealthy ranchers and remittance men newly arrived from England. It wasn't long before he turned to politics, representing this eccentric constituency in the territorial assembly in Regina, wherever possible standing up to the Montreal and Toronto companies the Eastern establishment favoured to develop the Prairie economy. That included the controlling hand of the Canadian Pacific Railway, whose vast land grants and an exemption from federal taxes had created what amounted to a government within a government on the prairies. The company was made the sole proprietor of a strip of land a mile wide on either side of all its railway lines, effectively giving it control of property development in every railroad community. Such a monopoly might as well have been a tyranny, dependent as communities were on CPR trains to ship their goods to market.

Haultain considered such favouritism an attack on the very essence of frontier society. The survival of small businesses, even entire communities, was now at risk. Western history had been turned upside down, influenced more by the directors of Eastern corporations than the men and women who had chosen to make the Territories their home. Advertising in Europe and Asia promising a cornucopia of riches kept CPR steamships and trains loaded to capacity, but the hopeful immigrants, some having travelled halfway around the world, discovered a frontier controlled by oligarchs in top hats and waistcoats. The idea of citizens governing a society of their own making — the Last Best West described on immigration posters — had been betrayed from the beginning.

As a result the stakes in the Woodstock debate were very high. Both the independence and the authority of regional government were at stake. Peggy wrote that the very idea of a frontier society, empowered to pursue its own destiny, hung in the balance. Haultain framed his argument with the importance of the recently discovered tar sands — the enormous impact that windfall would have on the future of the territory. Like other provinces, the citizens of Buffalo should be able to control the development of that resource themselves. Oliver argued that for reasons of efficiency, it should be managed by the federal government. Both the vision and the passion of Haultain's argument were reflected in the editorial Balmer wrote the next day in the *Sentinel Review*. There was no question in his mind who spoke for the West that night.

But led by Oliver and the Department of the Interior, in the year ahead the federal government not only refused Haultain's petition for the creation of Buffalo, but effectively removed him from the process of province building in the West. That accomplished, the Liberals handily won Alberta's first election, widely rumoured to have been fixed by Oliver's gerrymandering of the electoral boundaries. Within days of the landslide (twenty-nine Liberals to three independents), Haultain, who had stood his ground against the party system, was removed from any role in the new provincial government even though he had been the premier of the Territories. The disfavour in which he was held became clear to Peggy and Balmer at the inauguration ceremonies in Edmonton. Among the swarms of dignitaries invited, Haultain was nowhere to be seen. Within days Alexander Cameron Rutherford, a lawyer originally from Montreal and lifelong Liberal, was named premier.

Haultain had fought all his adult life for provincial status and had won the trust of Albertans as he negotiated the enabling legislation for the new province. Yet he was left out in the cold, a measure of the power and corruption of party-based partisan government. With strong ties to the CPR, the treacherous Oliver could now proceed unopposed with his land development schemes and the removal of the First Nations from reserves they had only recently been awarded.

Peggy and Balmer were devastated. After all, it had been Haultain's vision of Alberta's future that had inspired the two journalists to come west. Their writing at the time contrasts the independent self-sufficient government Haultain had fought so hard to create with the hinterland Alberta was to become under the Liberals, a branch-plant economy governed from distant boardrooms. In the years ahead the colonization of the province's resource sector would only accelerate, the tar sands becoming the prototype for giving away what rightfully belonged to the people of Alberta.

> At about twenty-four miles from the Fork are some bituminous fountains, into which a pole of twenty feet long may be inserted without the least resistance. The bitumen is in a fluid state, and when mixed with gum, or the resinous substance collected from the spruce fir, serves to gum the canoes.

These are the words of explorer Alexander Mackenzie, written as he descended the Athabasca River in 1788 in search of a "western ocean" that would lead to the treasures of China. "Mackenzie's river of disappointment," as Balmer described it in one of his editorials, turned out to flow north, not west as the explorer hoped. But along the river's shores lay untold riches, far beyond what the Asia trade might have offered. Massive oil sands refineries have been built at the cost of billions of dollars to process the bitumen Mackenzie once collected in a bucket.

Tragically, in addition to their role in global warming, those refineries are a source of polycyclic aromatic hydrocarbons (PAHs) carried downstream into the drinking water of twenty-three

Indigenous communities. In Fort Chipewyan, a community on the shores of Lake Athabasca, PAHs have been linked to an abnormally high incidence of cancer since the oil sands began to be mined.

When I worked in Fort Chip in the 1970s, making my first film, *Death of a Delta*, the only access was by river or the bush plane that brought the mail once a week. The streets were unpaved and the water, cold and clear, was delivered door to door by a horse-drawn wagon. Across the lake from the town, where the Athabasca ends its long journey through the oil sands, myriad channels and sloughs fan out into what is known as the Peace–Athabasca Delta. To the west another great waterway, the Peace, feeds the complex of lakes that has formed. The delta is a World Heritage Site, one of the richest wildlife habitats in Canada and home to the traditional hunting, trapping, and fishing culture that sustains Fort Chip. Balmer made the same trip in 1910, but never reached his destination. In a sense I was finishing the journey he had been unable to complete, following the northern rivers the Métis had navigated as they fled the aftermath of their struggle for independence in 1885.

At the heart of *Death of a Delta* was a larger-than-life Métis trapper, Frank Ladouceur — in French the name means "sweetness" — whose trapline bordered one of the channels of the river, close enough to the oil sands that he could hear jets landing on the airstrips the multinationals have built on their massive leases. Frank's family had fled to the delta from northern Saskatchewan, seeking refuge from Middleton's troops. A fighter in the tradition of Gabriel Dumont — short, broad-shouldered, quick-tempered — he once pulled the local Hudson's Bay manager across the counter when the man tried to cheat him on his furs. "I was going to finish him good," Frank told me, "before my wife stepped in. She's the negotiator in the family."

Before I arrived in Fort Chip in 1971, Ladouceur had led a campaign to stop the construction of the W.A.C. Bennett Dam upstream on the Peace River in British Columbia. Like the oil sands, the dam was a massive engineering project to provide energy for the south. And like the expansion of the strip mines and refineries to come in Fort McMurray, it threatened to cut off the spring floods that sustained Frank's life as a muskrat trapper.

I remember sitting with Frank in his beat-up outboard one evening in 1975, drifting across Mamawi Lake, where the Peace feeds the delta from the west and the Athabasca from the south. We are drinking tea he has made on his tiny propane stove, at that moment precariously balanced on the boat's prow. The surface of the lake is smooth as glass, broken only by the reflections of billowing white summer clouds rising in the heat. An unseen current moves this vast water-land north toward the Rivière des Rocheurs, and ultimately to the Slave and the Mackenzie; together they form Canada's longest river system. Above us, the sky pulses with the wings of migrating pelicans, ducks, and geese. The moon rises to the east; then Venus appears directly overhead. An hour later, all is quiet as the birds settle for the night. We are floating in a time and place as ancient as nature itself, far from the world of hydro dams, strip mines, and pipelines. My thoughts returned to Peggy — here was the kind of spirit place she had searched for all her life.

A hundred years ago, Ernest Thompson Seton marvelled at the bird life that gathered along these shores:

> The morning came with a strong north wind and rain that turned to snow, and with it great flocks of birds migrating from Athabasca Lake. In addition to flocks of ducks and geese, in the hundreds of thousands; many rough legged Hawks; hundreds of small land birds and snow-birds in flocks of 20 to 200 ... passed over our heads going southward before the frost.

Today Kevin Timoney, a wildlife biologist, calls this same flyway a "mortality sink," as the delta funnels the birds south over the tar sands refineries. Thousands disappear on the journey. The vast tailings ponds look like lakes from the air, and no matter how many deterrents the companies put in place, the birds keep trying to land on what looks like water. Year after year, the migrations at which Seton marvelled have gone silent.

We return to Fort Chip by the light of the moon, Frank threading his way through the maze of channels with an invisible map passed down from his father and grandfather. GPS would be hopeless here. The delta is five hundred kilometres wide, yet often less than a foot deep, with countless places to run aground. Well after dark, we finally see two shadowy figures on the shore ahead. Frank's father, Modeste, fiddle in hand, greets us at the dock. With him is his grandson, "Big Ray" Ladouceur, armed with a bottle of whiskey.

Inside the Ladouceur cabin, the old man's moose-skin moccasins sparkle in the firelight. Each is stitched with the blossoms of an intertwined Alberta rose, beaded in a traditional Cree design. As he tunes the fiddle in the kitchen the neighbours begin to pour in. Modeste obviously has a reputation. As the old man's gnarled fingers fly up and down the strings, his feet tap out the beat of a Red River jig on the cracked linoleum. Soon the furniture has been pushed aside and a party is flowing from room to room. Sweat pouring from his brow, Frank dances with each of his twelve children. Big Ray towers above his dad but his feet move like quicksilver. This night the Ladouceur kitchen echoes with music carried into exile from the Métis homelands of 1870 and 1885. "The St. Anne's Reel," "Ciel du Manitoba," "Riel's Farewell" … each brings with it the memory of a prairie nation won and lost, an elegy for the republics mixed-blood people established on the Great Plains.

Many of the Ladouceur kids eventually took jobs in the boom towns of the south, but Ray remained in Fort Chip. After Frank's death in 1989, Ray took over the family trapline, eking out a living like his father. But a new wave of devastation was in store for the Delta. Not only the expansion of the tar sands mines, and the release of more toxins into the river, but a second massive B.C. hydro project on the Peace, the $15-billion Site C dam near Fort St. John. Scheduled to be completed in 2024, the dam will once again restrict the flow of the waters on which Fort Chip depends, the natural world with which Indigenous Peoples have co-existed for millennia looted for the profit of the south.

In October of 1907, Pauline Johnson — Tekahionwake — still living between two worlds, found herself in Edmonton, part of a national tour to release a new book of poetry. When her train arrived, she went in search of her old friend, finding Peggy in a trapper's cabin that bore little resemblance to a newspaper office. She was reassured when she saw Peggy's Brantford oak desk in the sunlight that poured through the front window. There was just enough room behind it for the battered press Balmer had managed to track down and on which Saturday's issue was being printed. When Pauline asked about the lead story, Peggy was quick to answer: Frank Oliver's cheating Indigenous people of their treaty rights across the river in Strathcona and what is now Mill Woods.

The Papaschase reserve was in theory protected by Treaty 6, but Oliver had convinced Ottawa to backpedal on its promises. In the *Saturday News* Balmer pointed out that the honour of the Crown had ceased to have much meaning in the new province. Treaty land belonging to the Papaschase First Nation had been auctioned off to land speculators in 1891 in collusion with Oliver and the federal cabinet. Pauline was flabbergasted: the treaties were supposed to last "as long as the rivers flow," not at the discretion of Ottawa politicians and the local chamber of commerce. The promises to the Papaschase people in Treaty 6 had lasted less than twenty years.

The sight of her old friend meant everything to Peggy. That afternoon she took Pauline on what had become her favourite walk beside the North Saskatchewan as it wound through the valley below the trapper's cabin. They crossed the meadow where in 1812 Marie-Anne Gaboury had built a cabin next to Fort des Prairies, later Fort Edmonton. An early settler from Quebec, via the Red River, Gaboury had been the first white woman in the region, a pioneer in her own right. The fact that Gaboury had also been Louis Riel's grandmother struck a deep chord with both women.

Peggy was interested in what was happening in Pauline's life. The subject of many rumours, her name was seldom out of the news. Travelling in the company of Walter MacRaye, an itinerant actor who performed a role in the recitation of the poems, Pauline seemed determined to offend the sexual mores of the day. In frontier communities like Edmonton, where such affairs were unheard of, she made no attempt to cover up the liaison. For Peggy, the product of a convent education, her friend's abandon was a revelation.

The hour's walk turned into an afternoon and an evening, Peggy realizing how much she had missed the company of a like-minded woman. She told Pauline about the river that flowed at their feet, the river that still occupied her dreams. This sheltered bend in the valley, broad enough to build a settlement and grow crops, had been a gathering place for Cree, Saulteaux, Blackfoot, and Sioux peoples for millennia. The banks of a nearby creek were composed of sacred white mud, kihcihkaw askî in Cree, known for its healing properties. The site had been home to powwows, sweat lodges, and talking circles, the ceremonies that settled conflict and drew the plains peoples together. A place to grow medicinal herbs, perform dances and foster alliances. Gaboury had understood the importance of such a place in building a relationship of trust with First Nations.

For Peggy and Pauline the river meant something more, the knowledge that the swift current followed a uniquely Canadian course, making its way northward toward the solitude of the Hudson Bay and the Arctic Ocean. Here in Edmonton the geography tilted away from the clamour of the United States, toward the silence of the barren lands, home to ancient Inuit cultures. With the bite of winter in the air, the clear waters of the Saskatchewan carried a sense of place that would distinguish the writing of these two unusual women.

On November 4, the last day of Pauline's visit, they attended a talk at a Canadian Club luncheon, presented by Ernest Thompson Seton, a friend of Pauline's. Known as Black Wolf to his followers, the naturalist and explorer had just returned from four months recording endangered animal and plant habitat down the Athabasca and Slave rivers, including a rare herd of wood buffalo that had survived the slaughter of the previous century. Seton was later described by the *Globe and Mail* as belonging to "that most distinctive breed: the eminent Victorian ... eccentric, strong willed, well travelled and tirelessly curious." Peggy never ceased to be amazed at the characters her friend had made the acquaintance of.

A member of the Mohawk Wolf Clan, Pauline considered Seton a kindred spirit, the two writers fighting to protect a disappearing wilderness. Seton's animal stories fascinated me as a boy, Krag the Kootenay ram, Raggylug the rabbit, and Silverspot the crow part of the animal world that peopled my imagination. Peggy was enchanted by the rough and ready naturalist that day, asking him to sign a copy of *Wild Animals I Have Known* for

Balmer, in whose library I was to discover Carcajou the wolverine fifty years later.

The visit was cut short when a message arrived from the office that a crucial bank loan to the *Saturday News* had been refused. Peggy hadn't told Pauline that the paper was on the brink of bankruptcy. She would have to knock on doors the length of Jasper Avenue that afternoon to sell more advertising. She barely had time to say goodbye to Seton and Pauline, both of whom were taking the evening train. The two women would never see each other again.

Eight years later Tekahionwake, still writing poetry, died in Vancouver of breast cancer. Peggy maintained that Pauline died as she had lived, trapped between two worlds. At her final poetry readings she would change from a Mohawk costume to a proper Victorian dress at the intermission. As the eulogies were read in a packed Vancouver church, it became clear Pauline had led a life of poverty. Ottawa's brutal regulation of the lives of Indigenous Peoples had made the life of an unmarried Métis woman precarious at best. In the years ahead her work would be attacked by both the Anglo and Indigenous establishments. Who was this daughter of an English woman to tell a First Nations story?

In the 1980s I collaborated with one of the province's most accomplished Indigenous artists, Métis filmmaker Gil Cardinal, who directed the film version of Rudy Wiebe's novel *The Temptations of Big Bear*. Cardinal and Wiebe believed that a writer's sense of place was at the heart of the creative process. Gil would understand the transcendent world of one of the last great Cree chiefs very differently from his Toronto or Los Angeles counterparts. Big Bear's vision of a distinct nation and culture, native to the prairies, in many ways anticipated Alberta's struggles with identity, of which Gil was a part, in the years ahead,

Having grown up in the vastness of the Great Plains, Big Bear had fought for a confederacy among First Nations, joining the 1885 Métis Resistance. A century later Gil had been placed in a foster home in Edmonton at the age of two when his mother died. His work had an orphan's sensitivity to the dislocation of Indigenous Peoples. With Wil Campbell and Dorothy Schreiber, he created Great Plains, one of the earliest First Nations production companies in Canada. The company produced a thirteen-part Global Television series, *My Partners, My People,* which included a portrait of Cree painter George Littlechild, who had also grown up a foster child in Edmonton. I worked on the project with Gil, aware that Littlechild's art was in the tradition of Pauline Johnson, representing the uniqueness of Indigenous culture to the outside world.

The documentary followed Littlechild as he searched for the lost legacy of his people, from Big Bear and Poundmaker, heroes of the Resistance, to his own parents, who had died in Vancouver in a flophouse on East Hastings Street. How had the story of this disinherited family travelled so far, from the Great Plains to skid row, from a proud culture to drugs and abuse? Littlechild set out to capture the journey in his paintings. The world his mother and father had abandoned haunted him, the beauty and drama of the horse culture that had once stretched from Red River to the Rockies.

In the 1990s I spent days with Gil Cardinal driving across the grasslands Tekahionwake had crossed in her travels, researching a film adaptation of her work. We imagined how strange the land must have appeared to her eye, empty of the great buffalo herds, the riders of the plains gone forever, living out their days on government reserves. Yet in that silence, where Pauline swore she could still feel the earth tremble where the hunting parties and the buffalo had once passed, I could still feel her love of this vast empty prairie.

Something so tender fills the air to-day
What it may be, or mean, no voice can say,
But all the harsh, hard things seem far away.

Something so restful lies on lake and shore,
The world seems anchored, and life's petty war
Of haste and labour gone for evermore.

Something so holy lies upon the land,
Like to a blessing from a saintly hand,
A peace we feel, though cannot understand.

I often thought of Peggy as I walked with Gil. An orphan herself, she too had set out to develop a distinct Alberta sensibility. The danger of frontier society, I realized, was forgetting who you were.

5

Peggy

Farther than vision ranges, farther than eagles fly,
Stretches the land of beauty, arches the perfect sky.
PAULINE JOHNSON

Despite the cash Balmer manages to raise from the sale of his share in the Woodstock paper, in its first year the *Saturday News* is still desperately short of capital. Balmer approaches his close friend Charles Cross, about to be appointed the attorney general of Alberta's first provincial government. Cross has the connections in the city Balmer has been desperate to find. Balmer hopes Cross will introduce the publisher to his cabinet colleagues, all potential investors. Things look up when Cross tells them Balmer was editor of the *Varsity*, the student newspaper at the University of Toronto. The fact that Mackenzie King, a reporter for the same paper in Balmer's day, has recently been appointed Laurier's minister of labour in Ottawa, confirms their interest. A number of cheques are written that night, but Cross warns Balmer the money will have strings attached — support for the policies of the new administration.

The problem, as usual, is Peggy. She has come west to write about men and women homesteading the frontier, not a fraternity of transplanted Ontario politicians. She informs Balmer that from this point forward she wants to be her own editor, refusing to write a "society" page for the wives of the investors. As if to prove the point, her first week is taken up writing about the Galician immigrants she met on the train. She has discovered them camped out in front of the land office down the street, each with a story to tell of the journey from their homeland.

Often with nothing but a suitcase to their name, the newcomers fiercely guard their place in the queue, eating and sleeping on the square yard of sidewalk they have claimed. They are waiting for the government agency to open the following week to grant title to quarter sections east of the city. There will be no charge, as long as the homesteader can clear ten acres within the year.

Moving up and down the line, Peggy is surprised at the variety of would-be settlers. From English remittance men, the disgraced sons of the aristocracy, to Scottish crofters displaced from the highlands, to American populists, rabble-rousers from as far south as Missouri, they share the dream of starting again on 160 acres of free land. But her attention remains focussed on the Galicians she describes as "sheepskins" from the coats they wear, the most ambitious of the newcomers, who have already scouted the land they hope to claim. When not holding their place in the line, they return to the tent city by the river to see to their children, many of whom have fallen ill. Sanitary conditions are so bad the health authorities suspect an outbreak of cholera might spread to the city at large. Referring to the immigrants as "undesirables," associated with European revolutionary movements, the attorney general sends the police to investigate. Peggy documents the whole affair in her column, prompting Cross to have a word with Balmer. Is it reasonable to cast the new government as a villain in its own paper?

The more Balmer advises Peggy to stay away from the camp, the more stubborn she becomes. She is determined to get to the bottom of why the government is providing so little help to the people it encouraged to come west in the first place. The articles tell the story of how families are somehow surviving the cold but make no mention of the flask of whiskey she carries in her purse to share with the most desperate.

... how you love it! How dear grows even the hardest grind of it; what good friends it brings you, what a fine broad outlook it gives you on life. For in the day's work you learn of much that is splendid and generous in humanity, even as you discover a vast deal that is base and cruel and heartless.

Correctly assuming she is referring to the government, Cross is once again on the phone to Balmer. The investors are becoming restless.

Ignoring the investors' warnings, every morning Peggy and Frederick go door to door collecting used clothes for families with young children. Most have come unprepared for the January storms that lie ahead. In the afternoons she deposits Frederick with Balmer so she can distribute the hand-me-downs in the tent city. For once Balmer is pleased she has Boozer for company. The dog has already established its reputation in the city by taking on a Great Dane twice his size at the corner of Jasper Avenue and 101 Street. No one will bother Peggy while the renowned scrapper is with her.

Boozer's favourite hunting ground is the Market Square outside their front door. Cats and mice abound in the open stables Peggy and Frederick frequent in search of donations for the tent city. The old clothes and blankets come largely from the first generation of immigrants, already established as farmers and merchants. Peggy is taken by their generosity, which in every case exceeds their means. My Uncle Ted, writing seventy years later, remembered those excursions at Boozer's side:

Market Square was the boiling point of much of Edmonton's life and Mrs. English's caravanserie [sic] was the only permanent structure standing on that full city block. Surrounding it, however, were streets solid with livery barns. Throughout the cold day there was a constant jangling of bells as tethered horses pounded their hooves on the iron earth to keep the blood coursing. Everywhere the clink of shoeing hammers, and the constant shouting of vegetable and livestock dealers fighting to be heard above a babel of languages.

The location of Mrs. English's boarding house is ideal for taking the pulse of the growing city. In the evening many of the immigrants show up at Peggy's door for a cup of tea, fortified by the plum brandy tucked away in their sheepskins. Frederick often falls asleep amidst an assortment of bodies gathered on his bed for lack of chairs.

Some days Smutty, the boy who sells the *Saturday News* at the market, becomes Peggy and Frederick's guide as they make their way through the maze of stalls. Peggy pays him her respects in one of her earliest columns:

> "Smutty" is a newsboy, so small your hand creeps to your pocket involuntarily; so unkempt and yet so cocky, you turn around to take another look at him.
>
> Smutty whistles constantly. Why shouldn't he? The thought has never come to him that he hasn't had a fair start. If he lives from hand to mouth, so do heaps of other folks! …
>
> Smutty is a little human castaway with the dirtiest face and the bravest heart in all the world.

Mrs. English shares no such sympathy for the human condition. She doesn't appreciate the constant stream of visitors, and Boozer has outworn his welcome. One morning, after a particularly late gathering, she puts her foot down, giving the family a week's notice on their room.

Secretly relieved, Peggy sets out to find an apartment. Five blocks from the market, at the far end of Jasper Avenue, the muddy main street, she finds the newly constructed McLean Block (today the home of Audreys Books). Although the Edwardian brick building is more than they can afford, she insists her husband put down a deposit. At first Balmer drags his feet, until Peggy reminds him he can always borrow the money from Charlie Cross. Surely it won't do for the publisher of an establishment newspaper to be seen living in a boarding house.

When the last carpenter has left, Peggy christens the new apartment Bohemia, in honour of a group of fun-loving immigrants from Prague, then part of the Austro-Hungarian empire, she'd met in the tent city. At last she can bring home the friends she makes on the street and offer them a chair to sit in. All her life Peggy will set an extra place at her table, for whomever she or Balmer might meet over the course of a day. As a journalist, people become her stock-in-trade.

She writes in "The Mirror" as spring approaches:

Bohemia is a triumph of the unconventional, little late suppers, unexpected guests, conversations about anything under the sun ... I could live forever in such surroundings ... If you are a new comer to the flat and are curious, you may later solve the dinner puzzle. The solution is Song Lee's little Chinese restaurant around the corner, whence emerge a celestial boy and a capacious basket ... Many an evening the apartment is full, old friends and new, strangers the hour before.

Peggy's piano fills the apartment with music, her guests dragooned into singing parts from shows popular back East. An old Irish music hall version of *The Bohemian Girl* soon becomes the house standard with Peggy singing the lead aria: "I Dreamed I

Lived in Marble Halls." The cast she assembles around her speaks for the eclectic nature of the community: the Chinese grocers from Toishan where she buys her food, Edmonton's first market gardeners; Mrs. Leondey, the Hungarian opera singer who some days can afford only a single orange to divide with her maid for supper, but who insists the peelings be saved to scent her bath; J. Burgon Bickersteth, the impeccably mannered Anglican missionary; Vilhjalmur Stefansson, the Finnish Arctic explorer who enlists Peggy's help to raise money for his voyage down the Mackenzie River; Townsend, the rakish remittance man, waiting for the cheque he can expect from his family each month as long as he never sets foot in England again.

Peggy's first prairie spring is a revelation. It's as if she has discovered a part of herself long in hibernation. Sparkling streams rush between melting snowbanks along the edges of the streets she and Frederick explore. The whole landscape seems to be tumbling toward the river. Huge flocks of snow geese, whistling swans, and sandhill cranes fill the sky.

From the market she and the boy hitch rides on hay wagons travelling to the rolling hills east of the city where her friends from the tent city have filed for homesteads. On every side a virtual army of men and women clears the forest for farms. In the small towns they gather to build one-room schools and churches from the logs they cut. Peggy describes:

> How the air transmits sounds, and what an awakening prophetic character all sounds have! The piping of birds from the nearby thicket, the distant lowing of a cow, the whirring of the wild ducks overhead, seem from out of the heart of Nature ...

One May evening, a larger-than-life figure, Peace River Jim Cornwall, shows up at Bohemia's front door, two snowshoe rabbits slung over his shoulder. Originally a bushwhacker like the rest, Cornwall has become one of the province's first successful entrepreneurs, instrumental in establishing railways, coal mines, and riverboats in the north country. As she always does, Peggy invites the stranger to supper. Cornwall offers to cook the rabbits in the fashion of the barren lands, stewed in a collection of berries he produces from his pocket. Frederick is transfixed to see the giant trapper strip the carcasses without the aid of a knife, his strong hands plucking the fur.

The meal is a triumph, and to Peggy's surprise Cornwall describes his friendship with the Métis boatmen who gave him the recipe, buffalo hunters who sought refuge in the north after Batoche. No longer Road Allowance People, the Métis are helping build towns along the route of the proposed Alberta and Great Waterways Railway, a government initiative that promises to unlock the wealth of the tar sands.

Peggy is surprised how much Balmer knows about the railway scheme. Thanks to Charles Cross, the publisher is already up to his neck in the suspect venture. With an election coming, the Liberals are preparing to promote the railway on the pages of the *Saturday News*. In the weeks that follow Balmer meets with the cabinet to discuss the railway, but a recent incident in Saskatchewan consumes the conversation. As Balmer recounts in his weekly editorial:

> The sensational feature of today's sitting of the Regina legislature was the uplifting by Premier Scott of the curtain over the events prior to the summoning of himself to form the first government of Saskatchewan. Light has been thrown for the first time on the circumstances surrounding the passing over of Haultain, then the Premier of the North-West Territories, for either the premiership of Alberta or Saskatchewan. On the night of the North

Oxford bi-election Mr. Haultain made his famous speech in which he said he would go back to the west, win one of the two provinces, and tear the constitution to pieces. Until then, went on Mr. Scott, the premiership of one of the two provinces had been intended for Mr. Haultain and he himself would have supported him in that capacity. But after his speech, it was impossible for the government to consider the Territorial Premier as a possible candidate.

The events Balmer described had taken place two years before in Woodstock, the debate between Haultain and Frank Oliver that two young reporters, Peggy and Balmer Watt, had covered for the *Brantford Expositor*.

In the cabinet controversy that followed, Rutherford and Cross supported the Saskatchewan premier, unwilling to attack a Liberal colleague, but Balmer was not so sure. To his mind the Saskatchewan premier had misled the House. As a reporter would, Balmer remembered the Woodstock incident clearly, both the letter and the spirit of Haultain's remarks, none of which were grounds for his dismissal by the Liberals. His editorial in the next issue of the *Saturday News* showed just how well he remembered:

> Mr. Scott's admission makes it plain that the choice was made in Ottawa simply for partisan purposes. The proper and constitutional course for the Lieutenant Governor to have taken would have been to retain the old Premier and wait for the people of the province to say whether they wished him to continue or not in an election. From the way Mr. Scott talks about 'tearing the constitution to pieces' one would think that Mr. Haultain contemplated a crime. If the constitution is a bad one, why shouldn't he tear it to pieces? There is altogether too much control exercised by Ottawa in these two provinces.

Rutherford defended the editorial in public: after all, it made the case for a more representative regional government, free from the control of Eastern mandarins. But behind Balmer's back, the premier was already beginning to question the dependability of the paper. A loose cannon on the pitching deck of frontier politics might not be such a good idea after all. To make matters worse, members of his cabinet were again expressing displeasure with Peggy and "The Mirror."

As their son Frederick later remembered, "For all that Balmer was a traditional Liberal ... he had quickly sensed disturbing wheels-within-wheels in the federal–provincial relationship." One can sense the presence of Peggy behind those words. She was bound and determined to protect the *Saturday News* from the influence peddling of Charles Cross. Essentially she had to protect Balmer from himself, not allowing his ambitions as a businessman to compromise his principles as a journalist. In this case she won the day, but she knew the future would hold more political pressure from Cross and the investors. It was a simple-enough fact: disinformation came with too much government influence on a newspaper. Cross had been able to convince the cabinet to stand behind Balmer this time. There was no guarantee that would be the case in the future.

Frank Oliver and the federal Liberal establishment were another matter. They would never forgive the outspoken editor for drawing attention to the skeletons in their closet. Henceforth they would do everything in their power to destroy the *Saturday News*.

6

The First Separatist

We are not urging a secession of the west from the east, but we are endeavouring to show that such a result must ensue unless a change in the system of colonial government is made in Canada.

ALWYN BRAMLEY-MOORE

Main Street of
Fort Macleod,
constituency of
Alberta advocate
Frederick Haultain

Alberta's first election had an effect on the province no one could have predicted. Twenty years after the attempts of the Métis to establish an independent republic, a radical friend of Peggy's was elected to the legislature on a separatist platform. Alwyn Bramley-Moore, a farmer from Fort Saskatchewan, was a frequent visitor to Bohemia, warning Balmer about the danger of forming too close an association with the Rutherford government.

The remarkable thing was that Bramley-Moore was a member of the Liberal Party himself. Throughout the campaign he had demanded that the province assume control over its own affairs, especially its natural resources, shaking off the paternalism and outright theft of the Ottawa bureaucracy: "separate geographical units [Alberta and Saskatchewan], regarded as colonies, are denied the most elementary rights of autonomy; it is a dangerous policy; grievances after a time engender bitterness and hatred...." Much of that hatred was already directed at Frank Oliver and the federal legislation that robbed the new province of the ownership of its oil and gas deposits. In 1907 Bramley-Moore wrote a prophetic book, *Canada and Her Colonies; Or Home Rule for Alberta*, stoking the fires of rebellion. In his argument for independence he describes what he thinks separation will entail:

A radical procedure, and rather a practical one in its way, would be to hoist the flag of independence, which would *ipso facto* make the province owner of her own resources. After a banquet or two and patriotic oratory the province might express a desire to be reinstated in the Confederation, and then she would be in a position to make a bargain. This seems the most sensible plan; there is no objection to forming a partnership with the Confederation, but there is objection to being used as a step-child and deprived of local autonomy.

Balmer takes great exception to the hare-brained scheme, accusing Bramley-Moore of manufacturing a level of discontent on the prairies that in fact does not exist.

As the arguments between the two men rage into the night, Peggy can only shake her head. To her mind the compromise of confederation is still the best path. The rhetoric of independence will only attract a lunatic fringe — people willing to jeopardize the give-and-take of Canadian politics. In the years ahead she will support a variety of radical political movements in the province, but her dedication to Canada will never waver.

One afternoon Bramley-Moore discovers a dead badger on the road as he drives into the city. When he stops he hears the cries of the mother's baby in the ditch. Knowing Peggy's love of animals, he wraps the baby in his coat and takes it to town. Over Balmer's protests Peggy immediately adopts the creature, christening it Badgie. As it grows to full size it becomes inseparable from Boozer. Together they form the most feared tag team in the city.

Within a decade Balmer's arguments with Bramley-Moore will be brought to a tragic end. When war breaks out, Bramley-Moore signs up to fight for King and Country, only to be killed by a sniper's bullet in France. Until William Aberhart in 1935, the spectre of Alberta separatism will lie dormant.

Peggy and Frederick continue to visit the tent city, exploring the remains of the racetrack by the river where Laurier declared Alberta a province. It is another bitterly cold day. An eclectic assembly of "new Canadians" gathers around campfires: Chinese railway workers, Scots-Irish sharecroppers, factory workers from the English midlands, Russian Jews fleeing the pogroms, and the ever-present Galicians. If surviving their first Canadian winter wasn't challenge enough for the immigrants, the world economy is moving into recession and jobs are scarce. Peace River Jim's American-brokered Alberta and Great Waterways Railway scheme, funded in part by the provincial government, a boondoggle engineered by Charlie Cross, promises to set things straight. But rumours persist that its financing is on shaky ground. Balmer is seldom at home before midnight as the government reluctantly turns to the *Saturday News* for damage control.

In the midst of the tent city, Peggy notices a man with an ungainly box camera documenting camp life. "Ernest Brown, Everything Photographic" is written on a suitcase packed with equipment, carried by a female colleague. The closer Peggy gets the more eccentric the man appears — frumpily dressed, his hair dishevelled, a cigar protruding from his mouth. If it had been ten years later he would have reminded her of Charlie Chaplin. When she introduces herself, he brusquely tells her he is from Middlesbrough, in northern England, where he was a trade union organizer. It is as if he is challenging her with the information.

His partner, Gladys Reeves, is young enough to be his daughter. She smiles at Brown's gruff manner before disappearing beneath the black cloth that covers the camera to take a picture of Peggy. Beside her is a case of eight-by-eleven-inch glass plates on which the images are recorded -a far cry from Peggy's pocket-sized Kodak.

Gathered around a campfire with Brown, Peggy recognizes the sheepskins of a new wave of Galician families. As she greets them, Brown introduces her to a stranger in their midst dressed in a tweed suit. The man introduces himself as Petro Svarych and explains he is the group's land agent, hired by the railway to see them safely to their destination. Of Ukrainian descent but educated in Vienna, Svarych has impeccable English. Like Brown he describes himself as a socialist, although he is an organizer for the Liberal Party, part of a small community of expatriates who see the frontier as the opportunity to create a new social order.

As she looks at the pale-faced children huddled around the fire, Peggy expresses her doubts about the practicality of his ideas. Brown comes to the agent's defence, describing the immigrants from many countries who are working together to construct an egalitarian society on the prairies. Many of the ideas come from farmers arriving from the United States, members of the Non-Partisan League. Disgruntled with the monopoly enjoyed by the railways and grain exchanges of Chicago and Minneapolis, they have come to Alberta to explore new ways to market their crops. Brown is quick to point out Svarych's ideas have emerged from this commonwealth of interests, not the class-based revolution of Marx and Engels. The encounter introduces Peggy to the radical ideas that swirl beneath the placid surface of the Edmonton establishment.

Peggy asks Gladys whether she can purchase one of her photographs to accompany the story she's writing. Brown wants to know who this suspicious-looking journalist is working for, "hopefully not the damned government." But once Peggy describes the threadbare newspaper she and Balmer are running, and her own aversion to the Liberals, Brown reluctantly agrees. In return she offers to write a story on the portfolio on immigration he is assembling, titled "The Birth of the West."

When Peggy returns to the office, Balmer is not pleased by the agreement she has made with Brown. Not only is the man

considered a pariah in the community for his relationship with
Gladys Reeves, but Cross has warned Balmer to steer clear of people
who could tarnish the reputation of the newspaper in the business
community — in other words, socialists. Peggy reminds her husband that it's *her* article in *her* column in which the image is to
appear. She'll choose whatever photograph she pleases.

The ensuing altercation is the beginning of a deeper rift
between the two journalists. Like Gladys Reeves and Ernest Brown,
Peggy fears the increasing control of big business on the frontier.
Her first intimation of what lies ahead comes on a spring morning
in 1908 when she photographs two old men enjoying a cup of tea at
the Catholic mission in St. Albert, twenty miles north of Edmonton.
On assignment for the *Saturday News*, she's writing a story about
the meeting of Father Albert Lacombe, the retired missionary, and
Donald Smith, whom she recognizes as the man who drove the last
spike in Canada's first transcontinental railway, the CPR. Smith has
since become the founder of Anglo-Persian Oil in London, later
British Petroleum, a major player in the energy economy worldwide.

As the two men talk Peggy realizes it was Smith who negotiated
with Louis Riel during the 1870 uprising in Manitoba, convincing
the Métis to withdraw their demands for independence. Likewise, it
had been Father Lacombe who convinced Crowfoot not to join the
First Nations alliance at Batoche in 1885. In both cases a place in the
rapidly expanding colonial economy was held out as the reward for
compliance. But as it has turned out, that economy was designed
for the maximum profit of an Eastern establishment, not the welfare of Indigenous Peoples. Railways, then oil and gas, would bring
short-term economic booms to the West, but in the long term society would continue to be divided between the rich and the poor.

Peggy realizes each man had been instrumental in winning the
West for John A. Macdonald. As a railway magnate on his way to
becoming an oil tycoon, Smith had become Sir Donald Smith, Lord

Strathcona, instrumental in transporting troops and guns from Ontario to crush the Resistance of 1885. Lacombe had chosen God as the messenger to convince the First Nations that they should cede their land to the Dominion.

Needless to say, Crowfoot's decision was a disaster, ushering in the tyranny of centralized government and the paternalism of the missionaries. There had been many promises, but as Peggy walked back to her car, the St. Albert residential school loomed above her, the real outcome for Indigenous Peoples. As she told Balmer that night, they seemed strange bedfellows — the Catholic Church and the petroleum industry — sacred and lethal. Balmer was not amused, once again reminding her they were running a business. Men like Donald Smith could make or break them.

When my mother, Naomi Rebecca — Becky — is born later that year, Peggy goes on leave from the paper. Balmer thinks it's time for her to get to know the better class of person arriving from the East, attracted by jobs in the new provincial capital. Thanks to Charlie Cross, the *Saturday News* is now the paper of choice among the men and women who matter in the city. It is high time Peggy recognized the fact.

But to Balmer's disappointment, the result of Peggy's leave is just the opposite. With time on her hands, she becomes a regular at Brown's studio, where experiments in "natural photography" are under way, Gladys posing naked in front of various backdrops Brown has painted, from classical Greece to *The Last of the Mohicans*. Peggy's heart goes out to Gladys. It feels colder inside the building than on the street outside as the young woman huddles in front of the camera. Brown explains they are having difficulty keeping up with the gas bills. Whatever the case, Peggy tells them she thinks the frost on the inside of the windows adds to the artistic effect.

Brown's helter-skelter projects are reminiscent of Peggy's early days at the convent in Toronto. Forever curious, she had studied poetry, elocution, drawing, vocal music, harp, and piano as well as turning the drawing room into a stage for an amateur theatre company. On graduation she had moved in with an aunt in Toronto so she could study at the Royal Conservatory of Music. She had set herself the goal of being the first woman to play the piano with the Toronto Symphony, but soon discovered the chauvinism of the day would make that dream impossible. She would have to find a more practical way of making a living. With the remainder of the trust money her grandfather had left her, she enrolled at the Brantford Ladies College, where the curriculum stressed the arts, especially writing. It would be the ideal preparation for a career in journalism.

But as in the convent, Bible studies were never far away.

It is earnestly desired that this institution may be distinguished for its religious influences and character … and that all the excellences of a noble Christian womanhood, with its needful safeguards, may be diligently cultivated.

For Peggy such admonition was beside the point. Within weeks she had met Balmer, and as her first romance caught fire, all the "needful safeguards" of the women's college fell by the wayside. As with everything else she had been denied in the convent, there would be no half measures.

Now editor of the *St. Thomas Journal,* her beau had moved into a small apartment in town. He confessed to his diary on January 5, 1898: "Gertrude has been visiting here and went home today. I have spent almost all my leisure time with her … in all my intimacy I have acted as a man, not a boy." By spring the love affair was in full bloom, the two journalists arranging their weekly assignments around the chance to spend time together.

And then disaster struck. Andrew Pattullo, Balmer's uncle, the owner of the *Woodstock Sentinel Review,* killed himself, forcing Balmer to return to Woodstock to manage the paper. Pattullo had been embroiled in a political intrigue in England, had run for political office to vindicate his name, but was disgraced by the result. When his will was read, to the shock of everyone present, the majority of shares in the paper went to his young nephew, Balmer Watt. It was an odd choice. Balmer had often provoked the displeasure of his uncle, maintaining that the paper was too beholden to advertisers and local politicians. Now it was the young idealist who would have to find a way to make the struggling paper pay. His decision to marry Peggy came as much from desperation as dedication. The challenge of saving the paper was far more than he could handle alone.

A year after their marriage at St. Andrew's Presbyterian Church in Guelph, Balmer still couldn't afford to buy Peggy a proper ring. Nonetheless, the two journalists had their first child, Frederick, and Peggy began to write a column for the *Sentinel Review.* From the outset, it was her goal to reflect politics and culture strictly from a woman's point of view. She had a habit of stirring the pot, attacking the men who ran the town, much to the chagrin of Balmer, who depended on their businesses for advertising. He begged her to tone down her crusade. Peggy wrote in her column the next day, "Candour is a virtue for which women pay most dearly."

It was little wonder she became a follower of Kit Coleman, the leading woman journalist in Toronto, eventually a fellow member of the Canadian Women's Press Club. Peggy was fond of quoting Kit's observation of the challenge women faced:

Why do men look ashamed if they are caught reading the woman's page in a newspaper? Are women utter idiots? Do men believe that there is not a word to be written for our sex beyond frills and fopperies. And besides: Literature would pay better if there were not so many dead men still in the business of hogging the customers.

In the years ahead Peggy would realize there were many such men in Edmonton, dead and alive.

Saturday

AN ALBERTAN WEEKLY REVIEW

INDUSTRY ENERGY ENT

EDMONTON, ALBERTA, SATURDAY, JANUARY 21st, 1911.

Miss Kathleen Parlow

Every-
tretch the
area. The
son's Bay
miles close
hich is all
a crime.
ch an ex-
d-George's
eal heare
privilege:
gives such
petus and
the spread
led social-
ize where
s. Great
or in any
requires,
these are
tem which
spring up

son's Bay
aking Ed
administer
g of the
ops four
direction

large expense t
many other de
sources, is not

The high lev
in the west end
there. In fact
owners in that
to have it buil
five years ago,
was the chair
Trade commit
strong recomm
fect. But the c
the citizens. T
mined to come
it is now buildi
to have high-
without standin
ly itself, it ha
railway's plans.
sent under co
access to the
part of the co
the river fro
should draw t
Edmonton and
one place, rega
nicipal union e
were the obje
prime importan
ing so recently
obligation in c
it does not loo
rush into anoth
the present tin
Considering

7

Balmer

A newspaper that is true to its purpose
concerns itself not only with the way things
are but with the way they ought to be.

JOSEPH PULITZER

Balmer's first
independent
newspaper on
the frontier

Although one would never know it from his quiet demeanour, Balmer shared his wife's contrary nature. He claimed he came by it honestly, from British patriots who had defied the American revolution and claimed sanctuary in the northern half of the continent. He took his name from his own mother, Rebecca Balmer, the granddaughter of United Empire Loyalists who had given up a respectable place in New Jersey society to choose what would one day become Canada. The family name had originated in France as *palmer*, a pilgrim who carried palms back from the Holy Land. Stubborn and excitable, his ancestors tended to pick fights on principle, and on that account often had to move their place of residence in great haste.

When I was a boy, Balmer showed me the diary of a distant cousin, Samuel Curwen, written as he fled the first shots fired in the War of Independence:

> April 23, 1775. Salem, Massachusetts. Since the late unhappy affair at Concord, finding the spirit of the people to rise on every fresh alarm which has been almost hourly, and their tempers to grow more and more sour and malevolent against those whom they see fit to reproach as enemies of their Country, amongst which number I am

unhappily though unjustly ranked ... I think it a duty I
owe myself to seek some secure asylum, if to be found
in America.

Curwen was a New England district judge with little regard for the
Paul Reveres of this world: "a people licentious and enthousiastic-
ally mad and broke loose from all restraints of Law." And yet he
was no Tory, his family having come to Massachusetts in 1638 to
escape religious persecution in England. He had a nose for tyranny
and a free-thinking perspective on the possibilities the so-called
New World afforded. He shared many of the reformist sentiments
of the rebels but believed that in respecting the traditions of parliamentary democracy the colonists could enjoy the best of both
worlds. Curwen was caught between the values his ancestors had
crossed an ocean to protect and an expansive, violent United States.
It would prove a difficult balancing act.

His father, Captain George Curwen, had led an armed expedition "to exterminate the Indians" inland from the coast, a precursor
of the century of slaughter to come. He had also been a judge at the
Salem witch trials, seeking to root out the "inherently sinful nature
of women, like the Indians susceptible to the devil and damnation."
The world of the Massachusetts Colony, in his mind, was divided
between the righteousness of good Christians and the devil worship
of aliens. Never did it strike him that *he* may have been the alien, as
Balmer was quick to point out as he recounted the family history.

But progress was possible. George had been a tyrant. Samuel
was forced into exile for defending a parliamentary tradition. But in
coming west Balmer and Peggy had sought to establish an entirely
new world, although once again it would be at the expense of
Indigenous Peoples. The idea of next year country, in Canada at
least, was to reach beyond the established power of a rapacious
economy that had stratified society and made inequality its legacy.
In moving ever westward, for a time history was a progressive force.

One of Samuel's duties as a judge was to ensure the enforce-ment of the Royal Proclamation of 1763, signed by George III, intended to protect the tribes of the interior from the merchants of Boston and New York. Despite the depredations of the colonists, the King and Parliament recognized the rights of First Nations to live undisturbed in their own territory across the Appalachian Mountains. Their sovereignty was as important to consider as that of the Crown.

The Proclamation was to be the cornerstone on which the treaty rights of First Nations in Canada would be recognized for centuries to come. Although it was ignored, even vilified in the United States, the document provided a legal precedent for pro-tecting the rights of Indigenous Peoples, to this day providing the power to keep oil companies off their land. Yet in the American colonies the Proclamation simply became an incitement to revolu-tion. Land grabbers and the agents of a genocide that would last for the next century became "patriots." The fact that the Crown made it illegal for traders and land developers to lay claim to Indigenous territory was an affront to "the rights of man." The blatant self-interest of manifest destiny, of "making the world safe for democ-racy," was about to be unleashed on an unsuspecting world.

The Balmers were fortunate to avoid attack as they made their way from New Jersey to what is now Ontario. As United Empire Loyalists they were given the protection of the British troops they encountered en route, but much of the time they were on their own. A loner by nature, Samuel Curwen had decided to chart his own course, catching the last ship from Philadelphia to London, bypassing Canada altogether. In years to come, his diaries recorded life on the margins of the English capital where the refugees from America had gathered. The eccentric cast of characters he docu-mented was of such interest that his diaries were published — to be discovered by Charles Dickens a century later. In novels like

Great Expectations, the Victorian novelist based his own displaced characters on the predicament of these exiles.

When the larger part of the family arrived in the newly created settlement of York, now Toronto, they were awarded a homestead grant by the British government. A quarter section of farmland just north of the village proper, at the corner of two country roads named Bloor and Yonge. It was a miserable location, with poor soil and nothing in the way of society to recommend it. Within a year they sold the property for sixty guineas to help start a newspaper in Brantford, ninety miles to the west. It was only later generations of the family that regretted the decision, when the land they sold became the most valuable single piece of real estate in Canada, the heart of the future city.

Fond of argument, the Balmers and the Watt family they married into found journalism a perfect fit. In the years that followed, they moved from one respectable town to another in southwestern Ontario, starting newspapers, selling them, starting others. They took pride in the tight operating budgets and the appetite for controversy they brought to the papers, often challenging the ruling Family Compact on political matters. They always sold their last investment for a small profit, "waste not, want not" having become a family tradition. It didn't always work in their favour. In Brantford they were neighbours to a fellow Scot, Alexander Graham Bell, who offered to sell them a ten percent share in a newfangled talking device. They declined. It seemed the family's fate was to remain outside the mainstream.

By 1908 Edmonton's population had grown to 24,000, most of them expectant newcomers. The massive High Level Bridge was being built over the North Saskatchewan, allowing a streetcar line, the Radial Railway, to connect the two halves of the city. The old fort had been torn down, to be replaced by a legislature building worthy of a European capital. Sections of Jasper Avenue had been paved for the advent of the motor car, and the *Saturday News* had moved to an office block that could house a larger printing press. With continued investment from Charles Cross and his associates, business was flourishing. Balmer convinced Peggy it was time to buy a house in a district adjacent to the Legislature on 107 Street. Uncle Ted described the change the move made in their lives:

> Within two blocks lived a number of the most vital and controversial figures in the soon-to-be stormy record of Alberta politics, men whose lives would be marked by unending conflict, and in some cases, by tragedy. Charlie Cross was one of them.

The change of address did nothing to improve Peggy's frame of mind. Balmer's defence of the establishment, especially Donald Smith and Father Lacombe, continued to rankle. And despite the attorney general's displeasure, she continued to keep the company of "that scarlet woman," Gladys Reeves, who had opened her own photography business down the street. It seemed that downtown was changing with every passing day, the sea of log cabins and livery stables replaced by orderly avenues. Architects had been brought in to design handsome brick buildings, laid out in elaborate plans befitting a capital city. As each new edifice reached skyward, Gladys would be hired to record its progress, making her the province's first female professional photographer. Soon she was collaborating with Peggy regularly, her pictures of the tent city illustrating articles in "The Mirror," much to the horror of the investors in the *Saturday News*. Peggy was both inspired by Gladys's success and increasingly disenchanted with Balmer's attitude toward her. Was the fair-minded journalist she married growing to be like the men she met every day, rough and ready entrepreneurs? God forbid, he had even joined the Chamber of Commerce.

"Miss Reeves" continued to live openly with Ernest Brown, a transgression that alarmed Judge Emily Murphy and the Daughters of the British Empire, guardians of the city's morals. Mrs. Brown and her son were living next door, only added to the sense of outrage. But despite the slander spoken against him, Brown treated Gladys with great respect, making her an equal partner in his business. Not that a share in "Everything Photographic" counted for much. The firm's heating bills still went unpaid.

I interviewed Gladys for the film *Ernest Brown, Pioneer Photographer* a year before her death in 1974. She remembered her last winter in the building:

> No amount of activity could keep the studio warm, and I had to put bricks in the wood stove to put under my feet while I sat retouching photographs. Mr. Brown came in one day and was very put out because his cigar had frozen in his mouth.

Peggy was increasingly fascinated by Gladys and Brown's "audiovisual" project *The Birth of the West,* a lantern slide presentation designed to teach Albertans their own history. Photographs projected on a screen were accompanied by Brown's narration as he operated a magic lantern. As the story of the province unfolded, the music of a live chamber orchestra underscored the drama — immigrants huddled in the tent city juxtaposed with Indigenous people moving at their will across the open prairie, navvies building the railways with the voyageurs of the fur trade — creating a pageant of inclusion like the chautauquas of the next decade. But as always with Brown, a broader political subtext informed the narrative — who gained the most from an economy managed by the cabal of bureaucrats and Eastern corporations he loathed?

Peggy soon realized that Gladys and Brown were not alone. Across Alberta populist movements were springing up to challenge premier Alexander Cameron Rutherford, Charles Cross, and the lawyers who ran the province. Men and women who realized they had been left out of the political system began to organize a de facto opposition, meeting in the schools and community halls they had built across the province.

In the years ahead, when his photography business went bankrupt, Brown would run for a seat in the legislature as an independent labour candidate in Vegreville, a constituency sixty miles east of Edmonton where Galician immigrants had settled. Gladys hoped their socialist politics would give his campaign an outside chance, and she and Peggy worked long hours, travelling down treacherous gumbo roads 'til dusk, knocking on the doors of isolated farms who had no idea of who Brown was. Worse, the long arm of the Edmonton establishment continued to follow the itinerant photographer wherever he went. Victim of a chamber of commerce smear campaign, including rumours of illicit nude photos, he lost badly.

But the campaign was an elixir for Peggy, getting her out of the city, putting her back in touch with ordinary Albertans and the landscape she adored. Sunrise to sunset she soaked up the green pastures and rolling hills east of the city. She was amazed at how quickly the homesteaders had established the Last Best West of their dreams, no matter how rugged the quarter section they had chosen. Each town had a thriving main street, merchants of every description setting up shop, and if you were lucky, you could even find a copy of this week's *Saturday News*. She wrote her aunt in Toronto:

> This year the paper is firmly established; kind friends are legion; Edmonton has become the dearest place in the world. I no longer utter a mental protest against the prairies as our final resting place. Our western life is too real, too vital to waste time in gloomy speculation. It is enough that you are alive and can take your chances in the great future that lies ahead.

8

Scandal

As the flight of a river
That flows to the sea
My soul rushes ever
In tumult to thee.

EDWARD BULWER-LYTTON

As her marriage to
Balmer collapsed,
Peggy was to
be found in the
company of the
community's most
eligible bachelors

Alberta booms in those first years always seemed about to bust. In 1910, as suddenly as it had prospered, the *Saturday News* returned to a state of crisis as once again the economy faltered. The collapse of international grain prices had thrown the region into deep recession. Balmer did his best to cut costs, but the ground gave way under him when a pressmen's strike reduced the paper from twelve pages to four. The decision forced him to turn away the majority of the advertising he and Peggy had worked so hard to sell. As revenues slipped further, against Peggy's advice he had no choice but to go back to Charlie Cross and the Liberal investors.

She warned him that each time he took their money it would come at a greater price to the integrity of the paper. This time the *quid pro quo* with Cross was for the paper to pull back on its coverage of a railway scandal that was embarrassing the government. The financing of Peace River Jim Cornwall's Alberta and Great Waterways Railway had been contracted to a Kansas City banker, William Clarke. The problem, at least as the opposition in the legislature saw it, was that the banker in turn had offered preferred shares to members of the government.

But with the latest round of investment in the *Saturday News* already in the bank, Balmer had little choice but to tell his reporters to back off the story. Peggy reminded him that human endeavours are begun by men with great souls and little breeches pockets and ended by men with great breeches pockets and little souls. She disliked Cross as much as he disliked her, a state of affairs that was beginning to play havoc with her marriage. Not only had Cross bailed out the paper; he had convinced Balmer to expand the business to include a printing plant capable of producing a daily paper to compete with the *Edmonton Journal*, which had been founded in 1903 by three Manitoba entrepreneurs. Essentially Cross was making his old friend more a publisher than an editor, a transformation that angered Peggy despite the increased revenue. They had come west to launch an independent paper capable of challenging the political establishment, not to run a printing plant. Yet Balmer persisted. Having seen his uncle's paper fail in Woodstock, he was determined to make the News Publishing Company a commercial success.

When the marriage least could afford it, disaster struck on the home front. Always hostile toward Peggy and her strange friends, a trigger-happy neighbour shot both Badgie and Boozer for trespassing in his yard. Here in one calculated personal attack was the other side of frontier life, the settler who saw both Peggy and the natural world as his enemy. Peggy tried to be philosophical. Balmer had warned her not to let them run loose. But as the days past she found herself devastated at the loss. Boozer had been her companion through the great changes in her life moving west, a constant presence in an ever-changing world. Like Peggy he was the veteran of many battles, a scrapper with every dog in town.

The next day she bumped into an old acquaintance on Jasper Avenue: William Aberhart, the Ontario preacher who one day would become Alberta's seventh premier. She had first met the rotund man of God in Brantford a decade before when they had struck up an unlikely friendship based on a mutual distrust of the burgeoning industrial society they lived in. He had no idea how important the hug he gave her that day was.

In 1904 Peggy had been in the congregation of Zion Presbyterian Church when Aberhart delivered a guest sermon on "the rapture," the wrath of God. The collapse of the Tower of Babel, expulsion from the Garden of Eden, return of the Great Flood to drown civilization — Peggy could only smile as the young firebrand listed the catastrophes to come. On second thought she decided it would make a good column for the paper, especially when he warned the sleepy Ontario town their world would end in the next thousand days. He assured the congregation that as good Christians they would all ascend to heaven, "leaving the forces of evil to destroy themselves and the planet in a final apocalypse. This glorious event is just at hand, understand me please, the Rapture of this church may happen tonight. You may never see another sunrise."

Aberhart was running a bible camp outside of Brantford, ironically called Tranquility. But the young preacher was making plans to move to Calgary before the conflagration descended. He told Peggy the chances of being among the saved were greater on the western frontier, where at least one could avoid being confused for an Ontario banker. Now here he was, a lowly high school teacher on the frontier marking exams for the Department of Education. The next year he was to become principal of the Alexandra Public School in Calgary and would help found the Prophetic Bible Institute, a forerunner of the Social Credit movement on the prairies.

As the press strike ends and the economy picks up, the *Saturday News* once again begins to pay dividends, encouraging Cross to complete the financing of a Liberal daily, the *Capitol*, with Balmer as its editor. Increased revenues will allow a business manager to be brought on board to oversee the expansion of the printing plant, and for the first time the editorial, managerial, and mechanical operations will be brought under one roof. Peggy is noticeably absent from the ribbon-cutting ceremonies.

The first edition of the *Capitol* rolls off the presses January 11, 1910. Charles Cross and Peace River Jim are the lead investors, and the Alberta and Great Waterways Railway is the lead story. Cross finally has the daily opportunity to advance the government's position on the controversy. But he has misjudged Balmer, who is still very much an editor as well as a publisher. The stories from the news desk document Liberal policy in great detail, but the editorial page, at Peggy's insistence, retains its independence.

Balmer has become an astute businessman, but he's still a newspaperman for whom the integrity of what he writes is paramount. Yes, the railway is crucial to the province's future, but it has been badly conceived and is being built on unsound ground, its tracks sinking into the muskeg north of the city. The cost overruns that result are the talk of the town — the paper can hardly avoid reporting them. In the days that follow, considerable tension develops between the editor and the *Capitol's* investors. As Peggy feared, to their mind the paper's editorials have already crossed a line, questioning the financial feasibility of the scheme in the first place.

Cross takes Balmer aside to tell him the railway is becoming as contentious within Rutherford's cabinet as it is in the legislature. A breakaway caucus from southern Alberta is threatening to split the Liberal party. In Calgary the bitterness over Edmonton having been chosen the capital is now out in the open. Cross insists that in the event of an insurrection among the backbenchers, the *Capitol* will have to support the premier. Balmer is caught in the middle, reporting events as they unfold as objectively as he can, but still beholden to Cross for the funds to operate the paper.

Fighting for his political life, Premier Rutherford announces in the legislature: that he will establish a Department of Railways and make it one of the most important departments of the government. If Ottawa will not help him, he will do it himself. Balmer worries about the competence of the new department. His reporters tell him that the construction through the muskeg country has become a disaster. It's clear the American contractors have little experience with northern geography.

Inside the legislature press gallery, Peggy watches Cross and Rutherford's backroom dealings become the centre of the province's first political scandal. The Conservative leader, Calgary lawyer and future Canadian prime minister R.B. Bennett, has discovered something amiss with the government bonds the Liberals have issued. He accuses the premier and the attorney general of exploiting their offices for personal gain. Under particular scrutiny is Cross's relationship to the government's American partners, William and Richard Clarke, whom Bennett maintains have made off with taxpayers' money.

Peggy writes in her column,

> Mr. Bennett is the matinee idol of the House. We of the gallery — well, he wakes us up, for which accept our thanks. You see, I am only a woman ... a voteless being, and, as such, I have direct orders from the editor to leave politics alone.

Cross warns Balmer that her column is going to have to go if she keeps up the backbiting commentary. The Conservatives have already called for an investigation into Rutherford and Cross's conflict of interest, and Calgary Liberals are joining demands for the premier's resignation. With a wholesale revolt within the party looming, Rutherford is forced to ask his attorney general to step down.

In the days ahead the Calgary–Edmonton split deepens. Rutherford barely survives a series of non-confidence votes led by his own backbenchers. Public support for the government evaporates, and a judicial commission is appointed to investigate the affair. Too late, Balmer tells his readers: "Never has a Canadian political leader shown such weakness in an emergency. The Rutherford administration is to all intents and purposes a thing of the past. A struggle of appalling bitterness has ensued."

As the Liberal caucus turns on itself in the spring of 1910, Charles Cross has a tightrope of his own to walk. When Rutherford finally falls, there's a moment when he might succeed him as premier, but Frank Oliver still wields enough power as Laurier's minister of the interior to block the appointment. On May 26, Lieutenant Governor George Bulyea appoints Arthur Sifton of Calgary as the new leader of the government, along with a slate of new ministers. Sifton, Alberta's Chief Justice, is an old-school Liberal Ottawa can trust.

But the scandal is far from over. William and Richard Clarke, the Americans who sold the railway bonds, refuse to testify before the Royal Commission. Balmer simply reports their unusual decision, trying to avoid the wrath of the government in his editorials. But even that admission is seen as provocative by Sifton. Within days the new provincial government joins Oliver in the campaign against the *Capitol* and the *Saturday News*. Everything Peggy and Balmer have worked for is suddenly in jeopardy.

My Uncle Ted remembered the strain on his parents as each night they sat in the kitchen recounting the day's events in the legislature. Across the street, in the sprawling mansion of the attorney general, the curtains are drawn. Balmer's principal investor, Charles Cross, no longer a friend, plots his revenge.

In parliament, separatist Alf Bramley-Moore questions Frank Oliver and the federal government's role in the railway scandal:

> As a member of the Alberta Legislature I could not fail from being deeply influenced by witnessing the total overthrow of the Rutherford government on account of their efforts to open up the northern portions of the province ... the injustice of a state of affairs by which a provincial government assumes the liabilities incident to the development of a vast country while the natural resources of that country are owned and controlled by a foreign government [Ottawa]. The province undertook to assist in the construction of a railroad into regions where every square inch of land, every stick of timber, every pound of mineral belonged to the federal government.

Laurier's inclusive vision of the nation in 1905 has been replaced by a politics of suspicion and mistrust. The seeds have been sown for a century of Alberta alienation.

On February 16, 1912, the resilient Charles Cross accepts Premier Sifton's invitation to be sworn in again as attorney general of Alberta. Under the headlines "The Issue Before Alberta" and "Northern Expansion of the Economy," the *Saturday News* and the *Capitol* express optimism that with Cross again in office the railway to Fort McMurray will proceed as planned, this time on a firmer footing. But Balmer's willingness to let bygones be bygones is not reciprocated by the attorney general. Peggy is convinced that Cross is advising his fellow investors against the new share issue on which Balmer's future depends.

Lack of funds has once again reduced the *Saturday News* to eight pages. The April 20 issue carries the news of the sinking of the *Titanic* and the death of 1,635 of its crew and passengers. An English investor Peggy had once taken to lunch is among the victims. She breaks down at the news, convinced it is a portent of what lies ahead for the paper.

Supporters like Alex Crosby, an old friend from university days who had moved to London, step up with additional funds, but they are few and far between. Likewise the well-wishers who go out of their way to buy additional advertising in the paper. When the situation seems beyond hope, Peggy raises the possibility of the publishing company declaring bankruptcy and making a fresh start — only to receive a polite smile and a shake of the head from Balmer. In his Scottish view of the world, debt is debt, something to be repaid regardless of time and circumstance.

It is only a matter of days before Cross withdraws his investment from the papers. Other Liberal investors quickly follow suit. Within a week the business is insolvent. Balmer gets on a train to Toronto in a desperate attempt to raise new money. Two days later, outside Flint, Michigan, a freight runs a signal and hits his train head on. The cars fly from the tracks and burst into flame. Balmer is knocked unconscious when he's thrown from his bunk. He wakes to find that the shattered engine has jack-knifed and landed upside down on the roof of his car. All around him its boilers are shooting clouds of burning steam into the sleeping compartments. He tries to force his way out, but finding no means of exit, climbs back to his berth to escape being smothered by the steam. The heat soon becomes unbearable, forcing him to reverse his steps. He stumbles half blind through the inferno until he feels a breath of air. On his last legs he makes for it, plunging through a broken window onto the tracks. Burnt from head to toe, he is the only passenger in the car to survive.

Balmer was taken to a hospital in nearby Flint. The prognosis the doctors telegraphed to Peggy was grim. As she boarded the first train east, another long journey across the Great Plains lay ahead. She had little reason to expect to find her husband alive. Yet three days later he woke up to discover her at his side. She remained with him a week, until he was out of danger, then caught the train home to do what she could to save the papers. In the September 10 issue of the *Saturday News*, she told "The Tale of the Yellow Journalist," a title conferred on her husband by his fellow patients because of his saffron colour following burn treatment with picric acid.

There was nothing Peggy could do to rescue her husband's interest in the *Capitol*. Cross and the board of directors had taken advantage of Balmer's absence to remove him as managing director. He no longer had any say in the future of the paper. A story on the front page announced that the business had been sold to Mr. William McAdams, who confirmed the next day on the editorial page,

> In order that there may be no misapprehension about the policy of the paper, *The Capitol* will be supporting the provincial Liberal Party. This explanation is made for the reason that there seems to be some doubt about *The Capitol*'s position and proprietorship.

One thing was certain: the paper would not represent the editorial policy of its original publisher, Balmer Watt, or the journalism of his partner Peggy. Independent views on the future of the province would have to be found in what was left of the *Saturday News*.

9

The Independent Mirror

The truth brings no man a fortune.

JEAN-JACQUES ROUSSEAU

Peggy prepares
for the leading
role in the play *The
Tyranny of Tears*

The report of the Royal Commission on the Alberta and Great Waterways Railway read as follows:

> The evidence reasonably gives rise to the suspicion that they have been actuated by some motive other than regard for the interests it was their duty to protect ... that motive is personal interest. Many of the facts and circumstances related are consistent with such a conclusion.

Frank Oliver insisted the premier and the attorney general resign over the scandal. Two of the three judges on the Commission had found the company itself guilty of no wrongdoing but took a dim view of the roles of Rutherford and Cross. Once again Balmer and the *Saturday News* found themselves painted into a corner. The journalist in him insisted he cover the report as it was written, but as a newspaper publisher he remained beholden to his investors. It was the double jeopardy Peggy had warned him against from the beginning.

By contrast, the *Bulletin*, Frank Oliver's paper, representing the anti-Rutherford views prevalent in Ottawa, gave full voice to the outrage in the community: "With the report of the evidence before them, only a scoundrel would declare the parties to have been absolutely vindicated and only a dunce could be made to believe it."

Peggy's disillusionment with the year's events was profound. Nothing illegal had been discovered, or at least the judges didn't admit as much, but as might be expected the Edmonton establishment was absolved of misleading the public. A failure of judgement seemed rather too polite a way of describing the double dealing that had characterized the bond issue. Whatever, the accused, each of them a "respectable" lawyer, maintained they still had the trust of the electorate, and the railway could proceed. Peggy summed up the situation in her diaries: "once again the good will of the ordinary citizen has been taken advantage of. The good land we came west to find is lost beyond recovery."

In the months that follow, Balmer spends all his time at the office, trying to save the *Saturday News* from bankruptcy. Bills from his creditors continue to pile up; Cross and the investors no longer answer his calls. But even with reduced resources coverage of regional issues remains a priority. What's politically at stake on the frontier may seem unimportant to the outside world, but it means everything to a journalist of the old school.

Then one rainy day, as strangely as it all began seven years before, the charmed life of the *Saturday News* comes to an end. Leaving a padlock on the door, the Liberal investors seize all the paper's assets, including the printing press. As if to rub salt in Balmer's wounds, even the trapper's cabin that served as the paper's first office is knocked down by Grand Trunk Pacific to build the chateau-like Macdonald Hotel. In the weeks that follow, Balmer calmly promises to pay back his investors, many of whom are family and friends. It will take him more than twenty years, but ever the Scot, he will never miss a payment.

But as Peggy realizes, something greater has been lost: the idealism that had brought her and Balmer to the frontier — the connectedness of East and West inspired by Laurier's vision of Canada's Century to come. The paper was to have been built on the foundation of the past, the continuity of a responsible press being the conscience of a nation. At Upper Canada College Balmer had been a classmate of B.K. Sandwell, the future editor of *Saturday Night* magazine and a champion of a distinct northern culture in the Americas. The two students had shared a deep commitment to confederation. At the heart of their vision was a *Pax Britannica* — the value of Canadian democracy, culture, and education on a continent dominated by the expansionism and consumerism of the United States. From the time his ancestors had emigrated to Upper Canada in 1776, to his student days editing *The Varsity* at the University of Toronto, to publishing the *Woodstock Sentinel Review,* Balmer and his family had pursued an independent course. Now as Balmer stared at the padlock on the door of the *Saturday News,* that legacy seemed to have come to an end.

I could never get my grandparents to talk about the betrayals that led to that fateful day. Peggy, much calmer at seventy than she had been at thirty, pointed out there are some things — like the broken promises of some of Balmer's closest friends — best not talked about. Balmer conceded he may have been naïve as a businessman, but at least as a journalist he had stood his ground. Maybe it was simply history that had conspired against the paper. He should have known Ottawa would never willingly give up its power over the development of the resource-rich western frontier. Frank Oliver would make sure of that.

As Alberta became as much a market as a culture, the distinctive character of the *Saturday News* had been harder to maintain. In an economy driven by business plans and revenue projections, local reporting was increasingly overwhelmed by vast newspaper chains headquartered in the big cities of the East. As their news services flooded the market with copy — as often as not shaped in the board rooms of corporations or government — the spectre of disinformation entered the world of the modern newspaper.

Balmer's idea of the press as an independent fourth estate, a gathering place for contending viewpoints was becoming an anachronism. Journalists who set out to discover what was really happening in the province were now few and far between. In the years ahead, with the rise of fascism worldwide, the media would become the propaganda arm of dictators who harboured a basic distrust of the truth. In the process Balmer's enemies would become a thousand times more dangerous, a threat to both his career and his life. In Alberta, the freedom of speech on which journalism depended would suddenly be at stake, and the world press would flock to Edmonton to report on the danger to democracy represented by the newly elected Social Credit government.

As the railway scandal passed into history, Peggy felt neither Alberta's courts nor its newspapers had done it justice. Journalism, in which she put so much faith, had proven ineffective in changing the course of events. Balmer might have made a difference, but his hands were tied. Whatever the case, she was unwilling to forgive him. For the first but not the last time in their marriage, she packed her bags and found an apartment down the street. With the money she had saved she would start a newspaper of her own, the *Independent Mirror*. On the front page would be a message to the reader:

> "The Mirror" is a journal of protest and conviction. A weekly paper that proposes to speak its mind without regard to any party's or any man's say so ...
>
> But why shouldn't a woman have views of her own and interesting ones at that.
>
> She has eyes for the little things that often escape a man.
>
> I believe she has fewer prejudices.

Her first column is titled "Through the Looking Glass," inspired by the Lewis Carroll fable she had grown up with. Signed "Peggy," it presents the world in a kind of reverse logic. Unlike Balmer's compromised relationship with his investors in the Edmonton establishment, the *Independent Mirror* would reflect reality as experienced by the ordinary Albertan. There is no trace of her husband on the masthead of the paper — from publisher to editor to business manager, the paper is the work of a woman of many parts. A reading of her columns in those first issues shows just how many:

- They say you can't sit on the Council unless you have a Liquor Man's support, or the Moral Reform League's backing ... if that is so, where do the great bulk of the voters get their say?

- "My dear Peggy, many thanks for the copy of *The Mirror*, and enclosed find my subscription. May you always turn the battery of your pen on those who deserve it."

- Twenty below today. The daily papers announced that the Lieutenant Governor would leave Government House accompanied by his escort at half past two. At three o'clock little groups of half frozen sight see-ers [*sic*] still kicked their feet to keep from developing into full fledged frozen statues, and still his honour came not ...

- I plan to publish a "Just Human Incidents" column. The little things one sees everyday on the streets and lets slip by, because they don't seem to fit in under any particular heading, and yet which somehow constitute half the interest of life ... a cowboy leading a string of mischievous western ponies, a mounted policeman dashing by on his well groomed steed, Galician girls in brightly coloured shawls ... any or all of these are silhouettes of what is moving in the streets today.

- I don't know anything that last week's issue reminded me of so much as an Irish stew. An Irish stew made by an

Irish cook who has an idea, and the result usually justi-
fies her, that the more odds and ends she can throw into
the conglomeration, the merrier and better the result.

• It is such a wonderful thing to have a new, and unsullied
as yet, career before you. To be able to begin afresh.

But there's no changing Peggy's mind about Balmer, no allowing the
anger to subside. When they pass on the street she won't even look
at him, instead writing letters that lay the blame for the collapse
of their marriage on his weeks and months at the office, precious
time when he should have been with his family.

But that said, Peggy also realizes it has not been the best time
to launch an independent newspaper. Across the continent editors
are thinking twice about the stories they publish as the commercial
class, alas mostly advertisers, begin to determine the papers' content. She shares her concern with her readers in one issue:

> *McClure's* magazine published a serial article by Miss
> Tarbell about John D. Rockefeller. The article was pub-
> lished in book form, but the entire issue was bought up, and
> copies never reached the public. Since that time *McClure's*
> has been struggling against a load that only its superb
> management and popular owner could cope with. Then
> there was *Hampton's* magazine, also a "muck-raker," so
> called, which trod the road from prosperity to the receiv-
> er's hands. *Pearson's* magazine offended the big interests in
> such a way that it lost almost all its advertising patronage ...

Why would Edmonton be any different?

Peggy's enemies have every reason to see her fail, most notably Charles Cross. The railway scandal has already blackened his
reputation; the last thing he needs is more investigative journalism. To his mind, the sooner the paper disappears the better, and

his ties to the financial community make it unlikely there will be any bank loans when Peggy's money runs out. Peggy writes to her sister in Ontario:

> I wonder if you have any conception of the rough row an editor has to hoe, who tries to run an independent sheet. The large cost of production. The interests who work so silently against you, but are there always to be reckoned with. Only the support of the Big Public can make a journal such as I hope to run possible.

Gladys Reeves and Ernest Brown provide whatever help they can, but their own photography business is next to insolvent.

By November Peggy is writing pleas to her readers and advertisers alike:

> This paper exists — or hopes to — on straight business principles. I want to pay my bills, and I want you to pay yours. I can't pay mine if I have to give away my very limited space. Already too, you know my oft-voiced theories that a thing that is worthwhile is worth paying for ... If my paper isn't worthwhile to you, go to one you think is. We are not a journal of rehash like the others. We believe we have a point of view of our own that will demand your sympathy.

Desperately seeking more readers, she asks Balmer to let her change the name to the *Saturday Mirror,* trading on their past association. He's happy to grant the request, relieved they are talking again. Peggy writes in her column on the front page: "Henceforth we will be known as the *Saturday Mirror.* In that dim land we call the future I hope and trust the name will stand for all that is just and honourable. That it will be a power in the land. That it will be a menace to the evil doers."

But the name change does little good; there simply aren't enough patrons for a women's paper in a small prairie city. The fifteenth issue, Saturday, November 16th, 1912, proves to be the last. Her final savings go to paying the rent as she shuts both her office and her apartment doors for the last time. She moves back into her and Balmer's home on 107 street as the Christmas season begins. Her high-wire act as a newspaper publisher has crashed to earth.

The collapse of two newspapers in the same year convinces Peggy the time has come to look for something completely different. She's determined to change her life radically, the only requirement that she be as far removed as humanly possible from the Charles Crosses of this world. Within weeks of closing the paper, she decides to return to the theatre, her passion as a young woman at the convent in Toronto. She discovers there are a number of amateur groups in Edmonton, looking not only for members but a proper place to meet and rehearse new plays. The house on 107 Street with its large drawing room proves to be ideal — not only the necessary space but Peggy's antiques as props and set decoration. It soon becomes a second home for men and women like herself, "fellow castaways," she likes to call them, gathered around the piano as Peggy plays the songs of her youth. Going through the song books one can feel the longing for a lost world. Titles like "I Think of All Thou Art to Me" and "When Will You Come Again?" speak more of the actors' lives than the plays themselves.

The city was building its own theatre, the Pantages, future home to the Edmonton Amateur Dramatic Society and travelling acts as famous as Sarah Bernhardt, Buster Keaton, and later the Marx Brothers. The actors who gather in Peggy's living room soon convince her to try out for the part of Lady Huntsworth in *Lady Huntsworth's Experiment*, a new English play that is to open the new season. Her debut is such a success that she soon finds herself cast as Lady Jessica in *The Liars*, then Miss Woodward, the lead, in *The Tyranny of Tears*, which the Edmonton group has decided to enter in a national theatrical competition. Balmer isn't exactly thrilled to see his wife cast as a romantic lead, but all things considered, it pleases him to see her occupied with something other than socialist politics and nude photography.

Earl Grey, the Governor General of Canada, had recently announced a Dominion Drama Festival in Winnipeg, with a trophy in his name awarded to the best play. The entries come from across Canada. The long shot of the festival, *The Tyranny of Tears* sweeps the top prizes — not only the Earl Grey trophy but Peggy herself as best actor. Her performance is hailed as "the great event of the week" by the *Toronto Telegram*, and Hector Charlesworth, later to become the first Chairman of the CBC, declares in his adjudicator's remarks that Peggy "could move to the professional theatre without trepidation. To Mrs. Watt must undoubtedly be awarded the honours of the festival."

The question was how unexpected stardom would affect Peggy's marriage to a beleaguered small-town newspaper publisher. The answer was not a happy one. Peggy's diaries and letters from this period show a woman not only changing career paths but stepping out from the bounds of the strict Victorian morality she had grown up with. Her fellow actors were a far cry from the nuns with whom she'd first performed, especially when it came to the passionate embraces of parlour room drama. As if to make matters worse, Edmonton's first cinema, the Dreamland, had opened on Jasper Avenue that summer. The steamy films it showed upped the ante for her performances. Peggy was soon competing for an audience with femme fatales like Edna Purviance and Mabel Normand. A note from an admirer who met her backstage shows the effect she had on men:

Pray cast me a melting glance, sweet Gertie mine,
From those dear haunting wine dark eyes of thine,
Deign but one watching smile, to indicate
Still sweeter greetings at a future date.

Balmer could only look on in horror as Peggy began to come home late or not at all. He now realized Peggy had been serious: his decision to launch the *Capitol* with Cross and the investors had left little time for his marriage. Peggy had decided to become as scandalous as he had become conservative. And never shying away from attention, she would make a public spectacle of the fact. As her diary testified:

> One day when my heart and soul were dusty through too long and intimate sojourning among correct folk, a man stopped me on the street. "Do you think you'd like to go for a drive this afternoon?" The man with his broad stetson and gaudily embroidered buckskin gauntlets took me away — out into the wilderness of things, past the funny little real estate signs at the edge of town onto the prairie, where I half held my breath for fear of kissing the earth. Now I know something of the wild, and the invisible hand that knocks at the doors of men. As we drove farther and farther beyond the fence lines, involuntarily I drew a deeper breath. The rosy light coming across the shimmering deserts of snow ... and the sense of driving you-know-not-where filled me with an intoxication for living that swept me off my feet.

There weren't many relationships, but those there were carried all the intensity that was Gertrude Watt. She had always pushed the limits of propriety, counting on Balmer to keep things within the bounds of reason. Now the lines began to blur.

It didn't help that she was never home. Some nights the

shouting matches on her return escalated to the point that my mother Becky, only seven, fled the house. Her bedroom was directly above the living room; she could hear every word they hurled at each other. Discovered hiding in the woodshed, she was put in the care of her brother Frederick. Some nights the only recourse for the two children was to crawl out his bedroom window onto the roof with their blankets. The last straw was Peggy inviting one of her leading men to live at the house. Balmer moved to a hotel the same night, taking the children with him. A week later he was back as they tried to reconcile. As her affairs became more entangled, the marriage broke apart, came back together, broke apart again, as if neither of them could summon the courage to leave or stay.

Hoping the discipline of a regular job might calm Peggy down, Balmer turned to an old friend at a community newspaper. Maybe he could convince Peggy to return to work. But the idea soon backfired. Her carrying-on didn't escape the notice of the paper's readers. Soon letters began to arrive on her desk calling out her personal life. Being Peggy, she couldn't resist replying:

> Last week, someone sent me an anonymous letter. It was a weak miserable thing — an attack on me, not my work. Was it sent to hurt me? It failed its mark. To frighten me? I don't scare worth a cent. Incidentally, I know you. Do not forget that once before I had the occasion to recognize your handwriting.

Now the whole city was party to her affairs.

Lewis Thomas, my history professor in the 1960s, was a student at the University of Alberta at the time. He remembered how quickly the gossip spread around the town, how stories persisted that the columnist received her callers "in bed," a purposeful affront to the Daughters of the British Empire who served tea and biscuits in their Victorian drawing rooms next door.

Townsend, a remittance man, was the closest Peggy came to taking up a permanent relationship. A homesteader in the Peace River country, he and his family lived alone, far from the nearest neighbour. But a man of many sides, there came a time when he had enough of the bush, and it was in Edmonton's only bookshop that he met Peggy. As she wrote in her diary:

> That he has a past you know; men rarely get that air of repression of having been and done things, who haven't knocked about and seen a great deal ...
>
> I met him once in an Ontario town. He had a wife, somewhere, children too, to whom I can honestly affirm he was rarely devoted. Few knew that even they existed. His days he gave to literary work and in his own Free Lance column of commentary, he was a peerless writer. When there was time he rode, swam, went shooting, did all and sundry that a live, healthy, able-bodied man may do — and in the evening he read and wrestled with his ghosts. He wasn't just the most sociable sort of man, not until you knew him. Then you grew to love his society. For a walk he was the prince of good fellows. Such a fund of information as he had, such a way of dispensing it. Always when you were with him you caught a little danger signal — Mrs Grundy was waving the red flag of warning. Behold here was a wicked man, a man with a past. To the average woman what a fascination! What child doesn't love to tamper with fire ...
>
> ... Throughout his conversation there was just that little touch of pessimism and an undertone of regret that added the charm of the unusual ... "He" is the man who is attempting to work out his own salvation with the illusive phantom — what might have been.

He looked nothing like a homesteader, dressed in a new suit he had purchased from Edmonton's best tailor. But when he came to town he rented a shack five miles downriver from the city, determined to get away from the frantic crowds of Jasper Avenue, travelling up and down the North Saskatchewan in a canoe. Thus it was that for one glorious summer Peggy became part of the river of her dreams.

Travelling on the water she came to know the various birds that nested on the shore, especially two herons who would follow her when she went to town alone. By summer's end she was an expert paddler and could negotiate the channels and shallows that came with the end of the snows in the mountains. She even discovered small islands on which she could pull up the canoe and be alone, writing essays about the life she had abandoned in the city, about Balmer and the sin of pride that had doomed his papers. Not recognizing the investors for what they were — not being willing to admit he'd made a mistake.

As the calm waters flowed through the green countryside on their long journey to the sea, she felt a deep sadness at what had gone wrong. She knew there would never be another Balmer.

It must have been a terrible time for the family. I remember my mother Becky in the 1960s, the week after Peggy's death, burning every letter, every diary, every scrap of paper Peggy or Balmer had kept from that tumultuous year. She would never forgive her mother.

But Balmer, the persistent Scot, was determined not to lose Peggy, welcoming her back to the house on 107 Street after each misadventure. He even offered to take her to the coast for a month to calm down, but again she couldn't make up her mind. Only when her beloved son Frederick ran away from home did Peggy come to her senses. As she and Balmer searched the city for the missing boy, she told her husband she would come home.

These wild birds proceed through the pathless
air, from where they winter to where they breed,
a distance of 2700 miles in a straight line ...
The question arises, by what means do the
wild geese make such a long journey with such
precision of place; the wise and learned civilized
man answers, by instinct. But what is instinct?
A property of the mind that has never been
defined. The Indian believes the geese are directed
by the manitou, who has the care of them.

DAVID THOMPSON, *THE NARRATIVE*

Book Two

1912–1935
THE PRECISION OF PLACE

10

Prairie Women

Civilization is standing at the crossroads; in
every heart there is a barely conscious feeling
of expectancy. In the silences it seems to us as
though great things were stirring in the womb
of time; we almost seem to hear the rustle
of great events rushing to us through space.
What is the old world about to bring forth?

IRENE PARLBY

As unpredictable as ever, Peggy had a new profession in mind, much more in line with the wife of a newspaper publisher: the buying and selling of antiques and works of art that had somehow washed up in the frontier city. In her first days in Edmonton she had frequented the secondhand shops on 101 Street, full of settler's effects, family heirlooms exchanged when desperate homesteaders found themselves out of cash. If a farm failed completely, all the family's possessions would have to be pawned for the fare home. I still have an oak chest Peggy found that had travelled around the Cape of Good Hope from Boston to Seattle and then overland to Edmonton by horse and wagon before there was a railway, only to be sold for next to nothing when someone's luck ran out.

Within a month she has opened an antique shop in her living room, convincing Balmer the revenue might help him repay the debts left by the bankrupt *Saturday News*. One of her first customers is a rancher from central Alberta, Irene Parlby, an organizer for the United Farmers of Alberta (although women are still not allowed to vote in its assemblies). Like many other farmers she regularly travels to Edmonton to petition the government for better grain and livestock prices.

The granddaughter of Captain Frederick Marryat, the well-known English author of nautical adventures and children's' stories, Parlby is an aspiring writer herself, penning pamphlets on country gardens as well as political tracts against the government. She is known in her district for riding a chestnut mare near and far to talk to farmers about their grievances. One day she will be only the second woman in the British Commonwealth to become a cabinet minister. But on this day she is just curious about Peggy's odd pieces of Wedgwood china, possible decoration for the plate rack in her new dining room. Collectors at heart, she and the now ex-journalist strike up an immediate friendship. Invited to supper, by evening's end she asks the entire Watt family to visit her ranch near the town of Alix in central Alberta. Balmer tries to beg off, but Peggy insists that he join her on the trip, reminding him he has not taken a day off in a year. Not that travelling with young children is exactly a holiday, as he discovers as they prepare for the train journey south.

The highlight of the trip is the recently opened trestle over the Battle River at Duhamel, the highest and longest wooden bridge in the world. Part of the Grand Trunk Pacific, it has been built in less than a year, an accomplishment that inspires Balmer's diary entry the day he returns to Edmonton: "Testimony to the spirit of industry and enterprise that has overtaken the province." Peggy is delighted to discover Alix, a charming village tucked into the lake district north and east of Red Deer. Named after the first white woman to settle the region, the town is home to a library, a music society, and a polo ground, where a game is in progress when they arrive. Frederick insists on stopping to watch, making friends with Parlby's young son, Humphrey, one of the grooms for the horses.

But behind the stables Peggy notices shanties thrown up by the district's homeless. One of the women in the doorways Peggy recognizes from the tent city in Edmonton. Although she tries to get the woman's attention, there seems to be an invisible barrier between the immigrants and the town. An impatient Irene gathers the guests for tea. Alix is as full of contradictions as Alberta itself. En route to Dartmoor, Irene's house atop a hill at the edge of town, they pass mud-covered wagons loaded with household goods. Barbara Villy Cormack describes the Alix immigrants in *Perennials and Politics,* her biography of Parlby:

> All sorts and conditions of them travelled down the Buffalo Lake Trail below the charming flower garden at Dartmoor en route to homesteads further east ... the hard luck family from the Dakotas looking for water for their weary horse ... the Cockney family driving their wagon to some possibly non-existent land which they had unsuspectingly purchased, sight unseen, in one of the spurious land deals of the time ...

Even in this progressive farm community Peggy is dismayed at the suffering she sees around her.

The next day, before returning to the city, Balmer convinces Peggy to accept Parlby's invitation to stay the week. He worries she has not got over the heartbreak of the past year, still blaming herself for what has happened to the family. Country life may be the tonic she needs.

In addition to the social whirl, Peggy is immediately drawn to the district's reformist politics. She discovers that Irene has as little patience with the Liberals as she does, including the impression that the new premier Arthur Sifton, the Chief Justice, has little time for women. Two warring organizations make up the United Farmers: the radical Canadian Society of Equity and the moderate Alberta

Farmers Association, of which Irene is a part. Together the two organizations set out to publish a newspaper, the *Alberta Homestead*, and approach Balmer to be the editor after his return from Alix. Given the demise of the *Saturday News*, he is quick to agree.

Peggy notices a credo framed above Irene Parlby's desk: "The greatest happiness of the greatest number is the measure of right and wrong." That evening she discovers that Irene's husband, Walter, has adapted Darwin's revolutionary ideas on natural selection to government. The biological theory of evolution, the idea that some life forms are better suited to their environment than others, has led him to believe that virtuous social organizations will with time prevail over less virtuous.

The Alix farmers are confronting a question that will haunt Alberta for a century to come: how to build an independent political culture at the grassroots, free from the manipulation of the urban elites? The issues in 1912 are grain prices, railway monopolies, and freight rates; with time they will grow to include control of natural resources and the struggle to resist being colonized by a global energy economy.

A young Peter Lougheed will ask the same questions in the 1970s when his government is negotiating royalty rates with the multinationals. He has to keep reminding the offshore executives at the table, "Don't forget who owns the oil." When I interviewed him for *The Life and Times of Peter Lougheed,* a CBC documentary, he reminded me that the United Farmers, led by people like Irene Parlby, had been Alberta's best opportunity to build a province from the ground up. The Leduc strike of 1947 and the opening of Great Canadian Oil Sands in 1964 had made it much more difficult for the province to maintain control of its own destiny.

A member of Irene's circle at supper that night is Oswin Creighton, the local Anglican minister who has come from England to work with the disadvantaged. Peggy's charm soon wins him over, much to Irene's amusement. Never one to judge, he is fascinated by this fallen woman suddenly in their midst. Although their relationship remains platonic, as the week passes Peggy spends more and more time in Creighton's company, finding a true friend in the altruistic young man, an echo of the Balmer she married.

Visits to Alix become more regular as the summer unfolds. Balmer is now preoccupied with the new paper and seldom home, leaving Peggy to her own devices. One project is to help Creighton build the replica of a small church in a railway caboose, which a horse can pull from farm to farm. The single room is just large enough for a family to gather for a service. Some days the young minister takes Peggy with him as he travels cross-country to the more isolated homesteads. She is taken with the gentle hills and plains stretching as far as the eye can see. Visiting a farm on the shores of Buffalo Lake she writes,

> Is there anything in the world one-half as appealing as a
> perfect summer day on the Canadian prairies? Across the
> fields one catches a flitting glimpse of a modest-thatched
> homestead ... amidst fields of wheat and oats that stand
> out of the fair June landscape, great green squares on a
> field of brown ... who wouldn't be a farmer on such days
> as these?

Creighton shows her the remains of the last Métis settlement in the region, from a day when these meadows shook with stampeding buffalo. Only a single family remains, the corral for their horses falling down, an ancient Red River cart abandoned in the front yard. Oswin advises keeping their distance when a man comes to the door of a sod hut, a rifle over his shoulder. Apparently there's bad blood with the neighbours, who still regard the family as Road Allowance People, not to be trusted. In Alix, Creighton tells her, they call them "one and a half people": one part Indigenous, one part European, one part devil. Peggy ignores Creighton's advice and gets down from her horse to shake the man's hand. But the Métis turns away and goes back inside the hut, shutting the door behind him. As Peggy turns away she notices one wall of the barn is composed entirely of buffalo skulls.

Peggy's respect for Oswin grows as the summer passes. Like Irene he embodies a spirit of inclusion and social justice. His work extends beyond the immigrant community to Indigenous people passed by in the march of progress the chamber of commerce advertises. His Christianity is free of denomination, celebrating the mixed congregation that gathers every Sunday at his church — "building the kingdom of God here on earth, not in heaven," in his words.

As winter approaches, there is always a hot meal waiting for Creighton and Peggy in the improvised kitchens of the impoverished settlers. Creighton attaches skis to his caboose church and extends his diocese even further to the east beyond Buffalo Lake — marginal land. The dwellings he visits there are mere huts, recently constructed from slabs of prairie sod, enclosing a single room and a few pieces of homemade furniture. Yet the generosity of their hosts impresses Peggy deeply, evidence of the populism that has taken root on the open prairie. The equal distribution of work necessary to prove up a homestead has made the women capable farmers, but that responsibility has also transformed them into political beings. As newfound "citizens" they are determined to have an equal say in building the future of the province. The fact that women still can't vote will not stop them. Working with organizations of farm women like Irene's in Alix, they have determined to form a political party that will contest the next election.

Peggy is amazed how well-read the women are.

> The first real achievement of the Countrywomen's Club was the establishment of a library. Irene Parlby had always been shocked at the paucity of books to be found in the average farm home, for to her books were the very breath of life. As Secretary she inserted a little notice in the *London Spectator* telling of this unfortunate situation, and asking for any books readers could spare. The response was much beyond her hopes. Two large mail sacks filled with books arrived, with contributions from as far away as Japan and South Africa.

Creighton distributes the used books to the more isolated farmsteads. Peggy loves to hear the farmers' simple proposals for solving the problems of the world. She notices an echo of Haultain in their thinking, a moral dimension to government, or "governance" as they prefer to call it, beyond the self-interest of party and politics.

One evening, as Peggy starts lecturing her new friends about the need to reach out to the urban voter, Irene politely interrupts. Speaking for the women of the district, she invites Peggy to join them in their coverage of central Alberta for the farmers' newspaper, the *Alberta Homestead*. With all due respect to Balmer, the recent issue had far too many men writing articles. Incorporating agrarian philosophy with radical politics, world affairs with recipes and gardening tips, the women intend to develop their own section of the paper. They are in the process of building their own organization, the United Farm Women of Alberta (UFWA), lobbying for equal status within the farmers movement, and they would appreciate Peggy's help.

Irene Parlby will become the closest friend Peggy makes in Alberta. In addition to being idealists, the two women share a practical agenda: to make men their allies in the fight for equality. In her first annual report as President of the UFWA, Parlby writes:

> The day has forever fled when woman can confine her interests within the four walls of her home. Our duties are ever pushing us out further into the great world. We cannot work there alone. We must have the whole-hearted co-operation of the men, to bring about the sane and Christian civilization for which the world is today in travail ...

But Parlby had no illusions. Later in a letter to Peggy she reflects further:

> We value our privilege of working on equal terms with men of our organization ... We have heard so much of the horrors of a man-governed world ... but heaven defend us from a world governed solely by women. "Man and woman created He them," not to work in isolated groups, but as the helpmate of one another, and the two points of view are necessary for sanity and wisdom.

But soon the early frosts of winter are on the ground.

Irene offers to accompany Peggy back to Edmonton. Maybe the two of them can convince Balmer to provide more space in the paper for their articles. Balmer tries to dissuade Parlby: the *Homestead* already receives twice the volume of submissions it can print. But he also realizes how much it will mean to Peggy to have a voice of her own again. He will do what he can, if nothing else watching their backs. The traditional male writers among the farmers are not going to take the challenge lying down. But within a month a new column appears on the front page of the *Homestead*, signed by hand, "Peggy."

Overnight the reborn journalist finds herself in the thick of Alberta co-operativist politics, a perpetual compromise between as many factions as there are farm communities in the province. The *Alberta Homestead* sets out to protect the interests of the small farmer, charting an independent course around the vested interests of corporate agriculture. Sifton and the Liberals are not pleased. Rural Alberta is an important part of their electoral support, and they fear Peggy will upset the apple cart if given the chance. They talk to Balmer, but he simply throws up his hands, thankful they are no longer his investors. In fact he is secretly pleased, relishing the fact Peggy will once again be a force to be reckoned with.

11

River of
No Return

The river dreams of its
descents yet to come
and never to be known

E.D. BLODGETT

Peggy never stopped trying to imagine the source of the river that had drawn her west. The North Saskatchewan in Edmonton, constantly in her view as it wound its way through the city, wouldn't let her forget the Paul Kane painting she'd seen as a girl. As construction on the Grand Trunk Pacific, Canada's second transcontinental railway, reached Fitzhugh (what is today Jasper), she saw her chance to travel to its headwaters.

Little more than a railway construction camp, Fitzhugh was on the Athabasca River, which flowed from the Athabasca glacier on the Great Divide. The Saskatchewan Glacier lay close by, an extension of the massive Columbia Icefield. Intrepid mountain explorer Mary Schäffer had told Peggy in an interview that the year before she had stood at the foot of the Saskatchewan glacier, surveying the North Saskatchewan on the first leg of its journey to Hudson Bay. Schäffer gave Peggy the names of guides in Fitzhugh who could help her travel up the Athabasca valley by horseback and then hike across the pass that separated the two glaciers to the headwaters of the North Saskatchewan. If she allowed enough time from Fitzhugh, she had a good chance of reaching the source of the river before winter.

The first Grand Trunk train from the east had arrived in Edmonton on August 13, 1909. At last the city had a direct connection to Toronto and Montreal, the business heart of the country. Peggy took Frederick to the edge of town to witness the great occasion. She took pictures for the *Saturday News* while Frederick convinced the engineer in the steam engine to let them hitch a ride back into town.

The railway was part of a 4800-kilometre national system, whose main line was now being extended from Winnipeg via Melville and Edmonton to Prince Rupert. It was a coming of age for the city, as Balmer described it. Frederick still remembered the day fifty years later:

> My father was waiting for us as the train pulled into the new station festooned with banners reading "The British Empire: Tested, Tried, and True". A brass band played *The Land of Hope and Glory* as the mayor and council waited on the platform. Balmer was pleased that Peggy had got the scoop and featured the story on the front page of the paper, heralding a new chapter in the city's development.

Three years later, among the passengers on the Grand Trunk was a young Anglican missionary, J. Burgon Bickersteth, brother of the man who was to become chaplain to the Queen. Ironically, Bickersteth believed in the social gospel, revolutionary in many of its programs, among which was the work he intended to do among the navvies building the railway west of Edmonton. As was so often the case with Peggy, he became an instant friend with whom she would correspond for the next fifty years.

I still have many of those letters and visited Bickersteth in Canterbury near the end of his life when he was the "keeper of the keys" to the cathedral. He was fascinated by the fact that I was making a film, *Ernest Brown, Pioneer Photographer*, documenting the period when Bickersteth had ministered to the rough-hewn men who were building the railway. He had published a book in 1914, *The Land of Open Doors,* an account of his journey to the Canadian West. We spent the better part of a week comparing notes.

Hearing the missionary's plans to travel to the mountains through which the Grand Trunk was being constructed, Peggy convinced Balmer to let her document the work camps Bickersteth would be visiting. The route would take her through Wolf Creek, Edson, Hinton, and Pocahontas en route to Fitzhugh. It would allow her to follow up the articles she had written on the tent city in Edmonton, the beginning of the western saga for many of these working men and women. No matter how harrowing the living conditions, many had little choice but to follow the railroad's progress into the mountains.

An early chapter of *The Land of Open Doors* describes the first bunkhouse Bickersteth and Peggy visited:

I wish you could have seen those men. They came in covered with mud from head to foot, and proceeded to divest themselves of their wet boots and socks and overalls, which they hung up in every conceivable corner. … The floor was soon as muddy as it was outside, with men coming in and out and, of course, everyone spat where they wished. When you see the conditions under which these men live, you could hardly be surprised if the outlook which many of them have on life is little better than a beast's. They work like horses, eat like pigs, and sleep like logs. Is it to be wondered at that after months of this they go wild when they reach the lights and glare of a city, and that the height of enjoyment is to be found in a whisky bottle?

Peggy is fascinated by the mining towns being developed to supply the railway with coal. The workers are paid even less than the railway workers but labour in equally dangerous surroundings. Unions are being formed to demand safer working conditions, but the mine owners simply fire the organizers. Strikes seem to have little effect; there are always more men looking for work.

Peggy and Bickersteth overnight at Pocahontas, a mining town at the foot of Roche Miette, the peak that marks the entrance to the valley of the Athabasca from the east. Nearly blinded by the coal dust that clings to everything, they make their way through crowds of immigrants looking for work to attend a clandestine union meeting. Peggy is surprised to find organizers from the United Farmers in the hall, seeking an ally to lobby the Liberal government in Edmonton for social relief. The union president opens the meeting with the story of a recent explosion, after which the mine manager's first question is "How many horses were killed?" The injured and dead men can be replaced within hours, but scarce horses are a much more serious matter.

Peggy realizes that night that the camps are not a safe place for a woman. Bickersteth's diary gives a sense of what a woman can expect in the desperate atmosphere they encounter:

> An end-of-steel town is a wicked place. Every other log shanty or tent that you see is either a gambling joint, drinking saloon, brothel, or pool room. The women make large sums of money, and are constantly going down to Edmonton to cash regular stacks of cheques. Some make 200 or 300 dollars a week. Men come in and give a girl a 15, 25, 30 dollar cheque for an evening, or perhaps even a few minutes, and then go back to the grade determined to make another stake.

There is a violence in the grim faces that makes Peggy shudder. Clearly a female journalist poking into these broken lives is not welcome. She has the good fortune to be offered a private berth in the caboose of the foreman of the railway construction, well away from the bunkhouses and the tents thrown up by the men looking for work. The railway boss advises her to stay away from the women who frequent the camps — there have been robberies and a murder. Peggy has little choice but to comply. The Grand Trunk would just as soon have her return to the city. She spends much of her days walking and writing with only the silent stone of the mountains for company.

Peggy has come to understand things will never be the same with Balmer. Yes, they have been able to resume the relationship, but their careers in journalism, fraught as always, provide a constant source of tension. Then there is the scandal of Peggy's affairs, still remembered by powerful members of the community like Judge Emily Murphy. Even the feminists have turned against her, excluding her from the ongoing fight for women's rights. Irene continues to involve her in the farmers' movement, but in Edmonton, "respectable" citizens consider her a pariah. And here on the railway frontier she can see the fate of rebellious women like herself.

Bickersteth travels up the line to an advance camp past Mount Robson, the highest peak in the Canadian Rockies. The railway has already left the Athabasca valley and climbed through the Yellowhead Pass to the headwaters of the Fraser River in British Columbia. Left on her own, Peggy sets out to find a guide to take her up the Athabasca to the Continental Divide. She convinces Joel Otto, Schäffer's guide in Fitzhugh, to allow her to join a party he is taking to the headwaters of the river, but he is skeptical she will be able to make it across the pass to the North Saskatchewan in the time available. Winter is moving into the high country, and he warns her it will not be an easy ride. Otto's backcountry survival skills are second to none, and Peggy is impressed, not least by the guide's civilized manner, a far cry from the leering reception that greets her in the railway camps.

The trip up the valley takes four days, as much riding as Peggy can manage, but Otto is right: the weather is turning against the small party. She has brought along Louis Agassiz's controversial book, *Geological Sketches*, a favourite from her years in the convent. Each time they pass a glacier, big or small, clinging to the side of the valley, she insists they stop and examine the moraines and banks of gravel the ice leaves behind. She explains to Otto how the presence of these features in Scotland, where no one thought glaciers had ever existed, led Agassiz to theorize that half the world was once covered by ice.

At the head of the valley waits the massive Athabasca glacier, which flows like a river of ice between towering mountains. The weather is turning as a blizzard sweeps down the valley. Otto is concerned. There is simply not the time to wait for the storm to blow itself out. Peggy can have an hour to photograph the glacier, and then they will have to turn back. Sensing her disappointment, Otto describes the Saskatchewan glacier, now inaccessible across the pass. It's one of his favourites for its s-bend, the double curve it traces as it winds its way from the icefields to the valley below. For an object so massive, the curve has a delicacy about it that few observers fail to see. To his mind it is one of the most beautiful sights in the Rockies. Peggy is deeply touched, telling him about the power of the ogee in her own life.

The photos Peggy takes of the Athabasca glacier are instructive today for those who measure the retreat of the ice over the last century. Looking at the images, one realizes that as much as half of the glacier is no longer there, melted by global warming. Like Agassiz a believer that catastrophes shaped the world, she had tried to convince Otto that the glaciers would do just the opposite, advancing once again to cover great stretches of the continent. But even in 1909 Otto had seen enough to know the opposite was true. As the party made its way back to Fitzhugh, Otto points out the falling water levels in the rivers they ford, tributaries of the Athabasca, each flowing from a receding body of ice.

In 2024, the Athabasca Glacier itself is nearly unrecognizable, its translucent blue face riddled with streams of meltwater. The broad valley the glacier once filled is now a moonscape strewn with discarded boulders. Year after year, as climate change intensifies, an entire ecology slips into crisis, victim of the emissions that overheat the biosphere. Not just the glaciers are disappearing, but the surrounding forests, decimated by pine beetles and wildfires. Birds no longer come to nest as the trees die, and fur-bearing animals have abandoned the valley for higher ground. Jasper National Park, created to protect this landscape, is defenceless against the industrial pollution at the root of the problem. The park is now part of a sacrifice zone scientists have predicted all of Alberta may one day become.

Bickersteth is late coming back from Tête Jaune Cache, leaving Peggy to her own devices in the camp. Once again she tries to talk to the railway men, with little luck. But when the missionary returns they visit the makeshift Fitzhugh hospital together. Here some of the injured men might be willing to answer her questions. She senses that the hope has gone out of them, immigrants so far from home in such hostile country. How much of their lives will they have to sacrifice to earn the money they need to prove up their homesteads? But this day the men are pre-occupied with the fate of one of their fellows from the construction camp, a badly injured Russian they have carried on a stretcher through the muddy streets.

Bickersteth's book describes the last hours of the man, whose head has been crushed by a falling rail.

> Nobody understood Russian, and he knew not a single word of any other language ... He made signs for a pencil, but was really too weak to write. We could only discover he came from Bessarabia, and the doctor was not certain that we even had his name right; so how can his parents be communicated with? ... During the afternoon we got a swarthy Russian, who had just come into Fitzhugh and could talk a little English, to come and see him. It was a curious scene — the little wooden room which served as a ward ... the sick man lying there gasping ... and on his knees by the bedside, his lips quite near the sick man's ear, the great black-bearded Russian. ...
>
> It was the most horrible death scene I have ever witnessed. The man was absolutely yellow in colour and fighting for breath. This fearful fight went on for nearly half an hour. ... One would never have believed that a man in his condition could have had the strength to fight so long. Then suddenly, with a gurgle, he seemed to give it up, and sank back dead. I said the Commendatory Prayer, or as much of it as I could remember, as he passed away, and then we tied up his head and wrapped him in a blanket. The doctor had already ordered a rough wooden box from one of the men at the station ... He was put into it, nailed down, and put outside; there was nowhere else to put him.
>
> Next day, after seeing the park ranger about a burial place, the doctor and I went down with four labourers on a hand-car to a place where there is a flat stretch of land near the Athabasca River. Here, where an Indian baby and a Finlander were already buried, we told the men to

dig the grave for the Russian. A more beautiful place no one could desire for a last resting-place...

Behind us, the forest-covered slopes ran right up to the rocky cliffs of Pyramid Mountain, and along the side of the hill went the great Transcontinental line, in the construction of which this man, like many another, had met his death.

... The men stood round with bare heads, and one of them threw earth on the coffin at the right moment. After the service was over, they did not take long to shovel back the sandy soil. Another fellow and I cut down some small spruce trees, put posts and rails round the grave, and made a cross. We wrote the date on the cross, but not his name, as we did not know it for certain. So there we left him, and another is added to the number of those who never return.

Stunned by the turn of events, Peggy walks back to town by herself. The experience of watching the Russian die, then burying him, has taken place in little more than a day, life at its most transitory. As she stares at the rushing grey waters of the Athabasca, laden with the silt of the glaciers, the whole world seems to be flying apart before her. The permanence of the steel railway, of man's mastery over the natural world, seem absurd. For the first time in her life the premonition of an uncertain future for the planet overtakes her.

For once the river offers no consolation.

12

Man Who Chooses the Bush

Our present "leaders," the people of wealth
and power, do not know what it means to
take a place seriously: to think it worthy, for
its own sake, of love and study and careful
work. They cannot take any place seriously
because they must be ready at any moment,
by the terms of power and wealth in the
modern world, to destroy any place.

WENDELL BERRY

Peggy's arrival
must have been
a surprise for the
boatmen on the
Athabasca River

In 1910 Peggy and Balmer travelled north on the Athabasca River for the first time to see the "tar sands" for themselves, long before any viable commercial process had been discovered to refine the tar (what today we call bitumen). Since the death of the *Saturday News*, Balmer had become a freelance editor. Much to his chagrin, one of his first contracts was to produce a brochure for the federal Department of the Interior promoting investment in the northern frontier. Nothing could have been further from his and Peggy's vision of the frontier, sustained by their hopes that a mutually beneficial relationship could be developed between the government and Indigenous Peoples — not simply to finance the further confiscation of native land by men like Frank Oliver. Balmer feared an oil and gas boom would do just that, a fear that was borne out by the tyranny of oil sands development in the century ahead.

Balmer never got to see the bitumen oozing from the banks of the Athabasca, however. Boarding a paddle wheeler in Peace River, he slipped on the gangplank and fell twenty feet to the rocks below. His leg fractured in three places, and he was sent to the Grande Prairie hospital to recover. The doctors insisted he stay put while the bones set, leaving him at the mercy of the Peace River mayor, whose daily visits were to ensure that the town would be well represented in the brochure. The leg prevented any chance of escape.

As had been the case many times before, it was Peggy who came to the rescue. First, in no uncertain terms she told the mayor to leave her husband alone — the content of the brochure had already been determined. Then she let her old friend Peace River Jim know of the accident. A regular in the town, he too had Balmer at his mercy as he promoted the benefits of the Fort McMurray railway. But he was the kind of company Balmer needed as he recovered — argumentative, opinionated, full of schemes for the future of the province. Cornwall's vision was of a robust, self-sufficient economy that would make Peggy's distinctive culture and society possible. Balmer that agreed Fort McMurray, at the time still an abandoned fur trade post in the middle of the boreal forest, would one day be at the centre of that vision. It was Peggy who saw the dangers that lay ahead.

Balmer's badly broken leg takes six weeks to heal. While he recovers, the ever-resourceful Peggy takes advantage of her time in Peace River to visit the grave of pioneer settler Twelve Foot Davis. The grave is high on a hill above the confluence of the Smoky River with the Peace. As she surveys the last of the great rivers in her life, the immensity of the landscape overwhelms her, stretching to the mountains fifty miles away. It is as if she's travelled back to the age when the ice sheets that covered half the planet carved this country into being. The time scale of a human life seems to have no meaning here.

Yet as she surveys the valley, Peggy can't get her affair with Townsend, the remittance man, out of her mind. This is the country in which he filed his homestead; his home must be one of the buildings she can see by the river far below. Part of her wants to visit him, but another part holds back. That chapter of her life is over. For better or worse she has made her peace with Balmer. She turns her back on the river and returns to town.

In the following weeks Peggy sets about tracking down the Métis families who moved north after Batoche in 1885. Peace River Jim Cornwall hired many of them to work on the riverboats he has built to supply the isolated communities downstream. She wants to write an article for the *Alberta Homestead* on the place of the Road Allowance People in the new northern economy. But the Métis suspect the motives of a reporter from the south and resent the way she assumes they share a history. What she calls the economy they regard as little more than land theft.

At Balmer's suggestion, she decides to continue further north and makes her way to the tar sands, completing the government assignment to document the resource. Her camera will provide the photo documentation crucial to the brochure. Peggy takes a riverboat down the Peace, then hitches a ride with a convoy of wagons, bushwhacking cross country until she reaches the Athabasca where she hails a ferry travelling downstream to Fort McMurray. From there she talks her way onto a barge taking supplies to Fort Chipewyan, known to the locals as Chip. From the deck she will have ample opportunity to photograph the tar oozing from the banks of the river.

When the barge overnights in Chip she meets the Ladouceurs, the Metis ancestors of Modeste and his son Frank, the trappers whose lives I will portray a century later in the film *Man Who Chooses the Bush*. The family are among the first free traders in the region, descended from Pierre Martin *dit* Ladouceur from Montreal and Josephe Suzette Cardinal, a local Métis woman. They speak Cree, French, and English. Perched on a rocky promontory at the southern edge of the Precambrian Shield, their cabin commands a view of Lake Athabasca, the eighth largest lake in Canada. The spectacular view makes Peggy wish she had brought her children with her.

To her surprise the Ladouceurs take her to a library in town, assembled by the various fur traders who have wintered here since the 1790s. She concludes that since Chip is one of the oldest European communities in the province, this may be Alberta's oldest library, a starting point for an article she has decided to write about the town. Among the books and maps in the one-room cabin that houses the collection is a volume of poetry, *A Shropshire Lad,* written by an Englishman, A.E. Housman, one of Peggy's favourites. A verse from one of the poems makes her think again of her estranged children, both of whom have spurned her attempts to patch things up since her return to Balmer.

> With rue my heart is laden
> For golden friends I had,
> for many a rose-lipt maiden
> And many a lightfoot lad.
>
> By brooks too broad for leaping
> The lightfoot boys are laid;
> The rose-lipt girls are sleeping
> In fields where roses fade.

Peggy had hoped the Peace River trip would allow her breakup with the family to become a thing of the past. But the damage has been done. Now in his teens, Frederick is determined to strike out on his own, signing up to work on a riverboat before Peggy caught wind of the scheme. Becky is so nervous in her mother's company that Balmer has enrolled her in Loretto Abbey, the convent Peggy attended in Toronto. Maybe the nuns can calm the nervous disorder that flares up at the least provocation from her mother. The children's future preoccupies Peggy on the long return journey to the Peace River as the wind and rain of a cold front descend from the north. The bleak prospect makes her feel empty and alone, where only days before the country had filled her with wonder.

The stories of Fort Chipewyan Peggy told me as a boy made me want to repeat her journey someday. From what I had read the community, accessible only by boat or bush plane, or an ice road on the river in winter if you were willing to take the chance, had retained much of its unique history. The month I arrived, a truck had plunged through the ice, drowning its driver. The town's citizens were still largely Métis and First Nations people, determined to fight the development of a hydro dam on the Peace River in British Columbia and the beginnings of tar sand mining upstream on the Athabasca, two massive projects that threatened the delta on which their livelihood depended.

In the winter of 1975 I spent a fortnight with Frank Ladouceur in his cabin documenting the cycles of life of a Métis trapper, seeking to understand the importance of place in a rapidly changing world. How this patch of forest, unmarked on most maps, *was* Frank, the way it had once been his father, Modeste. How a person can become a place.

Sakaw Pimajowen, "Man Who Chooses the Bush," was Frank's description for himself in Cree. Each evening he would scrape kinnikinnnick from the stems of bearberry bushes to smoke in his pipe as he contemplated the silent river outside his door. Then it was back to assembling a pair of snowshoes from the tall tamarack he had felled nearby, steaming the frames over a kettle on the fire. On the ceiling hung their webbing, cut from the guts of a moose.

At the crack of dawn, even though the thermometer read twenty below, Frank fed his team of sled dogs chained outside with fish from nets he pulled up from the river. The rest of the day he would make his living setting traps for muskrats along the shore of the Athabasca. Before supper there was time to begin the construction of a new sled, crafted from a stand of birch behind the cabin. I was fascinated to watch him cut each board from the trees, measuring everything by eye, the pass of the saw's blade always true to the image he carried in his mind. He might have been an engineer making the finest calculations on a computer, but it was simply the tradition of bushcraft he had inherited from his father. I wished I could stay long enough to see him carve a new fiddle from the aspen along the river, a project planned for the spring when the sap would be flowing.

A flock of migrating geese lands on the river, the swish of their wings a whisper. They make me think of the "precision of place" David Thompson described in his *Narrative* when he first arrived in this northern wilderness:

> These wild birds proceed through the pathless air, from where they winter to where they breed, a distance of 2700 miles in a straight line ... The question arises, by what means do the wild geese make such a long journey with such precision of place; the wise and learned civilized man answers, by instinct. But what is instinct? A property of the mind that has never been defined. The Indian believes the geese are directed by the manitou, who has the care of them.

I am reminded too of Peggy's account of her journey west, tracing the canoe routes Thompson had followed into what seemed to her a wilderness. But she was soon to find there was a society here that had lasted millennia. This land, in which she set about making a home, grounded her, located her, removing any doubt of where she belonged. Whether it was the Athabasca or the North Saskatchewan, the rivers of Alberta now flowed through her veins. From the camps of the continent's first human inhabitants to the great migrations of cranes and geese that marked the coming of spring, a path forward had always made itself known — a pattern woven from water, land, and sky with which she could chart the course of her own life.

When I returned to Frank's cabin, I could make out the sound of the distant strip mines to the south, the low-decibel rumble of destruction, a round-the-clock reminder of the multinationals stripping off the forest to mine the bitumen that lay below its roots. This is how the energy frontier moves inexorably north, into the land of Carcajou the wolverine, who was still part of Frank's world. Small contractors dig up the overburden of muskeg, sand, and gravel, exposing the oil sand for excavation by the heavy machinery. The trucks into which it is loaded stand many times the height of a human, so massive that each cab must be accessed by ladders. The ten-ton payloads they carry are taken to nearby upgraders for processing before pipelines deliver the final product to the power stations of Canada and the United States.

In Fort McMurray, sixty kilometres upstream from Frank on the river, tens of thousands of imported labourers flood the work camps, here to take the huge salaries on offer, then return to a home place in a different province or country. Few stay in Alberta, content to be cogs in the machinery of a temporary society. The measure of Alberta has turned from the social value of the pioneer to profit.

Suncor's Millennium Mine moves thousands of tons of northern Alberta soil each day to keep up with the demand for oil. Overhead, sleek executive jets from New York, Houston, Calgary, and Beijing fly in to inspect the oil sand leases, landing on each company's private airstrip. A new generation of absentee landlords, here for a tour of the site, a few handshakes from compliant politicians, then back to head office to map out the next lease.

Outside the door of Frank's cabin, the Athabasca flows silently north, joining the Peace to form the mighty Mackenzie. The current carries toxins as far north as the Beaufort Sea, above the Arctic

Circle. The Inuit still call the river's broad estuary *Kuukpak,* "Great Water." But like so many other Canadian rivers, its poisoned waters can no longer be considered part of a sustainable planet.

Four decades after the gathering at the Ladouceur cabin in Fort Chipewyan, Big Ray, Frank's son, takes up his father's fight against Big Oil. The tar sands have become an issue for the world beyond the borders of Alberta, but Indigenous people are still left on their own to fight the global corporations destroying their land. Ray's grandfather Modeste had died in 1978, Frank in 1990, long before the citizens of Fort Chip had begun to suspect their water was being poisoned by the same toxins that were deforming the fish. One of the last muskrat trappers and fisherman left in the Peace–Athabasca Delta, Ray took me to the place where Frank had made us tea on Lake Mamawi. What was once an expanse of turquoise water, teaming with waterfowl, was now an abandoned mud flat, empty of life. "Not enough water left to fill a kettle," Ray pointed out bitterly. Lakes were so low throughout the region that trappers had to resort to dog teams to drag their boats across the dried mud in search of water.

A world apart from the Ladouceur cabin on the Athabasca, at Jasper Park Lodge the Outlook cabin, a three-thousand-square-foot, six-bedroom log palace, was the summer headquarters of J. Howard Pew of Philadelphia, the owner of Great Canadian Oil Sands, the company that opened the tar sands to the world market. The rush for spoils had begun, as new technology and rising international oil prices made refining bitumen profitable. Pew had arrived with an entourage worthy of a maharajah, led by the first electric golf carts to be seen in Alberta, a fleet of which transported his household around the mountain course — stopping regularly for scones and tea sipped from the lodge's finest china.

As well as an oil tycoon, Pew was the founder of the evangelical magazine *Christianity Today*, which suited the Social Credit government that had brought him to Alberta to a tee. A friend of Barry Goldwater and Billy Graham, Pew worked closely with Premier Ernest Manning to launch the first successful large-scale tar sand operation, Great Canadian Oil Sands. As the Pew empire grew, Great Canadian became Sun Oil, with head offices in Dallas, which in turn became Sunoco, determined by Forbes Global 2000 to be the 252nd largest public company in the world. Along the way it swallowed up Petro Canada, "the people's oil company" funded by the federal government, and through a hostile takeover, the majority share in the giant Syncrude project the Alberta government had helped get off the ground.

"Let the big dogs eat" is a familiar phrase in the fossil fuel industry, reflecting the power and reach of multinational corporations — what Kevin Taft calls "oil's deep state." In Balmer's day, such concentration of ownership was just a sign of the crisis yet to come.

For Balmer it was a time to take stock. Committed to saving his marriage — he would never stop loving Peggy — he set about finding a permanent job. Strangely he felt a sense of relief when it became clear there was no hope of saving the *Saturday News*. He realized at the last he had sacrificed too much for the paper. From this point forward he would try to put his family's well-being before the demands of whatever newspaper he worked for — a resolution he was to discover was easier said than done. Sleeping for two days and nights after the bankruptcy, he awoke with the composure of a man who knows he did everything in his power to save the business. Now he could move on.

The following month, after their return from Peace River, Peggy tells her husband that another local paper, the *Edmonton Journal,* a conservative-leaning daily owned by an American, Bob Jennings, has been purchased by William Southam of Hamilton, Ontario. Already a patriarch of Canadian publishing, Southam has the financial clout to make the paper top dog in the Alberta market. Within a day Balmer is surprised to discover Bob Jennings at his door. Southam has convinced the publisher to stay on as editor, and Jennings in turn is now looking for an associate editor, someone who knows the ins and outs of Alberta politics. By the time the meeting is over, Balmer has signed on to an affiliation that will last the final thirty-six years of his newspaper career. He regrets leaving the *Alberta Homestead*, but here is an opportunity to return to mainstream journalism. He will start immediately and within two years will be the editor of the paper.

As neither Jennings nor Southam is well disposed to the Liberals, Balmer is given free rein to write about the government as he pleases. None of the Liberals' recent backroom dealing impresses Balmer in the least. His editorials continue to question the byzantine nature of the party, seemingly divided against itself — Calgary versus Edmonton, urban versus rural — and how it mysteriously maintains its electoral stranglehold on the province.

Travelling town to town in rural Alberta for the *Homestead*, Peggy the reporter is hearing a different story. Knocking on doors in search of new subscriptions, she hears complaint after complaint, rumblings of discontent that don't bode well for the government in the upcoming election. A belief is growing that the only way to change things for ordinary Albertans is to vote Sifton's "party of privilege" out of office. Support for R.B. Bennett's Conservatives is limited to Calgary, and the leader of the United Farmers of Alberta

(UFA), Henry Wise Wood, refuses to run candidates. Even though polls show the UFA to be the most popular organization in Alberta, Wood fears what power could mean to the sense of purpose that drives the membership. A fundamentalist Christian from Missouri, he is unwilling to expose his reform movement to the corruption of party politics — a point of principle reminiscent of Frederick Haultain. Peggy recognizes the UFA as the only legitimate hope for change in the province and tries to convince Irene Parlby to stand as a candidate. But it will take ten years of grassroots organizing before Parlby will be in a position to defy Wood and run for office.

It is an important juncture in Peggy's life. From this point forward her sympathies will lie with the radical face of Alberta, anchored in the upstart farmers' assemblies and coal-mining unions like the one she encountered in Pocahontas. Balmer quietly reminds her that his position working for the Southams as an editor, someone who is paid to see all sides of an issue, is a far cry from her emotional outbursts on behalf of prairie populism. He can't resist suggesting she take a more national perspective in her writing, balancing her regional perspective with the concerns of the country as a whole. As usual Peggy is not convinced. Whose national concern is he talking about? Bay Street's? As for populism, it will be an argument that will plague them all their lives. Balmer equates the word with reactionaries, both on the right and on the left — a threat to the due process of democracy. As years go by, from fascism to communism, the term become even more associated with extremism. Peggy will have none of it, holding on to the original meaning — a grassroots political movement to return power to the people — the antithesis to the rule of the establishment.

The political battles between the two journalists seem to know no end, but they are the first to admit that without this battle of wills, each of them would likely perish from boredom.

13

A Distant War

Evolution cannot be brought about
by the use of dynamite.

IRENE PARLBY

Grave of an
Indigenous
person near
Marlboro, Alberta

Co-operation *Is The Principle Which Is To Save Society* reads the banner headline atop an issue of the *Alberta Homestead*. Irene Parlby believes that each occupational group — farmers, miners, teachers, nurses, lawyers, factory workers — should organize to protect its own interests. When the Co-operative Commonwealth is finally attained, a truly democratic government will emerge, composed of delegates sent from all participating groups. The whole apparatus of general elections and parties will be rendered obsolete. The farmers are at war not just with governments in Ottawa and Edmonton, but with the parliamentary system itself: "If one then asks: how can one bring this about, the answer will be simple, by showing the merits of co-operation and the evil of competition."

The paper's first issues give a sense of the down-to-earth yet oddly elevated society the farmers envision. Books on philosophy, economic theory, and the natural sciences are offered with each subscription — Hegel, Herbert Spencer, Jeremy Bentham, Charles Darwin. Yet the articles themselves tend to follow the practical issues the farmers face: "How to Increase the Capacity of Your Well"; "Learn How to Get a Good Yield in a Dry Year"; "A Drought Will Mean Nothing If You Read *Campbell's Scientific Farmer*." Ads concentrate on increasing the circulation of the paper itself, critical if the venture is to survive: "A $100 building lot to the first person sending in 100 yearly paid-in-advance subscriptions to *The Alberta Homestead* by March 1st." Notices of the upcoming meetings of the various women's auxiliaries appear, although women still don't have a vote within the UFA: Morningside, Beaumont, Bluesky, Blindman, Gull Lake, Wildwood, Garden Plains, Bon Accord. Each gathering takes place in a community hall or one-room school, often miles from anywhere — outlying constituencies to which Peggy will somehow have to find a means of transportation if she is to report on the night's discussion. Yet by 1920, the organization will have thirty thousand paid members, far and away the most influential advocacy group in the province.

To Balmer's amazement the fledgling farmers movement attracts the attention of newspapers around the world. In 1913, the *Westminster Gazette* in London sends renowned poet Rupert Brooke to report on the rise of populism in this faraway world. Annotated with Balmer's notes, Brooke's articles have a prominent place in the scrapbooks.

> The most interesting expression of the new Western point of view, and in many ways the most hopeful movement in Canada, is the Co-operative movement among the grain-growers of the three prairie provinces ... an advanced Radical programme of a Chartist description. And it is becoming powerful. Whether the outcome will be a very desirable rejuvenation of the Liberal Party, or the creation of a third — perhaps Radical-Labour — party, it is hard to tell.

When they meet, Balmer tells Brooke the former is unlikely: the Liberals are too protective of their urban power base to change. All the same, Brooke is both fascinated by Alberta. But as much as he admires the farmers, Alberta's cities confound him:

I travelled from Edmonton to Calgary in the company of a citizen of Edmonton and a citizen of Calgary. Hour after hour they disputed. Land in Calgary had risen from five dollars to three hundred; but in Edmonton from three to five hundred. Edmonton had grown from thirty persons to forty thousand in twenty years; but Calgary from twenty to thirty thousand in twelve. "Where" — as a respite — "did I come from?" I had to tell them, not without shame, that my own town of Grantchester, having numbered three hundred at the time of Julius Caesar's landing, had risen rapidly to nearly four by the time of the Doomsday Book, but was now declined to three-fifty. They seemed perplexed and angry.

As Brooke notes, for the chambers of commerce, riding the boom means development at any cost. As railway schemes are dreamed up by the banks, land speculators follow in their wake, flipping properties and creating the illusion of prosperity. But Brooke is also aware of a discomfort amidst the buyers. Will the land hold its value as the international economy once again slides toward recession? A fellow doubter, Balmer maintains in his editorials that the growing weakness in the stock market favours no nation, renewing old hatreds, setting country against country, the world drifting toward war. He hopes sanity can prevail, reminding his readers that Alberta can create its own place in history, that the frontier with few established institutions can mediate the conflicts that arise. But few Albertans favour his ideas. Rather, as Brooke describes,

Pavements are laid down, stores and bigger stores and still bigger stores spring up. ... Hordes of people ... inspired with the national hunger for getting rich quickly without deserving it — prey on the community by their dealings in what is humorously called "Real Estate." ... all devoted to the sale of town-lots in some distant spot that must infallibly become a great city in the next two years ...

By the summer of 1914, as tensions rise in Europe, Peggy notices a transformation in Alix itself. Once a model of co-operation among its citizens, grassroots democracy is being replaced by the swagger of commerce and empire. The result is that the men and women Peggy once befriended in the tent city are being arrested as "undesirables." Even though they are Galicians of Ukrainian descent, they are considered potential traitors for having grown up within the borders of the Austro-Hungarian empire. Sent to internment camps in the Rockies, these new Canadians have once again become "bohunks." German neighbours have met the same fate, branded as enemy aliens. The opera singer Madame Yolande, an Austrian, one of Peggy's oldest friends, is deported.

As hostility intensifies, racism poisons the spirit of a greater Commonwealth in which the West has been settled. Across the Atlantic Bertrand Russell records his impression of the men and women who gather in anticipation of England's declaration of war:

> Those who saw the London crowds during the nights leading up to the Declaration saw a whole population, hitherto peaceable and humane, precipitated in a few days down the steep slope to primitive barbarism, letting loose in a moment the instincts of hatred and blood lust against which the whole fabric of society has been raised.

Even communities like Edmonton, home to many nationalities, turn ugly, hosting racist demonstrations. Peggy and Irene Parlby despair at the turn of events.

On July 28, 1914, war breaks out in Europe. Over the next four years, nine million soldiers and thirteen million civilians will die in the War to End All Wars. And although it will be fought thousands of miles away, Alberta society will be shaken to the core.

The province soon boasts the highest enlistment rate per capita in Canada, Union Jacks and "King and Country" banners draped over every available lamppost.

Within a matter of weeks, four thousand men have signed up in Edmonton alone, and Frederick runs away from home to join a regiment. A distraught Peggy blames herself and combs the city for the boy to no avail. Days later she and Balmer receive a telegram from the west coast. Frederick has ridden a freight to Vancouver, lied about his age, and enlisted in the navy. Peggy buys a train ticket to find him, but Balmer intervenes. He has discovered that the young sailor's ship is scheduled to sail for England from Victoria that day.

In one of Peggy's scrapbooks a photograph remains of a town called Empress, near the Saskatchewan border. A crowd is gathered on the town's only street, just a block long, an empty landscape stretching away on all sides. The townspeople, dressed in their Sunday best, are cheering a brass band and a small contingent of uniformed troops preparing to embark for the front. The soldiers march back and forth on the street in a ritual repeated across the province. The young volunteers, no more than boys, do their best to exude the confidence of men. Sixty percent of them will never return.

Used to running his own paper, Balmer gradually adapts to working for the Southams. Answering to a high-handed owner is harder for Peggy, who does little work for the new paper.

William Southam is a self-made man in an age of self-made men. His career reflects the classic example of a fortune made from hard work: a publisher who started selling newspapers as a boy and ended up running a media empire. Balmer has great respect for Southam's work ethic, but the war will strain relations between the two men. Southam is a patriot, Balmer a doubter. It won't be easy to find a middle ground.

As he has done for years, Balmer walks the path that skirts the rim of the North Saskatchewan to gather his thoughts. Sitting by the river, he writes a poem to his departed son, the boy who has grown up so much faster than a father could have imagined.

Little Boy Blue, come blow your horn
And mount your steed this summer morn
Your hobby horse is a charger bold
That takes a strong little arm to hold.

You take my hand and from our street
Familiar to your tiny feet
We pass along through foreign parts
To where the dear green country starts.

The river bank, the daisy field,
The wooded nook, what joy they yield!
The warbler's note 'mid leafy shade
Allures us further up the glade.

It's time for home; you cry "No! No!"
But when we turn our pace is slow;
And ere we reach the beaten track
You're glad to climb upon my back

Big Boy Blue the years have sped
And now you tower above my head
Another hour and you will slip
Away from home to join your ship.

You go alone, no more we two
The King has need of men like you
His call has come to eager ears
See how my pride has dried my tears.

In Gwynn Dyer's book *Canada in the Great Power Game,* my mother, Becky Watt, recalled how as a girl she watched the send-off of the troops in the first months of the war. How the streets were suddenly empty, as if an earthquake had hit the city: "They would have little flags in the window. I can remember one house with three flags, that [meant] they had sent three people overseas. One flag for each son or husband." Men who had not enlisted were publicly shamed, forced to wear yellow ribbons on their lapels.

My mother would often help us sort through the scrapbooks when she arrived to collect me at the end of the day. As she reviewed the articles, she was careful to point out that not every family supported the war:

> A mounted policeman once told me of the boys who had gone way deep into the Peace River country or the Athabaska [*sic*] country and hid out. He would be searching around, and find them in a cabin someplace or other. And I remember him telling me of a mother that practically scratched his eyes out — she had three sons hidden around the country, and saw that they got food.

Balmer recalled that it was a difficult time, communities divided, families not speaking to each other. Newspapers were required by the government to present a united front. To do otherwise was considered treason.

William Southam had no such misgivings. He worked with Lieutenant-Colonel John Alexander Gunn of the 24th Infantry Battalion in Hamilton to produce a book of marching songs to lift soldiers' morale. Gunn compiled the songs and Southam had them printed at his personal expense for free distribution to the 619,636 men who enlisted in the Canadian Expeditionary Force. Bound in khaki covers and small enough to fit in uniform pockets, the books included hymns, a prayer, and the text of Lord Kitchener's message to British troops: "Do your Duty Bravely. Fear God. Honour the King."

Peggy had gone silent, in shock from the turn of events, especially the departure of her son. As she travels the countryside covering farmers' assemblies called to discuss the war, an unearthly stillness lies on the land, as one by one the farms are abandoned. Often whole families sell their belongings and return to Europe. The Last Best West has lost its meaning.

Days after Frederick's ship sets sail, Peggy receives a letter from Oswin Creighton telling her he has resigned his position as Anglican minister in Alix and joined the army as a chaplain. He cannot stand by and watch the men of his parish go to the front without his support. In the fall of 1914, he makes a farewell tour to his congregation in the far country beyond Buffalo Lake. Remembering a sunlit day crossing the prairie with Peggy, Creighton writes,

> My final visit to a most delightful family, just a father and two sons, but rejoicing in life and in each other's society. I have seldom felt so absolutely at home; they were so delighted to have me ... They kept a spare room, where the bed even had a sheet and I was most comfortable. The next morning we had the service at 10:30. I arranged a nice altar, went into the workshop and made a wooden cross for it, picked a few wild flowers, and it looked quite like a little church.

Like most of his parishioners, the father and two sons were packing their bags, returning to "the old country" to enlist in the war. Creighton regrets the loss of the community he once knew as he packs his own bags and prepares to join the troops in Calgary.

The W. Parlbys went down on the same train with me,. and in the evening I dined with them and they took me off to the theatre, where we saw quite an amusing play. It seemed a frivolous thing to do, but I was glad of it, as I had been feeling very depressed all day, and could think of nothing but the war. It was very difficult saying goodbye.

Having helped Balmer man the phones at the *Edmonton Journal* as the casualty lists come in from France, Peggy arrives in Alix too late to see Creighton. Irene is on the next train from the south with news of his departure for the front. The two women collapse in each other's arms on the station platform.

The next day the Alix marching band plays at the station as young conscripts board the Edmonton train. Peggy recognizes the same Métis family she met with Oswin that summer's day at Buffalo Lake. Standing alone in a corner, Irene tells Peggy they're heading north to the Peace River country to join their exiled people. From their long faces it's clear this is not their war.

Peggy's mind goes back to Fort Chip and her time with the Ladouceur family, a far cry from the horror of the coming war. The Métis had come to represent what Canada should be fighting for — a meeting of minds and cultures, not the clash of empires. The tragedy of the Resistance of 1885 had never left her. The idea of the inclusion of Indigenous Peoples in a great nation. Now Canada seemed to be returning to the militarism of its colonial past.

By the time two million men had died or been wounded in France and Belgium, Frederick was in the North Atlantic on a small Canadian corvette, escorting merchant fleets through U-boat infested waters. One of his poems describes meeting a young sailor from the Alix district who had joined a sister ship.

I went aboard his ship the night before
We set out on our lonely long patrol;
We talked of all the things we loved ashore
And quite forgot the cruel North Sea's roll.
He told me of his acres in the west
And what he'd do when we had won the war;
I marvelled at his pioneering zest
Four magic words, he said them oe'r and oe'r
"When I get home."

The sun went down and with the dark came wind;
It swept the salty sea and murky sky;
And ever swiftly on we steamed behind
Our leading ship, whose stern lights all burned high;
And then there came a loud report, a flash;
We looked towards where the guiding lights had shone
"God help the lad," I cried, for with the flash
I saw our leader's gleaming points were gone,
"He'll not see home."

One night in the dead of winter, Peggy wakes up screaming as images of a sailor struggling to escape a burning ship fill her dreams. The nightmare is so vivid she insists Balmer go to the office to see if there is any news of their son's convoy. A week later news arrives that Frederick Watt has been seriously injured in a U-boat attack in the North Sea. His body has been crushed in an exploding passageway, but he is alive.

In May of 1915 a troop train makes its way across the Alberta prairie, dwarfed by the immensity of the landscape. Occasionally one can hear the refrain of a patriotic song from an open carriage window, only to have it carried away on the wind. Alone in the corner of a car overflowing with uniformed men, Oswin Creighton, now an army chaplain, cannot avoid thinking that history is bending back on itself, sending men to die in a world they thought they had left behind.

Creighton's train is bound for Halifax, where ocean liners commandeered to transport enlisted men to England are standing by. At stations along the way the exuberance of the troops is dampened by the presence of officers with billy clubs, sent from England to make sure the colonials maintain order. The Canadian Expeditionary Force will prove itself in battle, but the British High Command will be slow to recognize the fact. Even when General Arthur Currie's elite assault formations prove to be the difference in key campaigns, the Canadian Force is undervalued. Alberta has sent the Princess Patricia's Canadian Light Infantry and the Strathcona Horse, the mounts stabled in freight cars at the rear of the train.

Among the cavalry, neither man nor beast is aware of what awaits them in the quagmire of France. They have been sponsored by oil and railway millionaire Donald Smith, now Lord Strathcona. Many of them, polo players like Walter Parlby, have been rehearsing cavalry charges on the close-clipped grass of home. Little do they know they're to be swallowed up by the two-year-long Battle of Ypres in Belgium, horse and rider moving in slow motion through the mud, just long enough to be shot to pieces by German artillery. The gentlemen farmers of Alix will be no more.

14

North Star

This is the most cruel pang that man can bear —
to have much insight, and power over nothing.

HERODOTUS

The homesteading
frontier moves north

A slow-moving engine pulls a single colonist car across northern Alberta, in the direction opposite to the troop trains speeding to Halifax and the front. Unlike the crowded interiors of the military carriages, the ramshackle coach is all but empty. Travelling alone, an odd-looking young man dressed in a tweed suit stands in the aisle, wrestling with a sack of schoolbooks. The other passengers, local farmers returning from a fair in Saskatoon, watch him with amusement. Just nineteen, Harold Innis will one day be Canada's foremost political economist, but this day he appears out of sorts. Maybe the high spirits of the passing soldiers have caused him to doubt his decision not to enlist, choosing instead to travel to an isolated corner of Alberta to teach.

Innis has grown up near the Ontario town of Otterville, south of Woodstock, where Peggy and Balmer published the *Sentinel Review*. His family are grain farmers of the same United Empire Loyalist stock as the Balmers. Peggy met him when she was student at the Woodstock Collegiate Institute. All her life she would read his essays on the destiny of Canada, sharing his conviction that it is in the "far country," the margins of a country's geography, that one discovers its distinct character. Innis's description of his boyhood recounts a time when much of Ontario itself was still a frontier:

> My father, William A. Innis, started out on a farm of
> 100 acres between the ninth and eighth concessions ...
> the old homestead, chiefly obtained in the early stages
> from lumbering and later, probably, from livestock and
> dairying. The early history of the farm must have been
> characterized by high development of domestic indus-
> try, the burden of which probably fell on the wife and her
> daughters. But gradually fields were cleared, grain was
> grown and the farm, particularly after the construction
> of the railroad, developed along specialized lines with
> products suited to a wider market.

The challenge Innis set himself as an economist was to understand
how the social and political forces created by such a change transformed the life of his country.

As a young man Innis attended a Baptist church in Otterville,
which taught that both a devout spiritual life and a robust
democratic system of governance are necessary if a community is
to thrive. Ontario history showed that the more isolated the congregation, the more freedom it was given to determine its own
course. The ability of families living on the margins to make up
their own minds made a strong impression on Innis and would prepare him for his time in the scattered settlements of the West. His
distinctive ideas about Canada — a country that took its character
from independent communities spread across a vast landscape —
were already taking form.

As the train approaches its destination, a mere whistle stop
beside the Vermillion River, boreal forest dips down to surround cultivated fields, the northern-most edge of agricultural land in Alberta.
The sight of tender shoots of wheat, the first green of spring, raises
the young teacher's spirits after the long journey from Toronto. But

he also knows how risky it is to plant a crop this far north — how the men and women he met on the train have invested their future in marginal land, gambling a good harvest and wartime prices will wipe out their debts. They have come from the United States, Ireland, Scotland, Greece, and Galicia, many the same families Peggy and Balmer had met in the CPR colonist car on their journey west in 1905.

When Innis gets down from the train, not having slept well in days, he expects there will be someone to meet him. But the platform is empty. Inside the station he finds a note from a farmer telling him to find a bed for the night at a farm down the road. A group of riders will be leaving early in the morning, a twelve-hour overland journey down a single-track mud road to the Landonville district in the valley of the North Saskatchewan. The overland journey will be a revelation for the young man:

> All this was a completely new experience; the dirt roads, the hills and valleys, the riding down hill at a terrific pace ... I had never realized that horseback riding was still the normal way of travelling and it was only gradually that I began to see the many features of a completely different way of life.

Even though Innis will be the district's first schoolteacher, he is still only a student himself, at McMaster University in Hamilton.

As the stage pulls into Landonville, Innis notices a rough-hewn prosperity to the one-street community. The war has meant increased profits for local farmers, feeding the largest armies humankind has ever known. But supplying such quantities of wheat and barley means ceding enormous power to buyers, the cartels and grain exchanges in Winnipeg and Minneapolis to whom the small farmer is now beholden. The continuation of preferential tariffs and low freight rates in wartime has given big business an enormous advantage over the small producer.

With so many men at the front, there's little help to plant and bring in the crops, always at risk from early frosts this far north. Hired hands, once in abundance among the immigrants, are a thing of the past as German U-boats patrol the Atlantic. As often as not Innis finds himself pressed into service when the day's teaching is done. As he works in the fields he is impressed by the commitment of every man, woman, and child to maximize the yield. But the nights are another matter:

> Almost any excuse was used to get up a dance. Those invited arrived at all hours of the night and finally proceeded to break up possibly at two or three in the morning, allowing us to get home by four or five. I can well remember seeing coyotes running along with the dogs and the whole party making its way at great speed towards home.

Innis dispenses knowledge as best he can in a crude one-room log schoolhouse named Northern Star, thrown up the week before from an adjacent stand of poplars. Andrew Semple, the chair of a committee of local farmers determined to educate their children, offers Innis $720 for the summer, but room and board will have to come out of his salary. The next day Innis meets the local chapter of the United Farmers of Alberta, who have helped raise the money. The farmers aren't shy about confronting him about the Liberal government in Ottawa, which they are convinced favours Easterners like himself. Neither are they short of analysis on what's wrong with the economy, having spent hours discussing capitalism and its discontents. Within an hour, Innis's head is spinning. Many of the Ukrainians are communists who expound on the revolution-to-be in Russia; social gospel Americans call on the teachings of Christ to defy the railroad monopolies; English Chartists argue for an alliance with the trade unions in a general strike.

The all-night arguments give Innis vertigo, but he soon understands this is a community built from the ground up, determined to decide its own destiny. Within weeks he realizes that this isolated settlement, on the margin of civilized society, is the frontline for grassroots democracy in Canada. Here along the shores of the North Saskatchewan, far from the corporate economy of banks and railways, the common good is being examined nightly. The ideas that will lead to the barnstorming Alberta populism of the 1920s and 1930s are taking root.

Dominion Day will be Innis's only real holiday, yet the outdoor dance and picnic provide little chance to rest. One of the few eligible bachelors in the district, there is no escaping the farmers' daughters whose young men are away at war.

> On July 1st a picnic was held in the district and this included a great number of hair-raising activities with which I had never been familiar. One of course was the bucking contest, in which the most obstreperous animals of the district were brought to the grounds and the prize awarded for the individual who succeeded in staying on the horse longest. This was no mean achievement, since the horses were accustomed to bucking, biting, and occasionally running straight through a group of trees with low branches which were certain to dislodge the occupant of the saddle.

I wonder whether Innis met Peggy that day, as she and Irene Parlby made their rounds of the various chapters of farm women in northeastern Alberta. Against the wishes of the Liberal government they were distributing birth control information long before it was legal to do so. At picnics they would always have a table at which they sold United Farm Women of Alberta cookbooks, into which they would slip the contraband instructions — all the while collecting recipes for next year's edition. Peggy had a tattered copy of the cookbook in her own kitchen until the end of her life, the pages spattered with cooking oil and inscribed with new ideas in the margins. She claimed she'd tried out every one of the sixteen recipes for pancakes and waffles and added six more.

I remember her formidable UFWA waffle iron steaming away in the kitchen of the "Big House," sitting like a battleship atop the stove. Wrapped in the padded silk dressing gown of her glory days, one eye cocked on the steaming batter, Peggy waited for the precise moment to lift the lid. She would be smoking her morning cigarette, all the while holding court on everything from the horse races to Chinese porcelain. Relishing the ritual, she would cook me as many waffles as I could eat, as long as I listened to her stories. Balmer had long since had his coffee and a piece of toast and fled to his study to read the morning papers.

With the rise of the farmers as a force to be contended with, Irene Parlby had become president of the UFWA, now a province-wide organization. With Peggy at her side, she travelled across the province promoting the idea of a wheat pool, a farmer-run marketing co-operative that promised to provide an alternative to the monopoly enjoyed by the grain companies. Because of their close ties to the American market, these Eastern-controlled businesses often worked against the interests of the Western farmer. Parlby insisted the wheat pool would provide the farmers a say in setting the price for the wheat they were growing.

The meetings were held in isolated community halls and one-room schools one could reach only by horse and wagon or sled in winter. Peggy often found herself huddled under a buffalo robe to survive the cold. It was not unusual for her to see the sun rising over the darkened fields as she returned to the railway station for the long journey back to the city. By the time her train pulled into Edmonton, her column was already written and ready to take to press.

At North Star, Innis would help wash the supper dishes in the schoolhouse transformed into a community hall, then watch as the children were put to bed, wrapped in blankets on the floor behind the piano. Then, as the coyotes howled at the rising moon, the farmers' general assembly would begin. The first item of business was to pass the resolutions the parent body of the UFA had prepared in Edmonton. Then the consideration of local initiatives like a dairy co-op, made all the more difficult by the depressed Alberta economy. But the farmers were never short of ideas. Solutions ranged from a universal minimum wage to nationalizing key industries to once and for all putting an end to war.

Innis realizes the UFA was not to be taken lightly. Its members would not let a day go by without enquiring about his lesson plan for their children; education isn't a responsibility they are willing to trust to just anybody. They would do everything in their power to give the rural child an equal opportunity. As Helen McCorquodale of the *High River Times* later wrote of her own UFWA chapter:

> There will be no difficulty in recognizing the Alberta women in Heaven. With pencils and notebooks they will be gathered in little groups beside the river of life, putting finishing touches to resolution B2894, urging that more rural children be taken into the heavenly choirs.

But by evening's end, talk among the farmers inevitably turns to the war. There is an opinion in the community, especially among the Americans whose country has not yet joined the allied forces, that the longer the fighting lasts the better. The shortage of wheat in a disrupted world market means prices can only keep rising. Such a sentiment is not appreciated by the Scottish and English families whose boys are already fighting and dying at the front. As the casualty lists grow, old animosities resurface, stretching back to the United Empire Loyalists who once opposed the American Revolution. Neighbours stop speaking to each other; fist fights break out at community dances; the United Farmers cease to be unified on key issues. Within months, the war in Europe, however distant, begins to tear the isolated community of Landonville to pieces.

The two trains that passed each other on the Alberta prairie that day in 1915 carried very different hopes and fears for a young nation. To the west lay the frontier, the prospect of a new world; across an ocean to the east, the horrors of a society that once again had turned on itself, whole countries reduced to rubble, battles consuming the best and the brightest of a generation. As Harold Innis the teacher disembarked in northern Alberta at the edge of a farmer's field, Oswin Creighton the army chaplain proceeded to Halifax to join the masses of Canadian troops being marshalled for the Great War. There he would join the contingent bound for Southampton, then Gallipoli, Winston Churchill's ill-fated Turkish expedition. One hundred thousand men would die in the campaign in the months that followed, including Rupert Brooke, the light-hearted reporter who had enlisted in the British Army soon after returning from Alberta.

Creighton would write to Peggy once the fighting began,

> It is so terrible seeing these young fellows go into action, so healthy and full of life, and then hear they have been killed in swarms in some great charge. And then the wounded. We had over 500 through our station in twenty-four hours. And one is so powerless to help them ... I don't mind the dead. They have got away from it all.

As news from the front worsens, Peggy spends more time on the Parlby farm. With a new baby, my Aunt Lois, asleep in a carriage beside her, she works in the garden Irene has built on the plan of her grandfather's country house in Devon. In addition to growing a winter's supply of vegetables, she has raised beds of flowers from seeds brought from England in her saddlebags. Hollyhocks climb the wooden arbor she has built herself; saxifrage covers the hill behind the house; lilies line the path to the lake. Irene's Christmas card to Peggy that year is a watercolour she has painted of a trellis bursting with new blooms. An inscription from Pascal is written under the painting: "Man is lost and found in a garden."

And yet the letters from Oswin speak of a world beyond recovery, the lives of millions of ordinary men and women sacrificed to the ambition of a privileged class. Peggy's older daughter, Becky, has returned from the convent to help Balmer, who is on the verge of collapse from lack of sleep. As the war drags on, his office at the *Journal* has become the only reliable source in the city for news of men wounded or killed. His reporters in the newsroom have taken the phone off the hook, yet people call at all hours to enquire about sons and husbands at the front. Balmer always answers his phone. The only sleep he gets is when Becky is able to relieve him by reading the latest casualty lists to the caller. My mother remembered:

> All the men seemed to have gone. You had a tremendous rate of enlistment here, and my father at the newspaper was working overtime all the time, and he would come home absolutely exhausted.
>
> You have to remember there was no TV, there was no radio, but a dispatch would come through that, say, the Somme battle was in progress. ... And the phone rang incessantly — these poor, anxious voices: "We're so sorry to bother you, but is there any news?"

So at the age of nine ... I was part of the chain of communication, because I would let my father rest. And I remember what a dreadful time I had pronouncing the names of these various battles. And Daddy would tell me what dispatch had come through, and I'd just repeat it.

Outside Balmer's office the crowds gathered around the billboard the paper had erected to post the latest news. But Becky knew the news everyone dreaded could come in many forms:

> The sight of a telegraph boy was a thing of horror ... because they [officials] were never allowed to phone bad news. And you'd see the boy come down the street on his bicycle, and you'd watch what house he stopped at. And then, later, probably my mother would go over, one of the neighbours would go over.

My mother never forgot the war. A full fifty years later she would tell me stories as if they had happened yesterday.

In the spring of 1915, as news from the front worsens, the North Saskatchewan overflows its banks, flooding the tent city and all of Edmonton's lowland neighbourhoods. Two thousand people are left homeless. As she did during the terrible winter of 1906, Peggy spends her time collecting clothes and food for the victims. She and Balmer are still estranged even though they live under the same roof. Her boy lies wounded in an English hospital. The *Saturday News* and "The Mirror" are bankrupt, and the *Homestead* seems poised to follow the same fate. Now she's been betrayed by the river itself, the forces of nature laying waste to the young community.

A frantic telegram arrives from Rocky Mountain House, one hundred miles upstream, saying the water level has risen a further ten feet in the last ten hours. Balmer works around the clock publishing a special edition, warning people of the floodwaters' progress. City Council is able to convince the Canadian Northern Railway to leave one of its trains on the Low Level Bridge to prevent the structure from being swept away. The debris piled against the bridge's pillars includes a house carried downstream by the current. As if by a miracle the weighed-down bridge holds. The city's lumber mills aren't as fortunate. Built flush to the shore, one after the other they're swept away.

For five desperate days the city can at least take its mind off the war in Belgium where Canadian troops are arriving at the front lines. At the second Battle of Ypres, a raw 1st Canadian Division suffers 6,036 casualties and Alberta's Princess Patricia's Canadian Light Infantry a further 678, many of whom are Edmonton boys. The phone never stops ringing in Balmer's office.

On April 9, 1917, Harold Innis, long since recruited from university into the British Expeditionary Force, is part of the Canadian attack on Vimy Ridge, the allied offensive against the German Sixth Army. Innis describes the challenge the Canadians faced:

> Our task, therefore, was that of bringing material to the front line so that a bridge could be thrown over the line immediately after the attack and that the guns would be moved over these bridges to a new front. This was highly speculative and dependent on the weather and became a complete fiasco because of a heavy snow fall on the night of the attack and the impossibility of moving the guns forward in the mud. Most of our time spent in carrying this material to just behind the front line meant heavy night work, occasionally digging into pools of mud with the German star shells illuminating the whole area ...

> The burial parties and ambulance corps had taken care to
> a very important extent of the wounded ... But the snow
> of the night of April 9th fell on great numbers of dead
> men whom we saw the next day.

By April 12 the Canadian Corps had captured the high ground,
forcing the Germans to retreat from their entire position, breaking a stalemate that had lasted a year. It was considered a great
victory, the first time all four divisions of the expeditionary force
had fought together. The Corps suffered 10,602 casualties: 3,598
killed and 7,004 wounded. On July 7, as the Canadians switched
their attention again to the muddy plain of Ypres, Innis was hit by
fragments of an exploding shell, shattering his right thigh.

> They had obviously spotted our group, since in spite of
> the fact that we rather hastened our pace, the next shell
> landed right into the midst of us. Two or three were
> blown over but I was the only one hit. A shell splinter had
> penetrated the inner side of my right thigh but had not
> gone all the way through the flesh. Blood began to pour
> out at my knee and the men immediately got out their
> Red Cross tackle and bound up the wound ... It is clear
> that I was protected from other shell splinters by my habit
> of carrying around great quantities of stuff in my ruck-
> sack. At least one shell splinter was stopped by a book ...

Innis was evacuated from the trenches and a series of operations
saved his leg. His war was over.

The battlefield was not far from the city of Arras where Oswin
Creighton was now stationed, his latest posting in what was now
a war of seemingly endless attrition. It's likely that Creighton met
Innis on his daily rounds ministering to the wounded. I wonder
whether the two men were able to share the experiences of their

youth on the Alberta frontier. Next year country must have seemed a world away.

That winter Innis was sent back to Canada with thousands of other wounded men on the captured German ocean liner *ss Vaterland*. The massive vessel, bigger than the *Titanic* by thousands of tons, had to cross the storm-tossed waters of the North Atlantic where Frederick Watt was stationed. He had recovered from his wounds in Halifax and was once again patrolling the ice-strewn waters searching for U-boats. It would be his job to protect the hospital ship from attack.

Meanwhile, Oswin Creighton spends all his waking hours on the front lines, trying to give some comfort to the dying men. On December 11, 1917, he writes,

> More and more the world seems to have lost its charm and to offer little worth living for. Often I have thought that the simplest solution to its many insoluble problems would be to be blown to pieces. But after all, that is really too simple — and also cowardly. I don't think we are quite normal in these days, and I can only hope we shall be forgiven for our many failings ...

The next day, December 12, Creighton is killed by an exploding shell.

In Edmonton, Balmer is the first to read the news, recognizing the name in the daily dispatches from the front. The walk home to tell Peggy is the longest of his life. Irene Parlby is heartbroken when the news reaches Alix. She writes that week in the *Grain Growers' Guide:*

> Today the world is bleeding to death in its efforts to conquer a false idea of nationalism, but the only true

nationalism, the only true internationalism, is a spirit of
mutual sympathy and understanding among all people —
in other words the spirit of unselfishness which is the
essence of this thing we call co-operation.

Long after the war, philosopher George Grant, known for his 1965
book *Lament for a Nation*, described the impact of those years on
Canada:

> Canadians from all areas and all economic classes went
> off to that war hopefully and honestly believing that they
> were thereby guaranteeing freedom and justice in the
> world ... When one thinks what that war was in fact being
> fought about, and the slaughter of decent men of decent
> motive which ensued, the imagination boggles ...
>
> First, it killed many of the best ... and left the survivors
> cynical and tired. I once asked a man of that generation
> why it was that between the wars of 1914 and 1939 Canada
> was allowed to slip into the slough of despond in which its
> national hope was frittered away to the US ... He answered
> graphically: 'We had our guts shot away in France.'

In Alberta the impact of the war was so profound that Lewis Gwynn
Thomas, one of Alberta's most prescient historians, concluded the
young province would never be the same. More than half his class
at the university in 1914 had been killed at the front. Many of those
who returned, wounded or "damaged in the head," had to seek work
in a country industrialized by the war; their skills were no longer
needed. Unemployment was at a record high due to a worldwide
recession, and the Winnipeg General Strike of 1919 threatened to
paralyze the economy. Similar protests followed in towns across
the prairies, but the broken men, desperate for work, were simply
rounded up by the police and sent on their way.

Having survived the war, Frederick returns to Edmonton. Peggy does her utmost to rebuild the relationship with her son, but the shell shock he has suffered makes reconciliation impossible. Balmer gives him a job as a cub reporter at the paper, but journalism now means little to the shattered young man.

15

Sacrifice Zone

There is a river flowing now very fast. It is so great and swift that there are those who will be afraid. They will try to hold on to the shore. They will feel they are torn apart and will suffer greatly. Know the river has its destination.

HOPI PROPHET ORAIBI

The Turner
Valley oil field
in the 1920s

When Peggy researches a story on the fate of the buffalo on the Great Plains — the attempts to save the last herd from extinction — she is surprised to learn how close to disappearing the species had come. Earlier in the year, the Pablo-Allard herd, scattered across the Flathead Indian Reservation in Montana, was rescued by the Canadian government. Two hundred and eighty animals were rounded up and shipped to Buffalo National Park east of Edmonton in the hope they could be protected. They are all that remain of the ten million animals that once populated the Americas.

As she travels to inspect the herd, Peggy remembers the flocks of passenger pigeons she had seen as a girl in Ontario in the 1880s, before that species went extinct. The sight of those last birds has stayed with her all her life. Her grandfather had told her of seeing a single flock of three million "passengers" fly over Guelph in 1866, only thirteen years before she was born. Their song had filled the air, an echo of life on the continent before the arrival of the white man. In the years ahead sportsmen would shoot thousands of birds in an afternoon, competing for record kills. Peggy had asked her grandfather how people could stand by as God's creation was removed from the earth? He had no answer.

In the 1980s paleontologist Peter Ward, from the University of Washington in Seattle, visited Alberta. Research in the heavily eroded badlands along the Red Deer River allowed him to study a mass extinction which had been visited on earth sixty-four million years ago. Buried among the hoodoos was evidence of a collision between Earth and a massive asteroid, the resulting crater recently discovered in the Gulf of Mexico. The impact had left a gash in the planet's surface a kilometre wide and deep and had set off earthquakes, lava flows, and wildfires across the Americas, eventually destroying eighty percent of life. The amount of carbon dioxide the collision spewed into the atmosphere changed the biosphere for millennia and led to the extinction of the dinosaurs.

The most conclusive evidence of the impact was the presence of the mineral iridium in the fossil record. Iridium is rarely found on Earth and is thought to be the result of contact with an extraterrestrial body. The more Ward studied the catastrophe, the more he wondered whether a connection existed with the evidence of environmental destruction scientists like David Schindler were uncovering in Alberta in the present day. With each succeeding year, carbon dioxide levels in the atmosphere were approaching a similar danger point for the planet. Did the impact of massive projects like the oil sands have a precedent in Earth's history? Would the scale of destruction caused by the fossil fuel industry one day be comparable to an asteroid collision?

Ward had spent decades studying the worst extinction of all time, known as "the Great Dying," 250 million years ago at the end of the Permian era. At that time, as the temperature of Earth's atmosphere climbed to unlivable levels in a global warming event, ninety-six percent of all life vanished from the planet.

Producing a documentary with Melissa Ruckmick for the National Film Board of Canada, I followed Peter to the Karoo desert of South Africa, where, as in Alberta, the Earth's deep past lay exposed. The fascination with science Peggy had passed on to me as a boy went with me. The film was based on *The End of Evolution*, Ward's groundbreaking book on the need to preserve biodiversity in the face of a modern mass extinction already underway. Most alarming was his growing suspicion that the principal cause of the Permian catastrophe was not an asteroid impact as he had suspected, but simply the presence of excessive levels of carbon dioxide and methane in the atmosphere. If he was right, it was global warming that had been responsible for such a drastic change in the life of the planet. The rising concentration of those gases during the Great Dying was not unlike the crisis unfolding on the planet in the present day. Ward concluded that "it's happening again, but now it's Volvos, not volcanoes causing the damage."

Around the world species are disappearing at a horrifying rate, in part because of the province's emissions. Scientists have discovered that today's extinction count is hundreds, even thousands, of times higher than the natural baseline rate. A million animal and plant species are now threatened with permanent elimination in the years ahead. Peter Ward expressed his concern in *The End of Evolution:*

> My greatest fear, for our world, is that an increased rate of extinction can eventually reach some threshold point, triggering a cascade of mass extinction, a free fall of death. Each species on the earth is like a tiny piece in a four-dimensional jigsaw, interlocking with other species, and is a tiny conducting part of the energy flowing through the living world. Life is a giant house of cards, each creature supporting other species in a small or large way, so that if enough species are kicked out of place by their extinction, the entire house falls down. Did that happen at the end of the Permian? Did enough species get killed off to bring down a sudden torrent of extinction, eventually destroying 96% of the earth's creatures? How far from that cliff are we today?

Peggy had a similar concern. In 1916, during a trip south to visit Irene Parlby, she ran into Charles Hazelius Sternberg and his sons, fossil collectors from the National Museum in Ottawa. The men were building a raft to travel down the Red Deer River, home to the bones of dinosaurs millions of years old. The valley's spectacular badlands had once been the shore of a giant inland ocean, its forests teeming with life. The decomposition of that vegetation, sometimes miles beneath the surface, produced the oil and gas that would make Alberta a world energy producer. But for the moment it was the dinosaurs that captured Peggy's interest. The journalist in her sensed a story in the making as she watched the Sternbergs' preparations.

The old paleontologist didn't appreciate the attention. Short on time, he was engaged in a race to recover the bones before a rival American expedition arrived in Alberta. Barnum Brown was working for the Museum of Natural History in New York, a cutthroat competitor of the Canadians. Peggy had stumbled on the first sortie in what would become "the dinosaur wars" between the two institutions. And she correctly suspected that the discovery of previously unknown fossils would provide headlines for newspapers around the world.

Peggy's interview with Sternberg's son George revealed a remarkable discovery made in Deadlodge Canyon. While uncovering the skeleton of a duck-billed dinosaur,

> I had traced the skeleton to the breast bone, for it lay on its back with the ends of the ribs sticking up. There was nothing unusual about that. But when I removed a rather large piece of sandstone rock from over the breast I found to my surprise, a perfect cast of the skin impression beautifully preserved. Imagine the feeling that came over me when I realized that here for the first time a skeleton of a dinosaur had been discovered wrapped in its skin.

His excavation of a complete dinosaur mummy the next day was to revolutionize paleontology. Yet there was something deeply disturbing about the find. The badlands provided evidence of a disaster so complete that only mammals the size of mice, safe in their tunnels underground, survived.

Sternberg's gruff manner reminded Peggy of the homesteaders she had interviewed in recent years, always to the point, insistent she not waste their time. She was surprised by the paleontologist's anger at the changes that were transforming the province, driven by the Turner Valley and Little Chicago oil discoveries near Calgary. The virtual army of drilling rigs marching across the prairie reminded Sternberg of Petrolia, Ontario, where his father had taken him as a boy. The towns springing up along the foothills, driven by industry and big business, were destroying one of the most beautiful landscapes on Earth.

Her curiosity piqued by Sternberg's description of the boom towns, Peggy continued south to Turner Valley. The shacks that had been thrown up overnight, each a madhouse of speculation underway, were evidence of the amount of money an oil boom could generate overnight. Such a bonanza would make fossil fuel irresistible to the politicians. What lay beneath the ground seemed to be of much greater importance to Ottawa than the society struggling to survive above it. It was now clear to her why Frank Oliver, the federal minister of the interior, had insisted on retaining rights to the province's oil and gas deposits.

When she got back to Edmonton, Peggy showed Balmer her article on the Sternbergs — the fact that life had come so close to extinction in the past. Her husband, ever the realist, was cool to the idea. He told her there was no evidence of either the ancient calamity she described or the danger to the environment today.

Oil was good for business. Advertising in Alberta papers had doubled with the boom. Now the editor of the *Edmonton Journal*, he passed on the story.

I tend to take Peggy more seriously.

A century later I am in a helicopter tracking the wildfires at Fort McMurray. The wolverine is long gone, downriver into deep bush. The helicopter swings back over the tar sands and bitumen upgraders, the Athabasca glistening in the evening sun. Ahead, the Clearwater River flows into the main channel from its source along the Methay Portage in Saskatchewan — the route the Ladouceur family followed after the Métis defeat at Batoche. Modeste Ladouceur, in his nineties when I interviewed him, remembered when a person could stand on a headland and watch the currents of the two rivers converge, forming one vast stream of moving water, a quarter mile from shore to shore. Today the channel is less than a hundred yards wide. A solitary moose stands in water that barely reaches its ankles. We can see its tracks, wandering across mudflats where broad channels used to run. People who live downstream describe the lowest water levels in the river's history. Scientists are concerned that as climate change destroys the glacier at the river's source, summer flow levels could drop nearly thirty percent.

In 2010 David Schindler hosted a press conference at the University of Alberta in Edmonton to make public the discovery of deformed fish in the Athabasca River downstream from the oil sands. The trapper Big Ray Ladouceur, Frank's son, stood beside him, describing how the commercial fishery in Fort Chipewyan was all but extinct. Even the locals wouldn't eat the fish, a dietary staple in the community for centuries. Had the fish been the first victims of a die-off that might extend to other organisms that live downstream from the refineries?

Watching Schindler and Ladouceur take the fight to the government, I thought of the Métis legacy that stretched back to Winnipeg in 1870 and Batoche in 1885. It was the same tradition of resistance that had distinguished Haultain as a politician and Peggy and Balmer as journalists — speaking truth to power.

A commercial fisherman as well as a trapper, Ray Ladouceur had taken the fish to government officials as far back as 2005. Eyes and cheeks had been eaten away as if by acid; tumours the size of baseballs protruded from the skin. When the officials ignored him, he took the fish to Schindler, who along with John O'Connor, the doctor in Fort Chip, researched the cause of the deformities. The test results pointed to the tar sands tailings ponds, full of chemicals from the refining of bitumen. Hastily constructed and porous, the dam-like structures were leaking poisons into the groundwater, which in turn was seeping into the Athabasca River.

As Schindler conducted exhaustive studies of rivers and streams of the region, O'Connor began to investigate the heightened rate of cancer in Fort Chipewyan. Could the irregularities in the fish be linked to unusual incidence of lupus and rheumatoid arthritis among the town's residents? Cholangiocarcinoma, cancer of the biliary tract, which normally occurs once among one hundred thousand people, had two confirmed and three suspected cases in Fort Chip, a town of two thousand people. Schindler's findings pointed to the water. Research in hand, he decided to visit the families most severely affected. Some scientists would have released the results in the *Globe and Mail* or the *New York Times,* but Schindler felt his first responsibility was to the people of the community. I remember being with him in Fort Chip in a packed community hall when he described the cancer-causing chemicals he had discovered in the water. As he warned that contamination would only increase in the future, a silence fell on the room.

As the meeting ended, the town rose to thank Schindler and O'Connor — "their doctors," not the government's. At last someone in authority had told the truth. Years of corporate public relations could finally be seen for what it was. The Alberta government, the multinationals, the Canadian Medical Association had all tried to sweep the community's concerns under the rug.

The ghost of Modeste must have been standing at the back of the room. If he'd been alive, he would have concluded the gathering with a fiddle tune, most likely a Métis call to arms written by Louis Riel, "C'est au champ de bataille" — the battlefield. The day put me in mind of Peggy and her time in Fort Chip in 1912. Here in the room was a community that had persevered in the face of a level of adversity hard to imagine; that had stood as one, expressing a "precision of place" that even the most powerful business interests in the world could not dislodge.

Rather than addressing evidence of the poisons in the river, a Canadian Energy Centre, "the war room," as the government called it, was established in Calgary to "better inform" the public. With a $5-million annual budget to attack critics of the tar sands, the Centre set out to destroy any doubts people might have about the fossil fuel industry — doubts scientists had placed in the public mind. Discussion of environmental issues was to be discouraged, especially when they involved activists or charitable foundations outside the country.

In an earlier era when Peggy documented the disenfranchisement of the Papaschase First Nation in what became Edmonton, she maintained it was not just the hunting, fishing, and trapping rights Indigenous Peoples had been promised in the treaties that were at stake. It was the sacred places, the meadows where the Elders once collected medicines, the access to the graveyards where the ancestors lay buried. As Alan Adam, the chief of the Fort Chip First Nation, lamented a century later in the film *Tipping Point:*

"We have a treaty with the Crown in which our traditional life is protected, we just don't have the lakes and forests and rivers anymore on which to live that life."

For not the first time in her life Peggy turned to the ideas of Harold Innis. A summer teaching at North Star School had convinced Harold Innis that Alberta's unique gift was its place at the edge of the world, a landscape where the imagination could take flight, where ideas on how to improve society could be given practical application. Like Peggy and Balmer, he understood the essence of the frontier, the elbow room needed to become your own person, to create your own society. The Alberta frontier was the best of all worlds — a place of inclusion, the level playing field Peggy had sought since the day she arrived. Her experiences in Fort Chip simply confirmed the fact.

For Innis, Landonville was proof that significant thought was not always generated by a formal education. Homesteading, breaking ground, planting and harvesting crops, building new communities — each in its own way elevated the human condition. Innis's time on the frontier was to become the inspiration for the idea that civilization in Europe and the Americas had always moved westward, toward the edge of the known world. To his mind, it had started with the ancestors of the Greeks migrating across the Aegean from Asia to establish Athenian democracy and had ended with the first English and French colonists landing on the eastern seaboard of America. But he must also have been thinking about the courage of this lonely assembly of Alberta farmers, taking their chances on the western frontier.

To the end of his life Innis would remember standing with these men and women outside North Star School after a town meeting, taking in the wonder of the night sky. Stars seemed to reach down and touch the roof of the log structure the farmers had built. It was the same self-made society that Peggy had experienced in the north. Alberta at the edge of history.

Innis's thinking was no different than Peggy's articles in the *Alberta Homestead*, gleaning both the agricultural know-how and the fierce commitment to politics that distinguished the United Farm Women of Alberta. Like Irene Parlby, he was relentless in lobbying governments to introduce legislation more favourable to struggling homesteaders. He argued that freight rates and the excessive influence of the grain exchanges crippled the West, causing many homesteaders to fail, defeated by the larger forces of history from the frontier itself. Innis blamed the monopolies that controlled the staples economy of Mackenzie King. But it was more than simply economic policy. A branch plant, colonial way of thinking had begun to erode the national character. Where Canadian culture had once been distinct, it was becoming derivative, aping the Americans at every turn. The isolation of the frontier, once a strength, now turned to a liability. Distant from the corridors of power, with little impact on national affairs, the West began to be little more than a market for Eastern and American producers. Peggy and Balmer could only watch as the idea of an independent Alberta slipped away.

Peggy feared the powerful voice of corporate media would drown out the many smaller conversations that had helped develop a distinct Western identity. In isolated frontier communities that dialogue had been an essential feature of grassroots democracy. As the ability to share ideas, largely through local newspapers, disappeared, communities and regions became isolated, paranoid, increasingly strident in their demands. Peggy's one-on-one political conversations with her readers in the columns of

"The Mirror," dialogues that could take months to resolve, had gone silent. Likewise, Balmer's editorials, attempting to understand contemporary issues in light of the larger history of the Canadian West. At the *Edmonton Journal*, increasingly it was John Imrie, the new publisher, who decided the direction of the paper. Speaking for the Toronto owners as head of business affairs, he encouraged a new breed of Western journalist, exploring a more continental agenda, consistent with Alberta's new place in the global fossil fuel economy.

Peggy must have felt the chill of the Alberta-to-come in her bones, where every home would boast a cable service or satellite dish or computer app to access mass-produced American programming — the Netflix of the soul. The exchange of ideas that once animated farmers' meetings in North Star School had been replaced by a homogenous view of the world, connected by an umbilical cord to Los Angeles and New York. The community of independent thinkers that had fascinated Innis would be replaced by a culture that did very little thinking at all.

16

The Rise of the Populists

I want to leave something behind when
I go; some small legacy of truth, some
word that will shine in a dark place.

NELLIE MCCLUNG

Irene Parlby and
the newly elected
United Farmers
of Alberta MLAs

In 1919, as troops began the long journey home, men who had been the cannon fodder of an imperial army would never completely trust their "superiors" again. The politics of consensus on the prairies, once open to the future, would splinter along religious and ideological lines as the economy faltered. Canada's corporate masters, nearly all located in the East, had feasted on the spoils of war. Coal, oil and gas, railways, grain exchanges, munitions factories had all made fortunes for their owners. Their profits could now be ploughed back into buying up what was left of a shattered prairie economy.

Peggy maintained the war had been fought along class lines. Albertans, who had once left Europe to escape inequality, found themselves fighting under the command of a contemptuous English aristocracy. When she travelled to Jasper Park Lodge for the opening of its new golf course in 1925, she discovered that the Grand Trunk Railway had invited Field Marshall Douglas Haig to preside over the ceremony. To many Haig was still the "Butcher of the Somme," the commander who had sent a million men to their deaths, many of them Albertans. Now in the post-war world of the wealthy and privileged, he had become an exalted figure. By contrast a high percentage of the returning soldiers had lost their farms or their jobs. To Peggy's disgust, when Haig died three years later, there was a national day of mourning in his honour.

There was no shortage of pushback to the post-war status quo: the general strike in Winnipeg; "Wobblies" — the Industrial Workers of the World — organizing coal miners in the Crowsnest Pass; war veterans leading marches of the unemployed. In Alberta Liberal rule was wearing thin. The administrations of Alexander Rutherford and Arnold Sifton had become increasingly identified with Eastern corporations. Farmers' co-operatives, workers' councils, and small business associations had sprung up across the prairies in opposition, led by people like Irene Parlby and the superbly organized UFA.

Mackenzie King, who became prime minister in 1921 and held the office longer than anyone else in Canadian history, was no help to the Alberta Liberals. A longtime friend of the multinationals, he was soon pursuing a continental economic strategy in league with the owners of Standard Oil. As Peggy worries, poor provinces like Alberta had little choice but to play along with federal policy. During the Great Depression, Alberta would become desperate. Mortally wounded by the war, swept by crackpot ideologies, her citizens swung wildly to the left and right, but found no escape from the straitjacket in which they found themselves. The province Peggy had watched set out its own course only twenty years before was returned to the dependence of a colony.

Far from centres of power, the Alberta economy in the years after the war repeatedly staggered, then finally fell. Lashing out at distant boards of directors and bureaucrats soon became an Alberta tradition. Abandoned to its fate by the vituperative Mackenzie King, who had no time for the renegade farmers, the province virtually collapsed, becoming the poorest in Canada.

The United Farmers of Alberta now had little to lose by entering the political forum. In 1919 the farmers' leader Henry Wise

Wood backed down from his non-partisan stance and conceded that the party should run candidates in upcoming elections. To his surprise a UFA candidate, Alexander Moore, won a by-election in the Cochrane constituency with fifty-four percent of the vote. He had campaigned to reduce freight rates and increase grain prices. The next year, Peggy covered the campaign of Robert Gardiner, who won the UFA a seat in the federal parliament. She used the victory to convince her friend Irene Parlby to run in the upcoming provincial election, scheduled for the summer of 1921. The first woman to run for political office in the province, Parlby faced an uphill battle. Peggy quoted her in a diary entry: "The only thing which seems to concern my opponents is that I am a woman — and worse, an Englishwoman who, although I came to western Canada when it was still an undeveloped wilderness, could not possibly know anything about it!"

Encouraged by their by-election victory, the UFA runs forty-four candidates in addition to Irene. To their surprise, they win thirty-eight out of sixty-one seats, enough to form a majority government. But the party is without a leader in the House. Henry Wise Wood, the movement's founder, has refused on principle to run in the election. Irene Parlby will be a minister, but who will be the premier?

Peggy spends more and more time with Irene as party members prepare for the upcoming session of the legislature. Having sprung from a non-partisan movement, the government is happy to choose members of the cabinet from the opposition parties. First they ask a Labour MLA, Alex Ross, to be minister of public works. He accepts. Then they ask the Liberal leader Charles Stewart, the previous premier, to remain in office. Astonished at the offer, he agrees to stay on temporarily. Ultimately, a relative unknown, Herbert Greenfield, is named the first UFA premier, even though he protests he is far too busy with his farm north of Edmonton.

After years of struggle, a government sympathetic to women has been elected. Parlby is named minister without portfolio, responsible for rural schools and the advancement of distance education. Before the session is over she sponsors the Minimum Wage for Women Act and works with Nellie McClung to advance the Persons Case in 1928, giving women the right to be appointed to the Senate. At last women are recognized as having equal rights to men — or at least non-Indigenous women are.

For Peggy, the existence of a Farmers government changes everything. Here finally is the spirit of the frontier that drew her west, challenging the established order. Used to managing co-operatives that sell eggs and milk, the greenhorn members of the legislature will now manage the affairs of an entire province.

Balmer doubts the Farmers government will last. Too many first-timers in the legislature, not enough expertise to govern the province. The *Journal* has begun to turn a handsome profit and he doesn't want to see the newfound prosperity threatened. Peggy accuses him of becoming part of the establishment just as democracy is about to have real meaning in Alberta.

As usual they agree to disagree, but to cheer Balmer, Peggy reminds him that one of the government's first bills will be to end Prohibition. Open sale of alcohol through community-owned liquor stores will begin within a month. The flask of whiskey he carries with him everywhere can at last come out of its brown paper bag.

But this return to sanity doesn't change his mind about the dangers of populism. He will watch the Farmers closely for the authoritarian tendencies he fears are inevitable in grassroots movements. The influence of fundamentalist religion is already evident in the barnstorming politics of men like "Bible Bill" Aberhart. With the world economy in crisis, accompanied by the appearance of

Hitler and Mussolini in Europe, there's every reason for concern. Peggy argues that he's confusing two very different social movements — surely there's room for a left-wing populism that does not sacrifice democracy to gain power. Balmer is not so sure.

Peggy realizes that John Brownlee, the attorney general, is the true leader in the legislature. In 1925 he succeeds Greenfield as UFA premier, leading the party to a second majority government in the 1926 election. Yet many family farms still face foreclosure. To help the drought-stricken south of the province, Brownlee legislates a *Drought Relief Act* providing farmers with financial aid to help farmers pay their debts or at least reach a settlement with the bank. The premier had earlier played a leading role in the creation of the Alberta Wheat Pool to stand up to the plutocracy of the Winnipeg Grain Exchange. The Pool has long been a plank of the populist platform. Peggy quotes Irene Parlby in a letter to her aunt in Toronto:

> I envisage a time when we will not only be marketing our grain and livestock through co-operative channels, but we will be milling our grain into flour in our own co-operative mills, processing our livestock in a great packing plant, eventually selling these products in our own stores, and even sending them across the seas in our own co-operatively owned ships. When consumers in the cities become more enlightened as to the advantages of the co-operative principle, they will set up their own wholesale houses and stores. Then we will have gone a long way towards a Co-operative Democracy.

At Peggy's insistence Frederick Watt interviews the new premier, documenting his reform of health care. Hospitals in rural Alberta are still few and far between. Many minor operations, like tonsillectomies, are neglected, placing young children at risk.

The Farmers soon organize a system of mobile clinics to solve the problem. Teams of doctors and nurses travel the length of the province, staying as long in each community as is necessary. Peggy accompanies Irene to Fort Vermillion on the Peace River, the farthest north the clinics have been able to reach. Working in a makeshift operating room, the medical team performs fifty-three surgeries in two days. Soldiers from the war who had been abandoned to their fate by the Liberals are given special consideration. Across Alberta the first steps toward the universal public health system we know in Canada today are being taken. The level playing field is becoming a reality.

But there are unsettling signs on the horizon. The boom/bust cycles of the Roaring Twenties have left their mark on the province, choking off investment and destabilizing the markets on which Alberta's staple products depend. As if to make matters worse, both domestic and international finance are becoming suspicious of the Farmers' government. Populism is seen as a threat to the capitalist establishment. Balmer, now an astute businessman, worries about his investments, predicting the eventual crash of the stock market in 1929 in his editorials. He writes that Alberta is particularly vulnerable to the aftershocks of the collapse, its agriculture and natural resources dependent on distant buyers, beyond the influence of its government. Peggy worries about the decisions that lie ahead for Brownlee and the UFA. What's more, for her the crisis comes on the heels of a personal tragedy.

Irene had introduced Peggy to an old friend, John Hornby, an eccentric explorer reputed to have walked the nine hundred miles from Edmonton to Yellowknife — without so much as a hat. In the spring of 1926 Hornby arrived at Peggy and Balmer's front door with two young companions recently graduated from English public schools. Hornby's aim is to explore remote regions of the barren lands even the Dene and Inuit avoid for lack of food or shelter.

As always, extra places are set at the table and the men invited to stay over. Peggy is taken in particular with Edward Christian, Hornby's cousin who confesses he has no desire to live in a tent for the year ahead. A gentle soul, Christian reminds her of Oswin Creighton. By contrast, Hornby has an edge to him, impatient, short with Peggy's concern about the boys. He is known in town as the "hermit of the north," obsessed with the desolation of the arctic wilderness, relentlessly seeking to be apart from society. Peggy worries it will prove to be a dangerous obsession.

But Frederick is fascinated by Hornby and offers to accompany the party to document their story for the *Journal*. Peggy will hear nothing of his joining the expedition. She has hosted numerous arctic explorers at the house, from Vilhjalmur Stefansson to Cosmo Melville, and knows the dangers involved crossing the barrens on foot, especially in winter. Another English guest, James Critchell Bullock, had nearly perished when he spent a year "living off the land" near Hudson Bay with Hornby, who adamantly refused to take supplies. Peggy can see that neither Christian nor his friend, Harold Adlard, has any experience with such extreme conditions. She tries to convince Hornby to go it alone. The boys can remain with her, or stay at the Parlby ranch and play polo, more their cup of tea.

The better Peggy gets to know Hornby, the more worried she becomes. The explorer, a veteran of the Battle of the Somme, had suffered terribly in the war and is haunted by the deaths of his two brothers and his father beside him in the trenches. There is something unhinged about the man, unwilling to listen to reason. She knows the symptoms only too well. Frederick, another casualty of the war, is much the same — a danger to himself, especially when he drinks.

As if to confirm her fears, the next week Hornby announces he and the boys are leaving to winter in the forbidding Thelon–Dubawnt River watershed in the Northwest Territories. Again Hornby proposes to live off the land, hunting the great herds of caribou that migrate across the barrens. But the caribou fail to come that winter. Lacking sufficient supplies, the party is forced to eat the undergrowth that surrounds the cabin they build. Before spring can come to their rescue, they starve to death. Christian, the last of the three to succumb, leaves a diary describing their last days. Hornby is the first to die. Now it is Allard who is failing:

> 4th May. Since I last wrote I have not had a moment, for Harold's condition grew worse, and so did mine. At 10:30 p.m. dear Harold passed away. After a bad relapse the previous night, he seemed to get better during the day, so I went out to cut wood and get water. When I came back he said he felt very queer and knew not what to do. He was in pain. By 10.5 he had gone unconscious and slept. As for myself now I am played out after no sleep and food for a long time so have managed to make up some soup from bones and have a cup of tea and rest. Today I must fix things up as best as possible, cut wood, dig in snow for scraps of fish which we are surviving on still and rest as best as I can and trust for a good day tomorrow. I cannot hunt, as walking around in soft snow is beyond my powers now, and the weather is bad.

Peggy could hardly bring herself to read the diary.

The bodies were discovered by prospectors who came upon the camp in July 1928, two months after the men's deaths. The following summer they were buried by the Royal Canadian Mounted Police on a ridge overlooking the vast Thelon River watershed — only this year the great herds of migrating caribou had returned.

In the years ahead the region will haunt Frederick. He convinces a bush pilot, Lee Brintnell, to let him ride shotgun on a mission to Thelon country. They explore the barrens from the air, spotting the Hornby cabin and land on the river nearby. As they climb the ridge to pay their respects to the dead men, the expanse of the tundra opens before them. Peggy has sent a ring to be left on Edgar Christian's grave. The memory of the boy's eager young face will never leave her.

Still fighting the bottle, Frederick would return to the area in the winter of 1930, prospecting the rocky promontories above Great Bear Lake. Pitchblende, the ore that contained the uranium used to build the first atomic bomb, had been discovered in the region: "My journey, motivated by need and hope, became something more than a prospector's adventure. It was a journey into a savage land, a country for which I was unprepared. And it became a desolate struggle, a passage into the dark landscape of the self."

As a journalist, Frederick is researching rumours of what the pitchblende will be used for, whether the massive amount of energy released by splitting a uranium atom can be used to build an explosive device. In the years ahead, a mine is constructed on the lake at Echo Bay, and by 1938 the first pitchblende is being brought to the surface. Dene labourers are hired to carry sacks of ore to barges on the lake at Deline, to be transported to Fort Resolution on the Mackenzie River. Some of the men will travel with the shipment, sleeping on the sacks over the course of the long journey, later to die of the cancers associated with radiation poisoning. It is as if Great Bear had cast a shadow over Frederick's life, the source of a tragedy far greater than the personal problems he carried with him. He would return to Edmonton a changed man, finally prepared to forgive Peggy for the betrayals that had destroyed his boyhood. He would never take another drink.

By the winter of 1932, Peggy's spirits are on the mend. As a new wave of immigrants arrives in Edmonton, many of them refugees from the coming war in Europe, she makes her living room a home away from home, notes from her piano once again floating above the river valley. The recent arrival of radio in the province provides a further outlet for the music she loves. The UFA government has purchased a struggling station, CFCK, to be operated by the University of Alberta Department of Extension as CKUA, the first public broadcaster in Canada. The mandate of the station is to provide distance learning, reaching out to isolated farms and communities, but in Peggy's mind it has the potential to be something more. She meets the new station's Program Director, Sheila Marryat, Irene Parlby's younger sister, and the three women resolve to expand the reach of CKUA programming to include the dramatic arts. Working with local writers and actors, they propose a theatre of the air to explore the pressing social issues of the day, conscripting local playwright Elsie Park Gowan to tell real-life stories of the frontier.

The station has a broad canvas to work with as the Dirty Thirties descend on Alberta. An extended drought, especially in the south of the province, has left rural communities devastated. As local businesses and family farms collapse, young people have no choice but to move to the cities — only to be greeted by record unemployment. Gowan is the voice of those migrants, portraying the drama of lives beset by unemployment, lack of adequate housing, and grinding poverty. Overnight she becomes the inspiration for a new breed of Alberta writer: "When I was a youngster growing up in Edmonton, all art and literature was from far away. A poem was what Mr. Wordsworth wrote about daffodils, a play was something produced in London and a book was always written about somewhere else. The world we saw reflected was never our own." Inventing radio drama as a virtual stage in living rooms across the province, Gowan set out to change that sense of displacement.

Like Peggy, Elsie Park Gowan took special interest in the fate of women on the prairies, held back by the renewed sexism that accompanied the Depression. Next year country, which had promised so much to both sexes, was in free fall, a far cry from the egalitarian society the frontier had promised. Gowan's plays present women trying to ward off disaster with little or no help from either their partners, government, or business. Characters reflect marital infidelity in *God Made the Country;* bigamy in *A Toss for Father;* the racism that greeted inter-racial marriage in *One Who Looks at the Stars.* Yet they also hold out hope: pacifism in *The Giant-Killer* and women's liberation in *Back to the Kitchen, Woman!* In a letter to the editor published in *Saturday Night* magazine, Gowan refused to apologize for writing what Eastern critics described as "kitchen sink" drama:

> Outside our best hotels and transcontinental trains, so many Canadians still live in one-room houses ... we misguided playwrights have tried to create a drama (from their lives) distinctively Canadian. We believed that the quality of our lonely land might be found in its far places ... that its reality might be best known by those who live close to its prairies and forests and mountains.

Over her career Gowan laid the groundwork for generations of prairie artists to come, storytellers for whom a sense of place would mean everything: writers W.O. Mitchell, Maria Campbell, Rudy Wiebe, Myrna Kostash, and Fred Stenson; sculptor Joe Fafard; painters Illingworth Kerr, Sylvain Voyer, and Harry Savage; musicians P.J. Perry, Tommy Banks, k.d. lang, Ian Tyson, and Corb Lund, to name only a few. In their work you can sense the bittersweet mixture of Western hope and Western despair that Gowan and Peggy shared.

17

Dust Bowl

The difficulty lies, not in the new ideas,
but in escaping from the old ones.

JOHN MAYNARD KEYNES

As drought
descended on
the prairies,
fields blew away

Not only did Elsie Park Gowan expose the underside of Alberta social relations, but her radio scripts dramatized a tipping point in the politics of the province, a time when populism and grassroots democracy teetered on the edge of fascism — Balmer's greatest concern. As people lost their farms, jobs, and homes, reasonable voices were drowned out by the fury of the mob.

But fascism was only part of the problem. No matter what causes her journalism championed, or what government she worked to elect, Peggy feared Alberta would never escape the long arm of Bay Street. It was as if Toronto held a mortgage on the province. And when prices for natural resources plummeted with the collapse of the New York and London stock markets on October 29, 1929 — "Black Tuesday" — the house of cards collapsed. In an editorial for the *Edmonton Journal*, describing the potential of a worldwide monetary crisis, Balmer warned that the financial failures that were sure to follow would swamp the fledgling Alberta economy. In such a time of need, the banks would not be the province's friend.

The growing corporatization of the Alberta economy had long been an issue for the UFA government. Fossil fuels — from coal to natural gas and oil — ranching, and farming were becoming the domain of big business — Eastern and overseas companies encouraged by the federal government to invest in Alberta on terms determined by Ottawa. The fact that the Liberals of Mackenzie King continued to control such a large segment of the Alberta economy angered the new premier, John Brownlee, who set out to take ownership of future resource development. He would work indefatigably for three years to build the legal and political case for the transfer of jurisdiction to the province.

Mackenzie King, on the other hand, would do everything in his power to maintain the colonial status quo, of which Southam Press was a part. Balmer, who had never trusted the federal government, sided with Brownlee against Mackenzie King. In their days at the University of Toronto, during a student strike, the future prime minister had taken the side of the administration, all the while pretending to support the students. As a reporter for the student newspaper, the *Varsity*, Balmer had seen the deception first-hand, a duplicity that would become Mackenzie King's trademark in the years ahead.

But Balmer knew he had one hand tied behind his back. Experience told him he could expect little support from the Southams. Mackenzie King represented the Liberals' corporate Ontario power base, of which they were a part. As often was the case Balmer's editorials negotiated some form of middle ground. He wished Brownlee well, but maintained that good government should derive from discipline, not the anarchy of the constituency meetings that had given the premier his mandate, donnybrooks that raged democratically into the night. Donnybrooks that Peggy relished. Balmer held firm: reform was one thing, but responsibility for social harmony belonged with the individual, not the anarchy of class warfare.

In 1929, Brownlee won the case, taking control of the province's future, most critically the Eldorado of oil and gas that lay below the ground. As his train returned from the final negotiations

in Ottawa on a freezing November night, supporters lit huge bon-
fires along the tracks outside Edmonton and across the High Level
Bridge. Three thousand jubilant supporters led the premier into
the city.

Riding the wave of popularity, Brownlee led the United
Farmers to a third majority government in the 1930 election,
despite a quickly deteriorating economy. Alberta would now have
to set about creating its own institutions to manage the windfall
that lay ahead. Irene Parlby, now one of the premier's most trusted
cabinet ministers, told Peggy that the government would have to
act quickly if they were to control the pace and scale of development. Jersey Standard (later ExxonMobil) was moving into western
Canada through its subsidiary Imperial Oil. With the vast deposits
in the tar sands, it was only a matter of time before they began more
extensive exploration in Alberta. If the Farmers government was
to stand up to the multinational, Brownlee would have to build an
infrastructure of his own, a public sector capable of managing the
resource.

For once agreeing with his wife, Balmer wrote an editorial
about what an unusual premier Brownlee appeared to be:

> One admires the careful way in which this cautious, clear
> thinking man approaches the problems of Alberta's
> development. He is a man of ability. What comes as a
> surprise is that he is also a man of imagination. He hopes
> to extend park areas, promote growth of music festivals
> with the help of government broadcasting … he would
> like to see art and drama carried to rural areas, especially
> schools. These are surely not plans one associates with a
> farmers' government.

But as Balmer had also predicted, trouble lay ahead for the mod-
estly spoken premier.

The failure of economies like Alberta's was accompanied by the rise of fascism around the world. From Germany and Italy to England and the American Midwest, extreme right-wing parties were growing. Alberta would be no different. The Farmers government was already under attack from a more extreme brand of populism, what in the years ahead would become known as Social Credit. By 1932, as Hitler and Mussolini attacked the democratic traditions of their countries, Europe was once again drifting toward war. The fragile peace created by the Treaty of Versailles was in peril. To uphold it, a world disarmament conference was convened in Geneva.

Irene Parlby, now recognized across North America as a spokesperson for grassroots democracy, was invited by the new Conservative prime minister, R.B. Bennett, to represent Canada at the conference. A fellow Albertan, Bennett hoped Parlby's lifelong experience founding co-operatives would be of value to a world in crisis. The invitation confirmed Peggy's belief that populism could be a constructive force in the world, as opposed to Balmer's fear that it led to totalitarian government. For the time being, it appeared she had won the argument.

Parlby agreed to attend the conference, as long as the organizers would give her time to visit the grave of Oswin Creighton. Through the war office she had learned he was buried with hundreds of thousands of other men in the fields of Picardy in northern France, where the Battle of the Somme, one of the deadliest battles in human history, had been fought.

After travelling halfway around the world by train and boat, Irene found the conference a great disappointment. Adolf Hitler came to power in January 1933 and set out to re-arm Germany and withdraw from the Treaty of Versailles, one of the treaties with the Central Powers that ended the Great War. Within days the disarmament agenda was seen as unrealistic by many of the conference delegates, fearing the aggression that might follow Hitler's election.

The accomplishments of a farmers' co-operative government half a world away were beside the point.

Undeterred, Parlby spoke out against the suppression of democracy and the increasing persecution of minorities. It became clear how out of touch she was when news arrived of storm troopers marching through the streets of Berlin smashing windows, rounding up Roma and Jews. Listening to Hitler screaming threats over the radio at night disturbed Irene deeply. The peaceful countryside of Alberta seemed farther away than ever. By week's end she was in a state of collapse.

There was now no question of visiting Creighton's grave, and Parlby had to be escorted by a nurse to an ocean liner in Hamburg for the return voyage. When the ship docked in Montreal she was hospitalized for nervous exhaustion. A fortnight later Peggy, with Walter Parlby, met Irene's train in Calgary and drove the couple to the farm. Within days Irene resigned her seat and became a virtual recluse, never to return to the legislature. It was a bleak day for the United Farmers, who depended on her steady hand and calming presence. She had been the human face of the administration, transcending sectarian rivalries, calling out the competitive egos of her male colleagues, settling the regional differences that had haunted the movement from the beginning. With Irene's departure, Peggy feared for the future of populist politics in the province, vulnerable as it was to extremism.

As the Great Depression deepened, a wide range of alternative parties had sprung up across North America: technocrats who believed in an energy theory of value where salaries would reflect real work, not profit; the End Property movement in California, led by Upton Sinclair; the Ginger Group of the Co-operative Commonwealth Federation, founded by Bill Irvine in Calgary, urging Alberta to adopt social policies similar to Roosevelt's New Deal south of the border.

Yet establishment newspapers, including Balmer and the *Edmonton Journal*, would find fault with radical movements every step of the way. The establishment might have its faults, but it was the keeper of law and order in an unsettled time. In his book *The People, No*, Thomas Frank describes the prejudice in the press against populist movements:

> the newspaper industry ... came together against the would-be dictator Roosevelt the same way it had united against [William Jennings] Bryan in 1896. The reason for journalism's overwhelming hostility to the president seems obvious in retrospect: the owners of the nation's papers were wealthy figures who regarded themselves as spokesmen for their local business communities; they also felt their immediate interests to be threatened by the unionization that the New Deal encouraged. Whatever the reason, their cohesion was remarkable. FDR himself believed that the press was 85 percent against him; the historian Arthur Schlesinger Jr. put it at 75 percent of the country's big city newspapers ...

When it became clear that the Southams would take a similar line, Peggy and Balmer would once again have to agree to disagree.

One of Peggy's favourite critics of the business community was Chester Ronning, director of Camrose Lutheran College. Ronning had been born in China, the son of missionary parents, and as a student in Fancheng was a friend of Zhou Enlai, the first premier of the People's Republic. In later life he became Canada's ambassador to the government of Jawaharlal Nehru in India. In Alberta he worked hard for the United Farmers, helping balance their rabble-rousing enthusiasms with a knowledge of the world. Years later, he described a Camrose by-election campaign in 1932:

> I was speaking at a town hall meeting when my opponent for the Liberals, Arnold Westvick, accused me of having been raised on the milk of a Chinese woman. The crowd appeared to be shocked. He went on to imply my judgement might have been impaired as a result. I admitted that my mother had not had milk for me, and had found a milk mother in a nearby town to nurse me. I assured the gathering the experience had had no ill effects on me. Then I turned to my opponent and said that I had it on fairly good authority that Mr. Westvick had been raised on the milk of a cow.

Irene told Peggy that Ronning was a stabilizing force within the government. His experience outside Canada gave him valuable perspective on the dark side of populism, the totalitarian forces that were disrupting European and Asian politics. He had come to recognize that the major challenges to the Farmers government would come not from traditional sources like the Liberals, but from the far right. Fundamentalist religious movements were entering politics as the Depression became more desperate. No one in the UFA would believe Ronning when he told the cabinet of the popularity in his constituency of a new party called Social Credit, the name referring to an obscure economic theory devised by an eccentric Englishman.

The work of Major C.H. Douglas, social credit proposed that governments circulate more money in the economy. The basis of its A+B Theorem was that prices rose faster than incomes. Douglas proposed to make more credit available to the average citizen, bending the arm of the tight-fisted banks.

Led by the same William Aberhart Peggy had known in Brantford, Social Credit was organized as if by divine right — God was about to provide a quick fix for the problems of Albertans. Ronning described attending a meeting in Camrose where a woman asked Aberhart to explain the party's indecipherable economic platform. The leader pointed to the light bulb that was illuminating the room and said that one doesn't ask how such a marvellous invention actually works but simply flips the switch. It would be the same with Social Credit: the voters would simply have to flip the switch.

Ronning was just the opposite, approaching a problem from as many sides as possible. As missionaries in China, his father, Halvor Ronning, had taught the principles of democracy at his mission school, challenging the tyranny of the Manchu dynasty, while his mother, Hannah, had been instrumental in unbinding the feet of women. After returning to Canada, Halvor founded a utopian Christian community, Valhalla, in the Peace River country. The congregation was part of a breakaway faction of the Lutheran church led by a lay preacher, Han Nielsen Hauge, who believed one should be judged by one's good work, not simply one's faith. Although not driven to impose his religion on others, Chester carried that belief through the tumultuous century that lay ahead.

The Social Credit agenda for reform that Ronning and the UFA had to contend with in the upcoming election was nearly entirely focussed on the pocketbook of the impoverished farmer. In its campaigning, Social Credit promised to issue "prosperity certificates," in effect providing spending money for the cash-strapped populace. Discussion of Major Douglas's policies spread like wildfire in town hall meetings across the province. Suddenly political debate was consumed by supply-side economics and the heresy of the godless UFA. But like Balmer, Ronning sensed a nascent fascism in the rallies, the judgement of individual farmers swept away by the crowd. Irene introduced Peggy to the rangy MLA at a Farmers rally, giving the journalist the chance to challenge the doubts Ronning expressed about Social Credit. Irene later told her she was grasping at straws. Ronning had the pulse of rural Alberta.

Aberhart was no Hitler. His only violence was in his rhetoric, but the promise of government dividends issued to every Albertan made him an overnight sensation. Peggy could only smile when she thought of his sermon on "the Rapture" twenty-five years before. Now he had taken on the task of elevating three hundred thousand Albertans to heaven. As George Orwell wrote in an English newspaper at the time: "The future, at any rate the immediate future, is not with the 'sensible' men. The future is with the fanatics."

For a time the sombre, efficient Brownlee government seemed safe from such a political outlier. But their ethical approach to issues provided no easy answers to a collapsing economy. By contrast the provincial Liberals, in the final stages of a fall from grace that went back to the Railway Scandal of 1910, decided to throw caution to the wind. The leadership of the party, still a cabal of Edmonton lawyers, set about manufacturing a series of sex scandals that would destroy both the premier and his government.

The Liberals' first target was Tony MacPherson, the popular young minister of public works rumoured to be a likely successor to Premier Brownlee. MacPherson's socialite wife Cora had left him for another man, the aide-de-camp to the lieutenant governor, who in turn fled to Winnipeg to escape Cora's incessant demands. Left homeless and distraught, the minister's wife was now a public spectacle, penniless on the streets of Edmonton. Sensing a political opportunity, Liberal lawyers offered to sue her former husband for abandonment, drumming up a groundswell of public sympathy. To win the case they would have to convince a jury that he had left her before she had left him, but given her dishevelled state it wouldn't be difficult to portray her as the victim.

The case had little merit under the law, but great publicity value. Frank Oliver was on his deathbed, but his Liberal newspaper the *Bulletin* splashed each day's court proceedings across the front page, conscripting a mob of enraged women to take to the street in protest. Within days Mrs. McPherson had become a "woman wronged," even as evidence continued to mount against her. By contrast Balmer waited patiently for facts to emerge that would prove the guilt of the minister. In the meantime he relegated the story to a single column on the back page of his paper.

Peggy knew all the individuals involved, including MacPherson's new wife, Helen Mattern, who had been married in a civil ceremony in her son Frederick's apartment. Frederick's wife Ernestine was Mattern's sister-in-law. Peggy also knew the lawyers prosecuting the case, former associates of Charles Cross. "An unsavoury pack of scoundrels," she wrote in her diary, "all with ambitions of office." Nothing came of the case, but in the weeks it took to make its way through the courts, the salacious accusations ruined MacPherson's career. One of the most respected members of the UFA cabinet was forced to resign, and seeds of doubt about the integrity of the government were planted. The Liberals, overnight the province's self-appointed party of moral rectitude, could smell blood.

Next it was the premier's turn. Allan MacMillan, the mayor of Edson, managed to find a job for his daughter, Vivian, in the Edmonton household of Florence Edy, Brownlee's wife. Edy was an invalid and needed assistance raising her two sons. The young caregiver was welcomed into the Brownlee home by the family until one day on the front page of the *Bulletin,* MacMillan accused Brownlee of forcing his attentions on her in the back seat of his car. According to the virtuous young woman, the abuse had been going on for months. The claim of non-stop sex seemed preposterous: Brownlee was as restrained and colourless as the government he ran.

Again the Liberal lawyers who had ruined MacPherson would ensure the case went to court. Balmer wrote in his diary the day the news broke:

> Back to the office before nine o'clock. Markets went further into the bad slump that started yesterday. Then was told the Brownlee story had broken ... *Bulletin* publishing *Extra* with all the horrible details. Our story was condensation of statement of claim and was accompanied by strong denial from Premier. Feel more certain than ever after reading alleged details that whole thing is political frame up. Would be easier to believe if so much had not been charged. Exceedingly tired tonight ... very discouraging.

When *Edmonton Journal* reporters could find no evidence of MacMillan's claims, Balmer again relegated the story to the back pages, along with everyday domestic cases that were being heard in small claims court. The RCMP had similar doubts about Vivian's testimony, but nothing could stop the Liberals. A highly politicized jury found for the plaintiff, the judge for Brownlee. But the publicity surrounding the trial was so damaging that the premier resigned on July 10, 1934, replaced by R.G. Reid, a nondescript member of his cabinet. The man whom many historians would describe as the best premier Alberta ever had was ruined. The purported scandal also ended many friendships. Peggy never spoke to a number of her Liberal acquaintances again.

To make matters worse for the UFA, the Great Depression only deepened over the course of the trial, leaving the economy in disarray. Canada's Gross National Expenditure had fallen by forty-two percent in 1933. Thirty percent of the labour force was out of work.

One in five Canadians had become dependent upon government relief for survival. Problems on the Prairies were made worse by years of drought, high winds, and hailstorms that decimated crops. Neighbouring Saskatchewan experienced the lowest price for wheat in its history, causing provincial income to drop ninety percent within two years. In Alberta some men had no option but to sign up at Unemployment Relief Camps administered by an uncharitable federal government. The pay was twenty cents a day for hard labour building roads with a pick and an axe. Then the soil began to blow away and a near biblical plague of grasshoppers descended on what was left of the crops. Men began to ride the rails in search of relief. But there was no such thing to be found.

As the months passed the UFA began to realize how vulnerable the province was, depending as it did on the international grain trade. Overabundance of supply and loss of traditional markets had left granaries and elevators overflowing with next to worthless crops. Balmer wrote that Alberta farm income had plunged from $102 million in 1928 to less than $5 million in 1933.

Before the scandal, Brownlee had turned down a top job in R.B. Bennett's government in Ottawa, then the chairmanship of Canadian National Railway board, to stay in Alberta. Charles Clark had written in the *High River Times* how

> many people depended upon his dignity, wisdom, and cool judgement, and though differing with him in viewpoint, felt he was sincere in his devotion to the province and its people ... He repeatedly refuses to better himself materially, choosing instead to share the lot of the people of this province.

As his salary as premier was only $8500, the sacrifice Brownlee made was real. George Ferguson, a Winnipeg journalist with the *Manitoba Free Press*, described Brownlee thus: "He has no sense of the spectacular ... there is no fanfare of flourish about his actions. He simply gets things done." And in a series of interviews with the premier for the *Edmonton Journal*, Frederick Watt mused: "a slow smile lighted up [Brownlee's] rather sombre features as he gazed out his office at the beautiful valley of the North Saskatchewan in all its autumn glory. In his typically understated manner he told me: 'It would give me a wrench to ever leave Alberta.'"

But a group of lawyers, members of the Liberal Party, some candidates in the upcoming election themselves, had other ideas.

It happened that a fire broke out backstage in a theatre. The clown came out to inform the public. They thought it was a jest and applauded. He repeated his warning. They shouted even louder.

SØREN KIERKEGAARD

Book Three

1936–1964
THE DARKLING PLAIN

18

Man from Mars

… the Antichrist must be revealed, and
the Battle of Armageddon must be fought,
and the greatest time of trouble the
world has yet seen has yet to come.

WILLIAM ABERHART

Family en route
to the Peace River
country, pulling up
stakes during the
Great Depression

Many Albertans realized that the sex scandals that plagued the United Farmers had been manufactured and would rather put their trust in Brownlee than the "pack of jackals," as Peggy called them, who had brought him down. But now there was a third alternative, the Social Credit party and its charismatic leader, reformer William "Bible Bill" Aberhart, the dark horse in the race. As he broadcast sermons each Sunday from the Calgary Prophetic Bible Institute, his voice boomed across the province, "the words of my roaring" as Robert Kroetsch called them. He was the one candidate who understood the revolutionary impact that radio, recent to Alberta, would have on politics.

Aberhart had promised to run sixty-three "honest men" (two of whom would turn out to be women) in the election. His campaign centred around the recovery of the economy, promising twenty-five dollars a month to everyone in the province if he were elected. He completely avoided the sex scandals that had brought down the UFA ministers, leaving them to the prurient campaign he knew the Liberals would run, and instead chose "I am my brother's keeper" as his election slogan.

On August 22, 1935, Social Credit relegated both the United Farmers and the Liberals to political oblivion, winning fifty-seven of sixty-three seats. The United Farmers, battered by the

Depression, did not win a single seat. Brownlee, MacPherson, and Irene Parlby, the best and the brightest of the populists, were gone, and there seemed to be no one in the rank and file to replace them. The collapse was particularly hard on Peggy, who remained faithful to the end.

Newspapers across the continent couldn't believe the result. The *Boston Herald* headline read "Alberta Goes Crazy." The *Montreal Star* warned: "They have voted for an untried man and policies whose workings he ostentatiously refused to explain before polling day ... They are in a frame of mind to try anything once. It is a dangerous frame of mind ...." The *Ottawa Citizen,* a Southam paper, surprisingly took a different tack:

> The Social Credit victory in Alberta is one of the most momentous decisions ever made by the people of a self-supporting state in recent times. It may sound the death-knell of an archaic financial system which demonstrably fails to fit the facts of modern production, and it will come as a stupefying shock to those in other parts who dismissed William Aberhart as a sort of comic character suitable for the barbs of their misinformed derision.

Balmer had to watch his step. Unlike his Southam colleagues, he had been skeptical about Social Credit from the start, arguing that the policies required to make the theory work were not suited to a democracy, that to implement Major Douglas's ideas required autocratic powers. Again he warned of the danger of fascism in his editorials, reminding the reader of Aberhart's inexperience in government. The new premier replied it was enough to trust Major Douglas, the master in London: "You don't have to know all about Social Credit before you vote for it ... we'll get experts to put the system in." The votes counted, he immediately sent a telegram to Douglas in England that bordered on panic: "Victorious! When could you come? Aberhart." No one in the new government had the slightest idea what to do next.

The Douglas hypothesis, expanding the amount of credit available in the economy, was being discussed by economists, but Alberta was the first government in the Americas to take the proposal seriously. Immediately a cry went up from old-school economists in Ottawa, Toronto, and New York — not to mention their corporate masters. The Social Credit victory set off a powerful backlash against economic reform in the corridors of power. It was little wonder because Aberhart had not spared his words in attacking the establishment: "It was the Lord Jesus himself who took the whip of cords and drove the money changers out of the temple, wasn't it? He didn't stand at the door and pray that God would put them out. He put them out."

Irene Parlby pointed out to Peggy that one thing was certain: Social Credit would take itself very seriously. Not only were party members economic reformers, but they regarded religion as the foundation of politics. For them, a person's ethics — renouncing infidelity, gambling, or drinking — were the measure of a responsible citizen. Well into the 1960s, as long as the fundamentalists remained in power, commercial airlines were not allowed to serve alcohol while flying over Alberta.

Yet by the 1940s the much-maligned Social Credit thinking on the economy was instrumental in rescuing the world economy. A shift toward Keynesian economics, in many ways similar to what Major Douglas had proposed, made a recovery from the Depression possible.

Like a prairie fire, a second populist wave had swept across Alberta. But this time a fierce fundamentalism had fuelled the flames. There was something of the apocalypse in the preachings of the Prophetic Bible Institute — politics as a reckoning for the sins of mankind. More a prophet than a premier, "Bible Bill" Aberhart had not run in any specific riding, assuring the crowds that his calling transcended the everyday requirements of government. Once again the province was without an elected leader in the legislature. A hasty by-election was called, giving Aberhart a second opportunity to rant against Bay Street and the Eastern-owned newspapers aligned against him — "the financial papers," as he now called them. The *Calgary Herald* had mocked his campaign as that of a deluded high school principal. Now this Elmer Gantry-like figure would have his chance to set the record straight.

He began with a series of radio commercials called "The Man from Mars" featuring an extraterrestrial who, having landed on Earth, can't understand why Alberta is governed so badly. The Martian visitor was a favourite of Peggy's. Excited by the possibilities of the new medium, she wrote that the weekly radio series was a work of genius.

Aberhart was a brilliant propagandist in the tradition of Elsie Park Gowan. Within a month the show had half a million listeners, more than half the province's population. John A. Irving describes the impact of the series:

> Meetings for the coming week would be announced. Then the audience would be informed that a very strange character, known as the "Man from Mars," who had just arrived on earth, was anxious to hear about the political and economic condition of Alberta ...
>
> ...
>
> He could not understand why people were not receiving enough food and clothing in a land where food and clothing were being needlessly destroyed. Why were some people driving around in big cars, well-fed and

prosperous, while others did not have even the barest necessities of life? Aberhart informed the Martian visitor that, if he could stay for the meeting, he would learn that Social Credit was the only way out of the present financial chaos, the only solution of the paradox of "poverty in the midst of plenty."

From the beginning Aberhart's appeals to Albertans had identified a ready villain. On most any issue one could imagine, Alberta's woes could be blamed on the Liberal leader in Ottawa, Mackenzie King. In 1935, he was returned to power with one of the largest majorities in Canadian history, sweeping the opposition away in every region except Alberta, where he managed to win a single seat. Never known for his modesty, the prime minister quickly lost patience with upstart populist movements like Social Credit and the Co-operative Commonwealth Federation in Saskatchewan, excluding them from any role in his new government. He then succeeded in alienating every farmer in Alberta with the comment that the drought-stricken province was no more than "a small part of the U.S. desert area. I doubt if it will be of any real use again."

Mackenzie King had been Laurier's minister of labour and a close ally of the union-busting Rockefellers in the United States. Ostensibly a "friend of the working man," he had betrayed miners when he turned his back on strikes in the Crowsnest Pass of southern Alberta in 1909. Instead of representing the interests of the workers, he allied the government with the mine owners, expatriate British coal companies who refused to pay a decent wage and cared little about worker safety. The result was an explosion at the Hillcrest Mine outside of Blairmore on June 19, 1914, where 189 miners died. Although his speeches were peppered with antiestablishment rhetoric, Mackenzie King represented the interests of the Ontario and Quebec manufacturers and industrialists who ran the country, not to mention the Rockefeller trusts he continued to advise in the United States. As Aberhart explained to the Man from Mars, Mackenzie King was no friend to the ordinary Albertan.

Peggy was not without sympathy for her old friend. Writing about Aberhart's rise to power, she quoted Irene Parlby:

> I do not think I should be very wide of the mark if I said that the older parts of Canada have for years regarded Alberta as a rather peculiar place, favourable to the breeding of extreme radicals, and peculiar political phenomena, and let it go at that. One wonders if it ever occurs to them that there are always causes and conditions which breed these things.

Balmer shook his head when he read the column. A rocky marriage was about to get rockier. Although he couldn't abide Aberhart, Mackenzie King did not fare much better in his opinion. Balmer recognized double speak as the essence of the prime minister's Liberal politics. Having witnessed Frederick Haultain be stabbed in the back by Frank Oliver and the first Liberal administration in Alberta at Mackenzie King's urging, as well the earlier experience at the *Varsity*, he had experienced Mackenzie King at his most devious. When power was involved, truth became negotiable.

Irene Parlby was philosophical about the Social Credit sweep. She had invited Major Douglas to her home on his first tour across Canada in the early 1930s. The UFA had even considered legislating his cure for the economy. As much as she would never forgive the Edmonton lawyers who had framed Brownlee, she realized the devastation of the Depression was simply all too encompassing for a government to survive. She told Peggy about the fate of the family of Senator James Lougheed, one of the founding fathers of the province. It wasn't just the farms in southern Alberta that had been seized by the banks, but Beaulieu, the Lougheed residence in Calgary. Once the pride of the newly independent province, it was now in the clutches of the Bank of Montreal. As was so often the case, Peggy was determined to write a story.

As a young reporter in Ontario in the 1890s representing a little-known, small-town newspaper, Peggy had interviewed the senator, appointed to represent Alberta before the province joined confederation. At one point a lawyer for the CPR in Calgary, Lougheed had impeccable connections with the Eastern establishment, enabling him to present himself as the unofficial voice of the Prairies in Ottawa. But Peggy always had a way of both charming and confronting her subject. After chatting about the senator's new responsibilities, she questioned his support of residential schools, a federal program being extended into the North-West Territories. A successful businessman who traded in real estate and newspapers, Lougheed was a strict conservative, believing the place of Indigenous Peoples lay within the customs and culture of the British Empire. He replied by asking Peggy if she had considered the alternative to the schools — the despicable American treatment of its First Nations, which in many cases amounted to murder.

In the years that followed, Peggy remained fascinated by the contradictions in Lougheed. As minister of the interior and superintendent-general of Indian Affairs in the government of Arthur Meighen in 1920 he was a strict enforcer of the Indian Act, which he felt was necessary to protect Indigenous Peoples from exploitation. His wife, Belle Hardisty, was of mixed blood, her own mother a member of the Chinook people in what is now Oregon. Peggy interviewed Lougheed a second time when she discovered that he had reprimanded Indian Affairs officials when they refused to allow

Blackfoot and Stoney participants in the first Calgary Stampede. He fought the decision and won.

A century later, I made a documentary for the CBC, *The Life and Times of Peter Lougheed,* in which the senator's grandson recounted his boyhood, especially the foreclosure of the family home, Beaulieu. The old mansion was being seized for back taxes by a Bay Street bank and the City of Calgary. After the senator's death, the family had fallen on hard times and could not prevent the foreclosure. As James Lougheed's library and furniture were sold for pennies on the dollar by the bailiff, the future premier resolved to one day see justice done.

Lougheed's memories in the film included the profound change the province had been undergoing during his boyhood — the rise of a populist brand of politics capable of challenging the Eastern establishment. The Social Credit and CCF governments that lay ahead on the prairies sought a democracy that could empower ordinary people, not simply vested interests. The wealth of big business in Toronto and the power of a massive bureaucracy in Ottawa were being challenged by the ideal of a fairer society, "the level playing field" Peggy described so often in her writing.

Inspired by an immigrant culture seeking a new life on the frontier, populists like Aberhart brought a home-grown radicalism to politics. The era of smug liberalism represented by Chief Justice and then Premier Arthur Sifton was over. Inspired by what was happening in the American West, where a range of alternative political movements were taking root, local societies across the province gathered under the Social Credit banner to challenge the establishment. Franklin Delano Roosevelt's "New Deal" had been an inspiration for what could be done to change public life. As Thomas Frank wrote many years later,

Populism was one of the first of the great political efforts to tame the capitalist system. Up until then, mainstream politicians in America had by and large taken the virtues of the system for granted — society's winners won, those politicians believed, because they were better people; because they had prevailed in a rational and supremely fair contest called free enterprise. The Populists were the people who blasted those smug assumptions to pieces, forcing the country to acknowledge that ordinary Americans who were just as worthy as bankers or railroad barons were being ruined by an economic system that in fact answered to no moral laws.

Yet Peggy realized populism itself was a contradiction, as prone to tyranny and betrayal as any political movement. In Alberta it had grown out of the hopes of the waves of immigrants who came west at the turn of the century in pursuit of freedom. Yet if they were to have any chance of success against the power aligned against them, the leaders would have to build a mass movement, and that is where the danger lay — the rule of the mob. Aberhart was a believer in the parliamentary process, but he was also a demagogue, the product of his church, where the idea of a prophet leading his or her people out of the wilderness was universal. The temptation to wield power, sometimes singlehandedly, for what one believed was the public good was considerable. New ways of thinking were clearly needed. But how to turn the ship around when it was already far out to sea? There were no simple answers.

When Peter Lougheed took office in 1971, his policies borrowed from the economic and social platform of the populist UFA and Social Credit governments. Like his grandfather, he campaigned in the barnstorming tradition of a prairie politician, bringing a wide range of Albertans inside the ever-expanding Progressive

Conservative tent. To address the oligarchy that controlled the oil business, his administration was able to call on the province's past, reviving the sense of place and ownership that had made a distinct society possible.

Lougheed understood the contributions to Canada of a province at the margin of the nation, close to the land, with visions of a more egalitarian society. The appeal he held for the electorate reflected the best of Alberta, the confident stride of next year country, the ability to think independently.

Ottawa had been slow to respond to the Great Depression. In 1929, as the markets crashed, Mackenzie King felt that the crisis was a temporary swing of the business cycle and the economy would recover without government intervention. The prime minister carelessly remarked that he "would not give a five-cent piece" to Tory provincial governments for unemployment relief. The opposition made sure he would never forget the remark, reminding him of the hardships of ordinary people for the rest of his career. When Mackenzie King travelled to Alberta, Peggy remarked that he was more comfortable giving King George VI a tour of the Banff Springs Hotel than visiting desperate Canadians whose farms were blowing away.

The prime minister's trip to Germany to visit Hitler won even fewer friends in the West. Mackenzie King commented in his diary that the German leader was "really one who truly loves his fellow-men, and his country, and would make any sacrifice for their good." The Prime Minister later forecast that the world "will yet come to see a very great man-mystic in Hitler ... I cannot abide in Nazism — the regimentation — cruelty — oppression of Jews — attitude towards religion, etc., but Hitler ... will rank some day with Joan of Arc among the deliverers of his people."

Alberta would become so impoverished during the Mackenzie King years that in 1936 it would be unable to pay the provincial debt, threatening the ability of the government to open its doors. As they were doing around the world, citizens took to the streets, demanding justice, protesting establishment indifference to their plight. Mackenzie King turned his back. Tragically, the contempt he showed to what was now the nation's poorest province would have serious long-term effects for Alberta's relationship to Canada. The memory of humiliation ran deep, even when prosperity returned. For decades the resentment of "sovereignty" movements like Social Credit would remain, their alienation passed from generation to generation.

By 1936, the province had descended to the level of a failed state. The exuberant face Albertans once presented to the world had become inward looking, insolent, even violent. Patterned on the Brown Shirts in Germany and the Green Shirts in England, the extremists in Social Credit formed paramilitary groups to patrol public functions. At one rally in Edmonton, armed with truncheons, they made it clear they would brook no criticism of Social Credit policies. Aberhart had lost control of his own party.

Yet as Peggy maintained, the premier was still a man of the people, defending "the little guy" against the banks and the railway companies. Around him party workers — true believers — were preparing radical legislation to confront the financial establishment, most notably the banks. They moved quickly, limiting debate within the party, ignoring the consensus approach to issues that had been the essence of grassroots democracy on the Prairies. Foremost on their mind was forcing a confrontation with Ottawa, a key element in Douglas's larger strategy. The battleground was to be the financial legislation designed to give Alberta more control over issuing credit. As Bob Hesketh, author of a biography of Douglas, observes,

On August 17, 1937, the Credit of Alberta Regulation Act,
the Bank Employees Civil Rights Act, and the Judicature
Act Amendment Act, 1937 (Second Session), were disallowed by the Mackenzie King government. Douglas was
elated! The war had been joined. By drawing the federal
government into the fray, the legislation of the second
session had more than fulfilled his hopes. Finance had
shown its hand when it petitioned the federal government, which, in turn, had irrevocably shown itself to be
Finance's ally by disallowing the three acts. The second
stage of his strategy, in which all Finance's allies would
be identified and the battlefront would be widened, was
already under way.

The disallowance was followed by Social Credit issuing a release
from its Publicity Bureau: "We the people of Alberta, are at war
with International Finance." Aberhart and Douglas were counting on Albertans rallying behind the Social Credit government in
its war with Ottawa.

To their disappointment, the majority failed to rise to the
occasion. Once again the Dirty Thirties had taken their toll. As
Hesketh describes,

The success of Douglas's strategy depended on an awakened, directed public will. Try as he might, like Aberhart,
Douglas would be unable to mobilize the public behind his
strategy. By late fall, enthusiasm for his confrontational
tactics had begun to ebb. The grassroots membership of
Social Credit had little taste for his war rhetoric.

For Peggy the return of the apathy of the Great Depression felt like
the ultimate defeat.

19

The Pulitzer

A journalist is the lookout on the bridge of the
ship of state. He notes the passing sail, the little
things of interest that dot the horizon in fine
weather. He reports the drifting castaway whom
the ship can save. He peers through fog and
storm to give warning of dangers ahead. He is
not thinking of his wages or of the profits of
his owners. He is there to watch over the safety
and the welfare of the people who trust him.

JOSEPH PULITZER

Peggy and Balmer
attend a reception
hosted by John C.
Bowlen (right), the
lieutenant governor
who disallowed radical
Social Credit legislation

For Peggy Watt, the Ottawa disallowances were just one more example of a Last Best West that had failed to realize its promise. Mackenzie King or John D. Rockefeller or the justices of the Supreme Court would determine the future. The unwavering influence of the banks, "the financial fascists" as Major Douglas called them, would remain central to that power. The greed that had brought on the Great Depression would go unchecked. Despite the suffering of millions of ordinary women and men, "finance" had carefully avoided taking responsibility for the catastrophe, and now carried on business as usual. When all was said and done, the rich only got richer.

Aberhart had not given up. In autumn 1937 his government rewrote the financial legislation Ottawa had disallowed and introduced a new bill designed to silence mounting criticism in the press. On October 5, 1937, Alberta's Lieutenant Governor, John Bowlen, refused to approve the Bank Taxation Act, the Credit of Alberta Regulation Act, and the Accurate News and Information Act, referring them to the governor general-in-council in Ottawa. Mackenzie King simply referred the three acts to the Supreme Court, which quickly concurred with Bowlen's decision, ruling the acts *ultra vires,* beyond the jurisdiction of the province.

Again Bible Bill refused to back down, creating the Alberta Treasury Branch in 1938 to protect farmers and small businesses against foreclosure from the Bay Street banks. The provincial bank could also give special credit to businesses who bought made-in-Alberta goods. In Peggy's eyes, the Treasury Branches, established across the province to free Albertans from the usury of Bay Street, became Aberhart's enduring legacy. To this day they perform a major role in the financial life of the province, supporting marginal individuals and businesses the established banks refuse to help.

To alleviate the suffering of the poor, Aberhart had promised to issue a twenty-five-dollar monthly dividend, a "prosperity certificate," to every one of Alberta's 425,000 adult citizens. (Today's equivalent would be over five hundred dollars.) But once in power the premier had discovered the provincial treasury was empty. There was not even enough money to cover basic operating costs. When he did try to issue the certificates to save face, they proved to be worthless. Because they weren't real currency, banks and merchants refused to honour them — either as deposits or as payment for goods — reducing the whole scheme to a farce.

The Man from Mars broadcasts had ceased to be heard across the province. There was no longer irony or humour to be found in Alberta's plight, only further desperation.

When the Supreme Court ruled the Accurate News and Information Act *ultra vires,* Balmer found himself in a precarious position. It had been the coverage of the new government in his own paper, especially the editorials he had written, that had angered the extremists in the Social Credit League to the point that Aberhart was forced to act. Under the provisions of the Act newspapers could be fined, their reporters even jailed, for failing to publish "accurate" news distributed in government press releases.

Balmer contacted editors and publishers across the province. If they stood together and refused to recognize the Act, the integrity of a free press could be preserved.

But it wouldn't be that simple. Many of the rural editors were Aberhart backers, and surprisingly even major papers in the East supported the government. Two of the sons of his boss William Southam, Fred and Harry, ran the prestigious *Ottawa Citizen* and were believers in the Douglas economic plan Balmer excoriated daily in his editorials. Maintaining that the Douglas proposals were the only way to save capitalism, the brothers had taken the initiative to invite the Major to Ottawa to address a committee of the House of Commons, arguing that the problem was not social credit but the out-of-touch, old-school economists employed by the federal government. This caused more than one heated discussion in the family. "We're like a bunch of people in a canoe going over Niagara," Harry would say to his father, who stood firmly behind the conventional thinking of the establishment.

By contrast, Walter Davenport, an editor with *Collier's Weekly* magazine in New York, attacked what he considered "the perversion of democracy" in Alberta. He had met Balmer in the press gallery of the legislature in the fall of 1935 as the first Social Credit policies became law. Davenport was convinced Aberhart's reforms would require a totalitarian government, much like Hitler's, to implement. When he went back to New York he asked Balmer to write a confidential "Alberta Letter" for the magazine each week, describing new developments in the populist saga. As *Collier's* was the leading magazine of investigative journalism in America at the time, Balmer was free to speak his mind — anonymously. The letters show his rising disenchantment with Social Credit:

March 10, 1936. A group of labour representatives tried to meet with Aberhart yesterday but were thrown out with great violence by a body of men wearing labels on which was printed "Special Police." They were not policemen and an investigation has linked them to the same "storm troopers" who were active on election day, part of the Hitler techniques adopted by the Social Credit organization.

March 24, 1937. Now that the 'prosperity certificates' have failed, they're calling for the licensing of all occupations and for the fixing of the prices of all commodities and the control of all marketing operations. The regulations have empowered the government to introduce as complete a system of regimentation as prevails in any totalitarian country. When people found out their plan, there was an immediate outcry.

May 5, 1938. Most of the Social Creditors, who were told in 1935 that the province would be converted into a heaven on earth if Mr. Aberhart was elected, are now thoroughly disillusioned. A farmer recently told me: "Our ability to speak our mind openly in these parts is sorely persecuted. There are spies even at the picnics and social gatherings we attend ..."

The Social Credit faithful must have begun to realize how difficult it would be to challenge the power of the establishment, especially Bay Street's control of the media. As Harold Innis, remembering his time in the West, was later to write,

The overwhelming pressure of mechanization evident in the newspaper and the magazine has led to the creation of vast monopolies of communication. Their entrenched positions involve a continuous, systematic, ruthless destruction of elements of permanence essential to cultural activity. The emphasis on change is the only permanent characteristic.

Small newspapers that had served the public for thirty years were as close to "elements of permanence" as Alberta history could provide. And like the *Saturday News*, many had gone bankrupt. Some local owners who had survived supported Social Credit in the party's fight against big business. But they too must have suspected they were fighting a losing battle. Mass media were on the rise across the country, reducing regional voices to a whisper.

For better or worse, Balmer's career would be decided within the Southam empire. He now had to answer to a publisher and part owner from Toronto, John Imrie. The fiery independence that had served him for so long was now suspect. The *Journal* had become a "revenue" paper, each succeeding year more dependent on advertising to drive its profits. Making waves was not its strong suit. Ironically, in the months ahead the paper would have little choice in the matter as Aberhart set his sights on the newspapers he considered his enemies.

The betrayal of the people of Alberta by its major newspapers was clearly on Aberhart's mind as the government approached its second anniversary. The premier complained that he had received letters from South Africa, Australia, and New Zealand: "[People] tell us that what is put in their papers about Alberta would make you sick. Not a bit of it is true, copied from this paper, and copied from that paper, our own papers." Aberhart claimed that the only purpose seemed to be to portray the premier of Alberta poorly to the world.

Surely, the caucus argued, the failure of Social Credit legislation was due to the fact the government had no influence over how issues were reported in the press.

The vituperation of the big papers against the government had become so extreme that Major Douglas suggested that the government would need an unchallengeable news-circulation system. Douglas stressed the administration would require the power to discourage "by suitable methods" inaccurate accusations that might be directed against Social Credit by the corporate media. A wave of authoritarian thinking began to take hold within the party. Douglas's "green shirts," from within the English Social Credit movement, continued to arrive in the province; they had little patience with the prairie populist roots of the party. In their eyes, after a certain point, democracy simply got in the way. They were determined to silence Aberhart's critics for once and for all.

Designed to block criticism of government policy, the legislation would force newspapers to print government rebuttals to stories the cabinet deemed inaccurate. The names of all journalists working in the province were to be supplied to the government. All media outlets would be required to print government-issued news releases and to reveal the names and addresses of the sources of their own reports. Failure to comply would result in daily fines of one thousand dollars. One of Balmer's reporters, Don C. Brown, was jailed overnight for a story he had written poking fun at a chiropractor in the Social Credit government. "From the sublime to the ridiculous," Peggy commented in her diary.

Balmer set out to rally his fellow editors to resist the legislation. As he cobbled together an alliance of Alberta newspapers, he turned to Peggy for help. He had never driven a car in his life and would need someone to drive him to visit the independent weeklies, scattered at great distances across the province. As rural Alberta was the heart of Social Credit support he worried the arrival of a big-city editor would automatically raise suspicion. He knew he would have to proceed with great care. The presence of a woman sympathetic to the government might help.

It was a journey into his and Peggy's past. Each town reminded them of their early days in the province, a time when they had been independent journalists themselves. Grand Prairie, Peace River, Blue Sky, Garden Plains — as the grain elevators appeared on the horizon, so did memories of the Alberta they had fallen in love with in their youth. Publishers writing their own stories, setting their own type, distributing the papers from the back of an old farm truck — frontier journalism. The contrary spirit of the editors, always spoiling for a fight with the establishment, reminded Peggy of challenging Frank Oliver in 1905. Yet now their anger was directed against the financial papers, run by big business, that each year took away more of their customers. Balmer was encouraged to find that only a few publishers gave him an outright no when he asked them to join the fight. Freedom of the press was essential to the grassroots democracy they were determined to preserve. It seemed there was more to unite than divide them.

Although the Supreme Court of Canada would rule the Accurate News and Information Act *ultra vires,* battle lines had been drawn. The Alberta Government took the case to the Judicial Committee of the Privy Council in England, where four months after the Supreme Court decision, a panel of five English Law Lords unanimously dismissed the Alberta government's appeal. Reporters from the *New York Times* and the *Washington Post* led an international press corps that rushed to Edmonton to report on the confrontation between a democratically elected government and the courts. Needless to say they framed the debate in their own terms. Could the fascism of Hitler and Mussolini gain a foothold in North America? Balmer continued to express much the same fear, assigning Frederick to report any signs of enemy aliens in the Social Credit party's ranks. Peggy predicted it would be a wild goose chase, and it was.

In response, radical Social Credit green shirts issued brochures accusing Balmer of being "a toady of the Eastern banks and business interests" — a danger to society. Aberhart himself attacked the *Journal* and its editor on his weekly radio program:

> I fear I am going to be forced to come to the conclusion that the caliber of the men who are managing these papers is so low that as to be unsafe to claim liberty at all. They shouldn't be at large! [Applause] ... I feel certain that the citizens of Alberta will come soon to the judgment that something should be done to curb the mad-dog operations of certain of the financial newspapers! [Applause] We license doctors, we license lawyers and schoolteachers ... Why shouldn't the newspapers be licensed also? [Applause] ... I hope they are listening in so they will know what is coming. [Applause]

Balmer replied in an editorial:

> If this bill should pass and stand, where then would be freedom of speech and liberty of the press? Where then would be the liberty of the citizen to free expression of opinion? The press bill now before the legislature is a dictatorial challenge to every freedom-loving Canadian whose home is Alberta.

The *Journal* editor again turned to coordinating the resistance of the province's small newspapers. Once again Peggy's small car was seen on many a country road. Within the month editorials across the province began to turn against the Press Bill. Balmer's calm demeanour, along with Peggy's passion for fair play, had carried the day.

Peggy wondered if it was the Mohawk legacy of their youth in Brantford — the importance of listening to as many voices as possible. Thousands of miles from the birthplace of Pauline Johnson, the belief that a society should be free to consider the widest range of ideas had been re-affirmed. The power of government should never be absolute.

Yet the whole affair angered Peggy. Yes, Aberhart had made a bad mistake. But amazingly the issue of who owns the media was seldom discussed outside Social Credit circles. In nearly all press accounts, the question of how absentee ownership of newspapers could compromise democracy remained unexamined. Little was said of how the forces of wealth and privilege had conspired against a reformist movement. The fear of the original populists — that the concerns of ordinary citizens would not be heard in a media empire controlled by big business — had come to pass. For the most part, the Alberta press had portrayed the Social Credit members of the legislature as an assembly of know-nothings, open to ridicule at every turn, not the government the people had overwhelmingly elected.

Peggy supported Balmer's fight for press freedom, but in the same breath she would defend Aberhart's social policies. She had never forgotten the callow young man she had heard preach in Brantford so many years before — like her, about to venture into the world. Aberhart may have been led astray by Major Douglas and the Green Shirts, but he had never lost the good heart she felt in him that day. He had told her that justice for all would be his mission, and in the most chaotic of times he had been true to that promise. The families he encountered in the streets, lined up for government assistance, were no different than the desperate immigrants Peggy had interviewed in the tent city in the winter of 1906. Only now, to keep commodity prices up, good food was being destroyed while children were starving.

Coming to the premier's side, Peggy championed the relief and public works programs he had instituted to find work for the unemployed. She defended the legislation that discouraged predatory debt collection and penalized banks that abused their power to foreclose on mortgages. To her mind Bay Street was still the scourge of the Prairies, punishing the misfortune of farms and small business, many descended from the original homesteaders with whom she had travelled west. She was incredulous when, at the urging of the Eastern establishment, the Supreme Court overturned further Social Credit banking legislation. To her mind, the phrase *ultra vires* had become a curse. In her overworked diary she wrote, "The Establishment does not oppose Social Credit because it will not work, but for fear it will work."

On May 2, 1938, the U.S. Pulitzer Prize committee awarded a special bronze plaque to the *Edmonton Journal* for its defence of press freedom. The committee also awarded special certificates to five other Alberta dailies and fifty weekly papers for their defiance of Aberhart — the first Pulitzers awarded outside the United States. It was John Imrie, the publisher of the *Edmonton Journal*, who went to New York to accept the award. Neither Balmer's name nor the names of the editors of the weekly newspapers were mentioned. But as Peggy would insist, at least the publishers of those newspapers knew who had deserved the honour.

Social Credit was re-elected in 1940, but with a reduced majority. Two years later William Aberhart died of cirrhosis of the liver in Vancouver. He had been in a state of collapse most of the previous year, his once booming voice reduced to a whisper. The doctors said the cirrhosis had been brought on by overwork and nervous exhaustion. He had never taken a drink in his life. Some said it was a broken heart, having watched so many of his hopes come to nought.

In Edmonton ironically it was Frank Oliver's old paper, the *Bulletin*, that paid the premier the respect Peggy felt he deserved: "Whatever his obsessions, whatever his political acts, whatever his economic creed — he loved his fellow man. That will be his final tribute, that everything in his life pointed to that fact."

But Aberhart might have added a footnote from one of his radio conversations with the Man from Mars: *I am glad there will be no newspapers in heaven.*

20

Firestorm

Ah, love, let us be true
To one another! for the world, which seems
To lie before us like a land of dreams,
So various, so beautiful, so new,
Hath really neither joy, nor love, nor light,
Nor certitude, nor peace, nor help for pain;
And we are here as on a darkling plain
Swept with confused alarms of struggle and flight,
Where ignorant armies clash by night.

MATTHEW ARNOLD, "DOVER BEACH"

Memories of the
First World War
haunted Albertans
as once again
war loomed

For the last years of Aberhart's life, Alberta had been at war. Once again trainloads of young men were crossing the prairies to board troopships bound for Europe. But this time there were no brass bands and shouts of "King and Country," just thousands of destitute men thankful to have a job. War had replaced the idea of social programs. As my godfather said, "The money they could never find to help farmers would always be there for armament manufacturers."

Boyd Cuthbertson, an old acquaintance of Peggy's, was one of the volunteers who signed up. Owner of a farm south of Calgary, watching the topsoil of his fields blow away, Boyd hadn't had a crop in three years. Most every week he went to meetings at a nearby school to discuss the crisis that faced farmers in the wake of the drought. Like North Star many years before, the building was a one-room log structure that doubled as a community hall. The farmers still spoke as a group, inspired by the legacy of the UFA. Why wouldn't Ottawa help prairie agriculture recover from the devastation the Depression had left in its wake? Why not grow enough to feed the unemployed, not simply the troops? Why not turn swords into ploughshares?

Like his father before him in 1914, Boyd soon discovered that families on a distant frontier could do little to change the course of history. Ironically, the armed forces had turned Alberta into a massive recruiting ground: overnight training camps had sprung up across the stricken countryside. Housed in barracks in the middle of nowhere, the disenchanted farmers were at least being fed. On weekend leave they would gather in Edmonton and Calgary, many finding their way to Peggy's Big House, at 100 Avenue and 116 Street. News of her love of a party had preceded her, and the front door was always open.

To Peggy's surprise there seemed to be as many young airmen as soldiers gathered on her front porch overlooking the river valley. The British Commonwealth Air Training Plan had chosen Edmonton as a major centre for war preparations. Blatchford Field, the home of Frederick's bush pilot friend Wop May, had been expanded to be the staging ground for shipping Lend-Lease aircraft to the Soviet Union, a recent ally against Hitler. Airmen from as far away as Australia, New Zealand, England, South Africa, even Poland were arriving to hone their skills for the battle in the skies over Britain and Germany. Balmer noted that according to President Roosevelt, the Air Training Plan had transformed Canada into the aerodrome of democracy, referring to the fact that the flyers were singlehandedly saving England from destruction by the Nazis.

For her part, Peggy regretted that the silence of the prairie had been replaced with the ominous drone of Halifax bombers. She found herself confusing distant formations of aircraft with flocks of cranes whose migrations over the city she anticipated each year. Overnight, runways were paved and aerodromes thrown up where young men who hadn't yet learned to drive a car would be trained to fly a deadly mission over Germany.

At the same time Edmonton became the hub for the building of the 2700-kilometre-long Alaska Highway, bringing convoys of American construction workers to the city. From a sleepy provincial town, Edmonton was transformed into a hectic wartime city, another chapter in the boom-and-bust cycle that haunted the province. For Peggy, these were bittersweet years. The fatality rate among pilots and navigators was staggering, many flying their first mission only a fortnight after leaving Edmonton. The Big House was lit up well into the night every night, a place where romances caught fire overnight as men and women faced the horror of war.

There was always food on the table, and before long the Heintzman upright piano in the corner would be rolled out to the middle of the living room by the boys in uniform. The parties reminded Balmer of their first apartment, Bohemia, in 1908, where the immigrants from the tent city had come to escape the freezing cold. More than thirty years later Peggy was still "Aunt Peg," as the flyers called her, and a bottle of Scotch always stood open on the piano. The Big House had become a port in the storm.

The most vulnerable young men often had no one to share their fears with. Some couldn't face the prospect of dropping bombs on civilian populations, German neighbourhoods no different from the one in which they now found themselves. Others were simply loners or misfits, unable to fit into the squadrons to which they'd been assigned. One by one they would gather with Peggy in the kitchen where she kept a pot of coffee on the boil, at last finding someone to whom they could describe their nightmares. Friend to them all, she wrote weekly letters to wherever they were eventually stationed. Many of the flyers would ask to use the house as their forwarding address with the war office, opening the door to a flood of letters. But that relationship also meant the arrival of notices from the front announcing the pilots' deaths in air battles over London and the English Channel. Peggy always feared the moment she spotted the mailman coming up the street. Frederick had enlisted for his second tour of duty in the frigid waters of the North Atlantic hunting U-boats. He too was in grave danger.

One of her most faithful correspondents was an armed forces chaplain in England, Ivor Daniel, who had been part of the Bohemia gatherings and had never failed to stay in touch. Daniel was amazed to discover Peggy had met Vincent Sutherland, a young English flyer training in Edmonton. Sutherland had contacted the chaplain for counsel when he had arrived at the front:

> We met in a bookshop and talked across the books and later over a pot of tea and some toast in a neighbouring tea shop. There was a certain compatibility of temperament, especially concerning bomber command ... and we met for lunch in Soho on the morrow. In the middle of Oxford Street, we halted, but I forget what we said ... a place and a person had been mentioned and it went home to both of our hearts ... the place Edmonton, the person Mrs Watt.

Sutherland was one of Peggy's favourites. Gay, he had been shunned by his family in England and found himself an outsider to the testosterone culture of the air base. He was training to be a navigator, which meant sooner or later he would be assigned to the bombing raids over Germany. He confided in Peggy that flying over the peaceful green fields of Alberta broke his heart. The small towns they used to get their bearings, the children in the schoolyards, the old men who would wave from their gardens. She asked if she could write his family about their meeting.

Peggy had promised Boyd Cuthbertson, now departed for the front, that she would visit his farm to make sure the livestock was being properly looked after. She decided to take Vincent with her on a drive to southern Alberta. For the first hour he said nothing, preoccupied with his assignment to an English aerodrome, only days away, but as the Rockies appeared on the horizon he began to come out of himself. As it turned out the young flyer had never seen anything remotely like the mountains that stood on the horizon, sparkling under a fresh snow. Vincent was enchanted by the location of Far Hills Farm, perched on a foothill that overlooked the Rockies. Now he understood what he had liked so much about Boyd, forthright, making his peace with what lay ahead, aware of his small part in the greater scheme of things.

All too soon the training exercises, fast tracked because of the Battle of Britain, were cut short. Late one night Vincent arrived at the front door to bid Peggy a rushed goodbye. To her surprise, two weeks later a letter arrived from the young flyer, now stationed at an aerodrome north of London:

> My very dear Aunt Peg. What am I doing? Much the same as anybody else, being possibly a little more cynical and frivolous and much naughtier. Isn't naughtiness the perfect antidote to boredom, restlessness and suppressed revolt? How much I wish I could come to you for tips. The grateful country gives me about 16/- for navigating a bomb laden aircraft to Germany which is barely sufficient to amuse one person. Between you and me, I don't expect to outlive this war, and I haven't too many regrets. I've loved a number of people possibly too much, and always want to see them once again, but other than that there's nothing to keep me alive.

The next to write was the priest:

> I was going to see Lord Alfred Douglas in Brighton, and Vincent jumped at the chance to join me. Lord Alfred was so charming to him, and signed his sonnets for him — it was wonderful to see them together — the splendid youth and the wraith of beauty in the dying man. Little did I think then that they were destined to leave their world together — and so soon.

Douglas, once Oscar Wilde's lover, would die within the month.

Sutherland had already flown his first mission, over the Ruhr. Only weeks before he arrived in England, the Royal Air Force had firebombed the city of Dresden, killing over a hundred thousand civilians in two nights. Incendiary devices designed to create a wall of flame consumed all life in their path. The young navigator's worst nightmare was that his Halifax bomber would be sent on a similar mission: "One thing I'm glad of, that our first trip was what I call 'clean'. It wasn't homes, it wasn't a residential area ... the odds were even." Vincent had often talked to Peggy about the morality of killing for one's country:

> I've little faith in human nature; this present war indicates to me how irredeemable is society ... with what extraordinary facility do we perpetuate brutality and ghastliness ... in my sober moments I will always hate my job and refuse as being untenable all arguments of necessity, provocation, 'for the best', good out of evil etc etc. Fortunately sober moments are few, but war is to me savageness that has no place in my mad unpractical scheme of things ...

Here he was interrupted in mid-sentence as the sirens sounded to call the crews to their planes.

Vincent Sutherland did not return from the mission that took him away so suddenly. When Ivor Daniel went to collect his belongings so a new navigator could occupy the room, the unfinished letter was open on his desk. Daniel sent it to Edmonton along with a note of his own:

26.3.45

My Dear Mrs Watt.

Last Monday I had a telegram to say that our dear Vincent was 'Missing' from his second operational flight. I needn't tell you what a blow it has been, even to one as used to such blows as I am. From the moment we met there was no barrier between us, we understood each other per-fectly. I shall never forget his delight when he found that I knew you, he loved you so much.

Oswin Creighton blown to pieces at the Battle of the Somme. Now Vincent Sutherland, swallowed up in the inferno over Hamburg. In two wars Peggy had lost the two men closest to her heart.

Balmer had his own concerns with the war. With little or no con-sultation, the United States had assigned thirty-three thousand troops and service workers to the Canadian northwest. Edmonton, with a population of less than one hundred thousand, was awash with American troops. Balmer's editorials pointed out that Alberta was becoming a country within a country — with Washington its new capital. Prime Minister Mackenzie King had failed to establish Canadian jurisdiction in the preparations for war on Alberta soil. Not that the residents of the city minded. My brother remembers the god-like status of the American soldiers to the children in the community. With rationing, the American PX was the only source of chocolate bars in the city.

His other memory was of extraordinary Russian women caus-ing a sensation on Jasper Avenue in their black leather flight suits. Pilots, they had come to ferry American aircraft across the Bering Sea to the eastern front of the war, part of an agreement between Roosevelt and Stalin. Balmer worried because between 1941 and

1943, the US Army and Air Force had operated virtually as a free agent in the province. His concern was later to be repeated by military historian J.L. Granatstein, who called the situation that developed a "fit absence of mind" on the part of Ottawa. Donald Creighton also chastised the federal government for its failure to defend the country's independence, maintaining that

> The Americans had forced Canadian consent ... They treated Canadian sovereignty and the interests of the Canadian environment and native peoples with equal impatience and neglect ... All too often they behaved as if they were on their own soil or on a separate but tributary and submissive part of the Empire of the United States.

Mackenzie King's chickens had come home to roost — the American Army was every bit as persuasive as the Rockefellers.

Balmer's editorials expressed concern for Alberta's future under such an arrangement. Through sheer neglect the province had been overrun by the Americans, it is little wonder that in the years to come Alberta's fossil fuel economy would be handed over to the Texas multinationals that succeeded Standard Oil. Calgary would soon be the Houston of the north, and the next year country of the homesteader would become the staging ground of industrial Alberta.

Peggy and Balmer retired in 1947. The family was at last together again, Frederick having returned from the war in the North Atlantic and Becky from London where her home had been a direct hit in the V-2 rocket attacks. Peggy set about converting the old stable behind the Big House into a cottage where Becky and her son Nicholas could live. Her husband, Dan Radford, was fighting with Canadian troops in Sicily.

Becky had learned to drive an army truck and set about collecting scrap iron to be melted down into armaments. Her helper in those daily rounds around Edmonton was Jennie Hurtig, the mother of Mel Hurtig, who would become the first nationally recognized Alberta book publisher. Later founder of the Council of Canadians, Mel carried on the tradition of independent western publishing that Peggy and Balmer had fought a lifetime to preserve.

Peggy sensed the wheel of fortune turning once again. On February 13, columns of flame exploded from under a drilling rig position on a farm south of Edmonton. As a crew of roughnecks scrambled to safety, "black gold" gushed to the surface, ushering in an era of wealth unimaginable in the province's past. Imperial Oil, now a subsidiary of ExxonMobil, had drilled 133 dry holes in the area when Leduc No. 1 struck oil trapped in a previously unexplored underground basin. What became known as the Nisku formation was the motherlode of the rush to come.

Within weeks, more than a dozen companies were drilling throughout the region, and by the end of 1947 there were thirty-one operational wells, twenty-four of them owned by Imperial Oil. My father, returning from the war, became the office manager for a small company, Canadian Drilling Ltd., which had a single rig working the Leduc field. Needless to say the company didn't own the mineral rights, merely leasing their equipment to Imperial. For a year we lived high off the hog, my dad driving not one but two Jaguars. The next year the company just managed to keep its head above water as Imperial consolidated its leases and brought in their own equipment.

It was not long before the company's lone rig began to fall apart, surplus to Imperial's requirements. I remember being taken out of school by my father to drive with him all the way to Bakersfield, California, to buy spare parts for the rig. A strike in Hamilton had cut off the supply of steel, putting small companies like Canadian

Drilling in jeopardy. Only Imperial Oil had the resources to weather the shortages. As multinationals took over the industry, Alberta-owned companies simply couldn't afford to compete. Two years later Canadian Drilling was gone. The American takeover had begun. By 2012, the American-managed energy sector represented twenty-two percent of Canada's GNP, as opposed to less than a quarter of one percent when Peggy first arrived in the west.

In his final years, Harold Innis realized that Canadian history was moving in reverse, from a path toward independence and self-government to a recolonized staples economy, dominated by agribusiness, oil and gas, and forestry. One of his students, A.F.W. Plumptre, remembers his lectures:

> Innis had an undertone, if not of pessimism, certainly of deep misgivings at a time when we undergraduates really thought the world was going to be all right ...
>
> Innis at that time was very much concerned with where industrialism was taking the world. I can remember him talking about something which in those days we'd never heard of — 'Frankenstein' — which later became famous, but at that time was still a novel by Mrs. Shelley. The mechanical monster that took over and ran its creator. [Innis] kept coming back to the worry that technology was going to do this to civilized man.

Balmer worried newspapers were about to experience a similar fate. Ironically, as new technology allowed the volume of pages to grow, mostly to accommodate advertising, meaningful content shrank. The exchange with readers that had once been at the heart of Peggy's columns was disappearing. Edmonton the community was becoming Edmonton the market.

As the continental energy economy transformed Alberta, a new wave of immigration flooded the province. But this time the workers were temporary, many of them roughnecks from the Texas and Oklahoma oil fields, come to make a bundle and return to wherever they'd come from. The drugs and alcohol culture they brought with them made short work of the moral strictures of Social Credit. Their arrival after the Leduc strike in 1947 was a first indication of the tar sands era to come, where airports would be jammed with men and women arriving from across Canada, the United States, and Asia to cash in on the boom — but seldom to stay. Peggy's idea of a grassroots democracy, built at the community level, had no place in this transient society.

My mother was working nights for a welcome wagon company, so it was up to my dad to collect me from my grandparents on his way back from the oil fields south of the city. Usually his co-workers, Texans and Oklahomans, tagged along for a poker game, introducing me to a deck of cards at an early age. Each evening I would quietly find a place under the gate-legged table where the men gathered. The roughnecks kept my secret — maybe they saw me as good luck in the high-stakes games that followed. On my mom's instructions I had to be very quiet so my dad could concentrate. She worried, quite rightly, that her husband was in over his head, playing with the grocery money. The cash pots that accumulated often exceeded a thousand dollars. Soon there would be no Jaguars.

When Leduc #1 was finally capped in 1984, it had produced over 240 million barrels of oil. As production grew exponentially, Alberta's two major cities saw their populations double. Peter Lougheed would later recount, "My generation knows if we didn't have Leduc and its consequences, we probably would be living elsewhere."

But the growth of the economy was not without its drawbacks. Alberta was turning into a branch plant economy, where buildings full of lawyers and accountants managed an industry owned and controlled from elsewhere.

In the countryside the province's original small towns shut down as people moved to the oil fields and the cities for jobs. Grain elevators, once a proud symbol of each district's character and independence, began a long decline. By the end of the twentieth century there would be only a handful still standing, dwarfed by the massive concrete grain terminals American corporations were building.

One of my favourite communities — largely because of its grain elevator — was the almost ghost town of Dorothy on the Red Deer River, named after the daughter of the first postmaster in the district. The elevator seemed to store the memory the town's last inhabitants kept of the frontier. In 1976 I documented a reunion of the district's farmers and ranchers for the National Film Board. The film *Every Saturday Night* recorded how homemade music had been the saviour of these families during the Depression. Dorothy was as far from life in the fast lane of urban culture as you could get in Alberta. Radio reception was so poor that you made your own entertainment. The community hall was still active even if the town had disappeared.

For that final dance — on a Saturday night, of course — oldtimers had driven from as far away as British Columbia to celebrate the town they still carried in their hearts. At one time or another the entire community took to the dance floor — waltzes, square dances, two steps, the occasional Schottische — a collective memory expressed in the music of their forefathers. As the evening drew to a close at dawn the next day, twenty fiddlers took the stage to play a farewell rendition of "The Water is Wide." The oldtimers near the stage joined in song:

The water is wide, I can't cross o'er
And neither do I have wings to fly
Give me a boat, carry two
And both shall row
My love and I.

As the golden rays of the rising sun slanted across the prairie, it felt as if a whole world had re-awakened. The return of next year country. If Peggy had still been alive, I'm sure her voice would have been the loudest.

When I was a boy, my grandmother would take me on walks along a path that followed the edge of the North Saskatchewan River valley. It was her way of escaping the traffic that had come with the Leduc boom. At the western edge of the city, she would take a second path down into the ravines and coulees that had been the meeting place of Indigenous Peoples for centuries. As we descended, springs of clear, cold water trickled from the banks of white mud, their healing properties making the valley sacred to its first inhabitants. Nearby were the rusting tracks of the Edmonton, Dunvegan and Yukon Railroad, whose rails had never as much as reached the outskirts of the city, two thousand miles short of their destination in the gold fields. The skeletal rails were the last trace of an imagined Eldorado that had brought men and women from around the world, another boom gone bust.

Along the streams that flowed into the river, squatters' shacks housed what remained of these Klondikers, still panning for gold, now just to make ends meet. As evening fell we would follow the flicker of coal oil lamps in the shacks, pinpoints of light to guide us home. Peggy worried that history was about to repeat itself. Might the madness that had left Dawson City a ghost town a century before lay ahead for Alberta?

We would always stop to visit the valley's other residents, the Chinese market gardeners whose rows of vegetables ran alongside the river. The old men and women who tended the fields always had time for a cup of tea and a game of mah-jong when she knocked on their door. It had taken them generations to establish the small farms, overcoming the discriminatory head tax the Canadian government had imposed on Asian immigrants at the turn of the century. Contrary to the fears of the racist Ottawa bureaucracy, these gardeners had become model citizens, feeding Edmonton for fifty years and assuming an important place in the social life of the community. Like the current of the river at our side, flowing to the horizon, these extraordinary gardeners were a reminder of all that had come and gone in Peggy's lifetime. The deep roots, put down over many generations, that gave the city its unique character.

In 1959 Peggy reads a story in the *Journal* that a Sun Dance is being filmed near Blackfoot Crossing, the railway junction where in 1905 she stepped down from the train to see the snow-capped Rockies for the first time. She tells Balmer she wants to be there and buys a bus ticket that afternoon. To her surprise she finds a thriving town, Gleichen, where Crowfoot's Siksika camp once stood. She is excited to hear that the dance is underway on the nearby Kainai Nation, the first observance of the custom in a generation. Colin Low, a young filmmaker from the National Film Board in Montreal, is recording the ceremony at the request of the Elders. Ever the journalist, Peggy tracks down Low, who turns out to have grown up in nearby Cardston and remembers the *Alberta Homestead*. A local rancher he had worked for as a boy, E.N. Barker, had collaborated with Peggy on a weekly column for the paper, "Sputterings from an Old Frying Pan."

Colin's Alberta films, *Corral* and *Days of Whiskey Gap,* were already considered classics. But it was his film on astronomy, *Universe,* that had captivated viewers around the world. Nominated for an Academy Award in 1961, the film was a journey into our solar system, an exploration of light and form and infinite space. Growing up in the lonely country at the foot of the Rocky Mountains, Low had spent his boyhood looking up at the stars that filled the night sky as he rounded up his father's sheep and cattle. As a filmmaker the technology he invented to recreate that sky was deceptively simple, but so true-to-life that Stanley Kubrick hired a member of his crew, Wally Gentleman, to design the special effects for *2001: A Space Odyssey.* Backlit chemicals dissolving in fish tanks became the origin of whole galaxies, their sense of drama and authenticity years ahead of the multimillion-dollar computer animation of the *Star Wars* era that followed. It was as if the universe were inside Low's head, a prairie boy still gazing at the Milky Way on a winter's night.

Peggy soon discovers that Pete Standing Alone, the principal character of the new film Colin is shooting, has much to tell her about the revival of First Nations culture in the district. Pete had been working as a roughneck in the oil boom, but the Sun Dance has drawn him back to the reserve. The timeless ceremony pays respect to the unity of all life, a blessing he hoped could heal the many fractures within the Blackfoot world. In the years ahead Pete would leave the rigs for good and return to the Blood Reserve at Standoff as a Medicine Man. There he protected the precious knowledge of Blackfoot sacred circles, becoming a member of the Horn Society and the Long-Time Medicine Pipe Society. When the tribe gathered for the Sun Dance, as a pipe carrier he would recite prayers to seven cardinal points: the Four Directions and the Above or Spirit World, the Below or Mother Earth, and the Centre or all living things. Pete explained to Peggy that for the Blackfoot life does not travel in straight lines:

The sky is round.
The stars and the earth are round.
The seasons form a great circle.
The life of man is a circle.
From childhood to childhood.

21

An Unquiet Land

It was one of the first things travelling Europeans
noted about those who had come to live in the
New World. Here people seemed to have an itch,
as if the living were uneasy, troubling, almost
frantic. It was as if those who had inherited the
fruits of exploration and conquest had been left a
troubled bequest, as if there was some unplacated,
unmet spirit of place dividing them from an
authentic and comforting possession here.

FREDERICK TURNER, *BEYOND GEOGRAPHY:*
THE WESTERN SPIRIT AGAINST THE WILDERNESS

Officers police
labour unrest in the
Crowsnest Pass

As the oil boom of the late 1950s transformed Alberta, Peggy decided to make a farewell tour of the province, a last chance to visit the people and places she had come to love before they disappeared. Visiting Irene Parlby's garden in Alix, she would pay her respects to the women who helped launch the *Alberta Homestead*. She would do her best to find North Star School and what remained of the legacy of Harold Innis. Exploring coal towns along the Rockies, she would visit the graveyards where her friends from the "tent city" had come to rest. But most of all she would pay her respects to the land itself, the vast open spaces and winding rivers that had cast a spell over her life.

She borrows my dad's old Hudson Hornet and, after a long day of driving, leaves the prairie for the wooded foothills that line the valley of the North Saskatchewan. Although she is only 150 miles upstream from Edmonton, the first thing she notices is how clear the water is this close to the glaciers and snow-covered peaks, the same intense blue she remembers in the Paul Kane painting she saw as a girl in Toronto.

The town of Rocky Mountain House lies ahead, mud-spattered trucks double parked on the main street, shiftless men gathered in front of trailers and clapboard hotels. She checks into the lone motel as night falls, the woman behind the desk offering little sign of welcome. In the nearby town of Nordegg, the Brazeau Collieries, which once employed eight hundred men on its coal face, has recently shut down. The American and British coal companies that once fuelled the expansion of railways across the continent have moved on to greener pastures. Appalachia and Australia now offer the cheap labour the immigrants of the tent city once provided.

When she arrives at the mine the gates are locked. No Trespassing signs mark the fields where militant workers once gathered to sing "The Internationale." Labour unrest over working conditions and wages had repeatedly shut down operations here, as they did along the eastern slope of the Rockies as far as the American border. Desperate for work, many of the immigrants died in explosions and collapsing mine shafts deep underground, where proper safety precautions were seldom taken by the coal companies. When the workers went on strike, the companies called in the police and immigration officials to deport the leaders. Years before Peggy had travelled to Blairmore in the Crowsnest Pass to hear Honore Jackson speak in support of the striking miners. Peggy was amazed to learn that Jackson had been personal secretary to Louis Riel during the events of 1885 and had ended up a union organizer in Chicago. He had never given up the Resistance and was compiling a history of the Métis nation he had fought to establish.

Many of the immigrant families Peggy had met in 1906 ended up in these mountain towns, including that of a young Italian, Filumena Lassandro, whose story Peggy has come to research. The miners had established vibrant communities with hospitals, schools, and libraries funded by the workers and their unions. The companies who profited from the mines invested little in the welfare of the miners themselves. In the 1920s Peggy had visited the towns often to portray that rough-hewn world, but also to report on Filumena's fate — the first woman hanged in Alberta for the shooting of a policeman in the Crowsnest Pass.

In the midst of prohibition Filumena had been the girlfriend of a Blairmore rum-runner, Emilio Picariello — "Emperor Pic" as he was known to the police. In a gunfight that followed the arrest of Picariello's son, officer Stephen Lawson was shot while Filumena watched in horror. The police claimed she was an accomplice to the murder. Peggy never believed Filumena was guilty and was suspicious of the young woman's accusers. Contemptuous of immigrants, Alberta Provincial Police officers cruised the streets of the coal towns with machine guns mounted on their patrol cars. The ethnic divide had become so great that when Peggy visited the accused on death row, Filumena refused to speak to her. After her execution, Filumena's body was not returned to Blairmore as her parents requested, but instead was buried in an unmarked grave on the outskirts of Edmonton. Peggy was appalled but powerless to help the family.

Now thirty years later, huddled against a biting wind, Peggy walks down the main street of the coal-mining town. Like so many turn-of-the-century communities in Alberta, the buildings are boarded up, any sense of the future abandoned. Peggy can feel the chill of what Balmer has described as an unquiet land, the promise of the town turned to dust. The level playing field the immigrants came in search of has been replaced by a top-down resource economy managed by multinationals.

Tim Buck, leader of the Communist Party of Canada, visited these communities in the 1930s, imploring new Canadians working in the mines to form unions to protect their families. In a local museum hand-sewn banners proclaim *Workers of the World Unite*. In these most forbidding of landscapes, the spirit of the original Alberta remains. In a film I made in the Crowsnest Pass in 2010, *Common Ground*, veterans of those struggles describe how they were arrested for simply attending union rallies. The police considered it a crime to be a labour organizer. Winston Gereluk, an

Alberta historian, describes how the authorities then tried what they called "enemy aliens" for sedition. A number of the "sheepskins" Peggy had met on her train journey west were among the workers stripped of their citizenship and deported.

Leaving the claustrophobia of history behind, Peggy drives east until she reaches grasslands that stretch as far as the eye can see. As she watches towering thunderheads build on the western horizon, she remembers crossing this country on horseback with the young Anglican minister Oswin Creighton, listening to him describe the Indigenous Peoples who once made it their home. On a day like today, she remembers riding for hours without seeing or hearing another human being.

As they were then, the fields around Buffalo Lake are alive with the song of meadowlarks, oblivious to the thunder that announces the approaching storm. Within minutes a fork of lightning strikes a nearby tree, forcing her to pull over as a curtain of rain sweeps across the highway. Soon acorn-sized hailstones bounce off the roof of the car like gunshots.

As she huddles from the cold, she is reminded of the nights she and Irene Parlby would be taken by sled cross-country to meetings in isolated community halls, beneath buffalo robes provided by the farmers to keep them warm. An abiding sense of place comes with the memory: midnight potluck suppers; collecting contributions for a new dairy co-op; sipping tea from fine porcelain brought from the old country. She can hear Irene Parlby plotting against the banks, promising resolutions that will become the platform of the United Farmers — an Alberta that resonates with the vision of next year country.

Now sitting beside the ivy-covered trellises of Dartmoor Farm with Irene, Peggy finds the reassurance she has been seeking since revisiting the Lassandro tragedy. The home-baked scones and preserves from the garden haven't changed in thirty years. Local members of the *Alberta Homestead* editorial board drop by to see an old friend. No one can account for how quickly time has fled. Was it the wars, or the Depression, or simply Big Oil that changed their lives so drastically? Communities like Alix, once at the vanguard of political thought in Alberta, have disappeared from national life. To be called a populist in Ottawa now is the ultimate insult, as John Diefenbaker has recently found out. What had become of the reformist spirit of the Prairies, of Aberhart's visions of a heavenly kingdom on this earth? So much has been sacrificed for the sake of an economy designed for the profit of others. The frontier of industry, not community. But as always, it is not long before Irene brings the conversation around to the growing of things. The spirit of the frontier has never left this remarkable woman, unchanged since the day Peggy first met her fifty year earlier.

As Peggy sets out the next morning Irene reminds her of the battles that still lie ahead: "The mind is not a vessel to be filled, but a hearth to be lighted." The old journalist recognizes the line from one of Irene's speeches in the legislature those first years of the Farmers Government — before the Depression shattered so many of their dreams.

Peggy approaches Landonville, where the young Harold Innis spent the summer of 1915 teaching school. The broad prairie begins to splinter as rig sites, survey roads, and industrial parks swallow the horizon. Piles of steel, stacked like cord wood, have replaced the wheatfields sown at the turn of the century. Everywhere the tyranny of oil and gas has descended on the landscape. On the site of North Star School, a lone steel pipe thrusts up from the ground, spitting a toxic orange flare into the sky. Despite her enquiries, the site's owners are nowhere to be found, most likely thousands of miles away in Houston.

But she does find out that the oil is shipped by pipeline to refineries in Edmonton, the massive structures she can now see burning every night from the porch of her house on the North Saskatchewan. In the fields where Harold Innis once helped with the harvest, hundreds of pumpjacks swing back and forth in mechanized monotony. The low-octave hum they emit is hypnotic, as if the entire landscape has come under a trance. Not only is the school gone without a trace, but the entire community of Landonville has disappeared. Only a cemetery remains.

The month after her final journey across the province, Peggy joins Balmer in celebrating their sixtieth wedding anniversary. It is the last of the countless gatherings she has hosted, from late nights with the "sheepskins" in Bohemia, to the young flyers who made the Big House their home. Peggy still refuses to install a lock on the front door: a guest is still a guest no matter what hour they arrive. As the room hushes Balmer toasts the bride by quoting from a song popular on the hit parade that year: "She may have been a headache but she never was a bore." Peggy only responds with a smile, but her appraising look sums up the sixty years. The two have weathered every storm. A week later she falls and breaks her hip. She will never walk again.

She is given a room in a Catholic hospital on the south side, St. Joseph's, in the care of a new generation of sisters. Balmer tells her it's as if she's returned to her childhood, and that pleases her. When Colin Low's *Circle of the Sun* is released later that year, Peggy insists my mother borrow a projector from the Film Board to screen the film on the wall of her room. The spirit of Pete Standing

Alone has never left her. Out her window she can see the North Saskatchewan River winding its way through the city, its valley a ribbon of green. Along its banks she can see the path she walked with Pauline Johnson so long ago — a day when all of their lives seemed to lie ahead. She shuts her eyes and can hear the voice of the Blackfoot Elder in the film: *The life of man is a circle from childhood to childhood.*

Her son Frederick remembers coming from Ottawa the next week to visit:

> I was surprised. She was still very much herself, propped up in bed … with her magnificent white hair perfectly coiffed and her eyes dancing as she told me the rector of the Anglican church Balmer supported had been in to give her Communion that afternoon. "He is a very nice man," she said, "and I didn't think it would be right for him to know that the St. Joseph's chaplain had given me communion earlier in the day."
>
> We talked of many common interests in the world outside the hospital's walls but by evening I had to say goodbye. I had a plane to catch to Vancouver. She said quietly, almost unemotionally, "When you come next time, dear, it will be to bury me."
>
> Five days later I flew back for the funeral. There had been no abrupt warning of the approaching end. She had simply started to slip away one morning and, as the word reached the wards — the sisters, the other nurses, and the ambulatory patients who had come to know her, dropped in to say goodbye. That evening, as peacefully as most of her years had been the very opposite, she was gone. The date was June 12, 1963.

With Peggy's death, Balmer moved out of the Big House to a modest apartment a block away on 117 Street, still within sight of the river. He was in no condition to look after himself. The family gathered around him as much as possible during the move, but soon Rochford Connelly, a distant cousin, had to come from the east to cook his meals and act as a live-in nurse.

On days that weather permitted, I would take him for a short walk along the trail at the top of the valley he had explored with "Little Boy Blue," my Uncle Ted. After a time we would just sit on the "Rest and Read The Journal" bench that had always been our lookout, taking in the sweeping arc of the river below, the first curve of the ogee Peggy believed could bend time. As we basked in the sun, he would recall the day in 1905 he had listened to Laurier declare Alberta a province at the racetrack down the road. His first scent of wolf willow, the song of a meadowlark, now clearer in his mind than all the speeches.

In the apartment, the small oak desk Peggy had brought west to start the *Saturday News* was in its honoured place beneath the window. The green velvet chair that had hosted guests to his news-paper office — Buffalo Bill, Pauline Johnson, Joseph Tyrrell, Grey Owl, Mackenzie King, Irene Parlby, J.S. Woodsworth, even Sarah Bernhardt on her farewell North American tour — stood alone in the corner. The scrapbooks were stacked beside the chair, and I would try to attract his attention with the clippings. But as the months went by he ceased to take notice. The onset of Alzheimer's had begun.

I was shocked how quickly a mind could deteriorate. The experience of Alberta, the adventure of that last great frontier, had come and gone. The old journalist simply stared at the valley out-side the window as if Peggy's river was all that was left of the world.

Balmer died on July 12, 1964. The news was covered in papers across Canada and — surprisingly — the *New York Times*. But the notice he would have appreciated the most appeared in his own newspaper, the *Edmonton Journal*:

> A. Balmer Watt, 87, died in an Edmonton hospital last night after a lengthy illness. His obituary is already inscribed, by his own hand, on the aging pages of 60 years of Edmonton newspapers — his record of the city he loved and chronicled since its pioneer days. *The Journal*'s editor emeritus was the kind of newspaperman who led his newspaper to a Pulitzer Award in 1938 for *The Journal*'s fight against the fledgling Social Credit party's Press Control Bills. But he also was the kind of newspaperman who was remembered by the hundreds who worked with him and for him as "a gentle man with a ripe and kindly wisdom, and that God-given art of looking sympathetically into human hearts."

EPILOGUE

Source of the River

There is a patience of the wild — dogged,
tireless, persistent as life itself.

JACK LONDON, *THE CALL OF THE WILD*

Peggy and
Balmer's
diamond wedding
anniversary,
sixty years of
perseverance

The spring I turned ten, in 1956, Peggy and Balmer decided to take me on a trip south and west to what remained of the old fort at Rocky Mountain House. They wanted to show me where David Thompson and his young Métis wife Charlotte Small had built their first cabin in 1795. It had been one of the first marriages between a European and an Indigenous woman. Peggy had decided it was high time I knew more about such things.

As we plan the trip, Balmer climbs on a step stool to retrieve a worn volume laid flat on the top shelf of the bookcase in his study. I can't help but notice the raised gold print on the binding, *The Narrative* — a special edition of David Thompson's diaries, published by the Champlain Society in Montreal. As he dusts it off, it's clear the book means a great deal to the old editor. He had been given it by Joseph Tyrrell, the geologist of tar sands and dinosaur fame, who had discovered a treasure trove of Thompson's maps in an abandoned trading post in northern Manitoba. Rescuing the parchment from the drawers of an old desk, Tyrrell was astounded by the maps' scope and accuracy — but no one knew who had drawn them. As Thompson had been lost to history, Tyrrell set out to find out who the mystery cartographer was, a job that would take him the better part of a decade.

Insisting I wear white cotton gloves to protect the fragile pages, Balmer carefully hands me the book. Tucked into the inside back cover are scale copies of the maps. I unfold one onto my lap, a section at a time, until it is the size of a small bed sheet. It has been assembled from the field notes and surveys Thompson and Charlotte collected from 1796 to 1812, he as a geographer, she as his guide and interpreter. Together they had explored the wilderness that stretched from Hudson Bay to the mouth of the Columbia River in what is now Oregon. The detail with which the map has been drawn is a revelation. Balmer carefully points out Rocky Mountain House, our destination.

Driving south of Edmonton, Peggy has to slow down for the town of Ellerslie. It's still the era when the two-lane highway goes through the middle of each community, giving us time to get our bearings. What we can't fail to miss are the huge letters painted on the side of an Alberta Wheat Pool elevator beside the train tracks. Their message has somehow survived from the Aberhart era:

Jesus said:
What shall it profit a man
If he gain the whole world
And lose his own soul?
Mark 8

We are now deep in the thirty-six-year rule of Social Credit, so it's not unusual to hear the voice of Ernest Manning, Aberhart's successor as premier, addressing Albertans on the radio. The *Back to the Bible Hour* is now in its third decade of Sunday broadcasts. Peggy is dismayed at the tone of what amounts to a sermon — gone is the warmth, the generous spirit of her old friend Bible Bill. She quietly turns off the radio and stares out over the open prairie as we approach Leduc. Although the streets are abandoned, a sign announces the boomtown as the oil capital of Alberta. Now every second farm has an oil rig rising above its fields of wheat.

One by one towns come up on the horizon: Wetaskiwin, Ponoka, Morningside, Lacombe, then finally our turnoff at Red Deer. My face glued to the window, I'm first to spot the Rockies, a faint line to the west. From the back seat, Balmer reads from Thompson's diary: "At last, the Mountains came in sight, shining white on the horizon. As we proceeded, they rose in height. Their immense masses of snow appeared above the clouds and formed an impassable barrier, even to the eagle."

That evening, as Balmer does his best to build a campfire, Peggy describes a Welsh orphan who arrived on the desolate shore of Hudson Bay in the fall of 1784. Only fourteen years old, Thompson was thankful to be at the end of a treacherous thousand-mile journey across the iceberg-strewn waters of the North Atlantic. He had been indentured by the Grey Coats School in London to be a clerk in the fur trade — a virtual slave to the fur trade. Yet he harbours a dream to be the first geographer to map the expanses of the new world properly. Ahead of him stands Fort Churchill, built by the Company of Adventurers Trading into Hudson Bay. The structure, standing alone on the barren coast, looks like a prison. As the ship prepares to leave for the return voyage to England, a bitter Thompson writes in the diary that will record his life on the frontier:

> While the ship remained at anchor, from my parent and friends it appeared only a few weeks distance, but when the ship sailed and from the top of the rocks I lost sight of her, the distance became immeasurable, and I bid a long and sad farewell to my noble, my sacred country, an exile for ever.

Peggy pauses to make sure I am still listening as she read from the *Narrative*, then recounts how the Cree and Assiniboine traders who come to the fort from the interior of the continent immediately catch Thompson's eye:

> In the years that lay ahead I always admired the tact of the
> Indian in being able to guide himself through the darkest pine forests to exactly the place he intended to go, his
> keen, constant attention on every thing; the removal of
> the smallest stone, the bent or broken twig; a slight mark
> on the ground, all spoke plain language to him.

Thompson soon discovers that far to the west these First Nations inhabit a land the traders call the Great Plains.

The following summer he finds himself part of a horseback party sent to report on potential trade routes along the rivers that flow from the "Shining Mountains," a translation of an Indigenous name for the Rockies. After months on the trail the party comes to the territory of the Blackfoot Confederacy, the powerful nation that rules the foothills country along the eastern slope of the mountains. By a twist of fate, the winter is too severe to return to Hudson Bay, and the boy is invited to spend the winter in the teepee of an Elder of the Peigan Band, Saukamappee. He writes in his diary:

> The Peeagan was an old man of at least 75 to 80 years of
> age; his height six feet, two or three inches, broad shouldered, strong limbed, his hair grey and plentiful, forehead
> high, and nose prominent, his face slightly marked with
> the smallpox, and altogether his countenance mild . . .

In the years ahead Saukamappee's counsel will lead Thompson to marry a Métis girl of fourteen, Charlotte Small, the daughter of a Cree woman and an Irish trader. Charlotte's knowledge of the land, passed down from her mother, will open the wilderness of the northwest to the young geographer. His detailed maps of the trade routes that follow the rivers of the western frontier will change the course of Canadian history.

Peggy wonders if we can find Saukamappee's winter camp, but Balmer says it's long since gone. Better to try to find the cabin Thompson and Charlotte built when they lived in this country. The diary records that it was built at the meeting place of two rivers, not far upstream from Rocky Mountain House on the North Saskatchewan. Peggy hikes along the shore from the site of the fort until we arrive at the place where a smaller river, the Clearwater, flows into the main current. And sure enough, as Thompson's diary has directed, there is the foundation of a cabin.

Showing me how to use her tiny Hawkeye camera, Peggy insists I snap a roll of pictures, scrambling up a hill to get as panoramic a view as I can. To the west the Rockies stretch to the horizon, the western edge of traditional Blackfoot territory. The Shining Mountains.

Over the course of a winter of deep snows, Saukamappee had taught Thompson various Blackfoot dialects, introducing him to the ancient knowledge of a hunting culture. Each night the old Medicine Man paid special attention to the sky, the home of the Great Bear, spirit guide to the Peigan. There in the clear mountain air, he relates the origins of his people, using the constellations as his guide. By contrast, Thompson, a student of European science, measures the position of each planet and collects the data from which he will construct his maps:

> My instruments for practical astronomy were a brass
> sextant of 10 inches radius and an achromatic telescope
> of high power for observing the satellites of Jupiter.

In the years ahead the First Nations will call him *Koo Koo Sin*, "the one who gazes at stars."

Saukamappee points to three stars in what Thompson knows as the Big Dipper. To the stranger the stars have no significance, but in Peigan cosmology, they are the hunters who pursue the Great

Bear, adjacent to the North Star. When fall comes, the hunters finally kill the bear, who bleeds over the earth and turns autumn leaves to red. Later the white grease under the bear's skin will fall as snow. For Peigan men, the colour red is sacred; for the women who render the bear grease, it is white that is revered. For Saukamappee the Great Bear is immortal. Even though the animal is the victim of the hunters in the fall and disappears from the sky, every spring she will return and resume her timeless journey across the heavens.

Balmer tells us that two days' ride south and east of the Clearwater is Iniskim Umaapi, built by the ancestors of the Blackfoot two thousand years before Stonehenge. A medicine wheel nearly a mile in diameter, the stones once measured the movements of the sun, moon, and stars. Over its central spoke the sun of the summer solstice would be seen rising, the sign that a new hunting season had begun. Knowledge of the stars would guide its builders in their movements across the plains, following the migrations of the buffalo, planting crops, and harvesting berries and roots in the forests alongside the rivers. Balmer thinks the medicine wheel may have also been a ceremonial site, a place where the gathering of knowledge itself was celebrated in a culture that had lived on this landscape for millennia.

As she sprinkles tobacco on the waters of the North Saskatchewan, Peggy explains that Thompson was one of the few Europeans on the western frontier to learn to live in the time-honoured way of its Indigenous Peoples. Then she recites the Navajo blessing she learned from Pauline Johnson half a century before.

This teepee will be a blessed teepee
It will be a teepee of dawn
It will be a teepee of mountain snow
It will be a teepee of crystal water
It will be a teepee dusted with pollen
It will be a teepee of long-life happiness
It will be a teepee with beauty above it
It will be a teepee with beauty all around it.

Mountain snow, crystal water. One can understand where the Clearwater got its name, most likely from Charlotte Small and the traditions of her people, although history attributes the naming to David Thompson, the map maker. As Peggy stokes the fire she explains why she has carried Charlotte and Thompson's story with her all her life. How, before she was too old to make the trip, she wanted to show me this place, the confluence of two rivers, sacred to the First Nations.

Today vast stretches of the Rocky Mountains have been leased by the world's most powerful coal companies. Mountain-top removal is becoming the new frontier of fossil fuel extraction. Australia's mining consortium, Valory Resources, one of the biggest multi-nationals in the world, has come to the Clearwater to strip the land. The property rights to the forests in which Saukamappee made his home have been sold to the world's richest woman, billionaire capitalist Gina Rinehart, who plans to dig a 16,000-hectare open-pit coal mine.

All along the foothills seismic crews identify new deposits of oil and gas as well as coal. The fossil fuel industry now holds the fate of a province in its grip.

As the current seems to quicken past, Peggy describes the danger of a society destroying its own birthright. How can it be that the river that has flowed from these mountains for millennia may soon be reduced to a trickle as the glaciers disappear? Again she remembers David Thompson:

> The Earth is also a divinity, and is alive. The Indians cannot define what kind of life it is, but say if it was not alive it could not give and continue to give life to other animated creatures. The Forests, the ledges and hills of Rock, the lakes and Rivers have all something of the Manitou about them, especially the Falls in the Rivers, and those to which the fish come to spawn . . .

We return to the remains of Charlotte's cabin so Peggy can leave a pouch of tobacco beneath the doorway. Feeling a chill, Balmer scuttles back to the car. It has begun to rain. As the clouds grow darker, Peggy announces that we should be on our way. Within minutes, walking back to the car, we are in the midst of a torrential downpour. Hurrying to keep up with her, I slip on the bank of a stream and lose one of my running shoes. As I go back to retrieve it, the first thing I see is an arrowhead, no bigger than my thumb, poking out of the loose rock exposed by the rushing water. I carefully bend down to pick up the fragile point before the current washes it away. In the palm of my hand the black obsidian glistens in the rain.

It's a painfully slow trip home. The gumbo roads have been chewed up by the huge trucks transporting oil rigs from the United States to the Leduc field. Each time a truck passes, gobs of mud are thrown up by the chains on its tires, exploding against the windshield. At last we reach the paved highway, and the storm blows itself out. The sky clears as night falls, and northern lights dance above the grain elevator at Ellerslie as our headlights catch the words *What shall it profit a man.*

Edmonton is asleep as only it could be in the Ernest Manning fifties, when the last bar shuts its doors at ten o'clock. Balmer wakes me as the car pulls up in front of the Big House. As Peggy unloads the trunk, my grandfather and I walk to the rim of the valley of the North Saskatchewan. In the silence it's as if the city around us has disappeared. Looking at the river far below, I wonder how many days it has taken the current to carry the waters of the Clearwater to where we stand.

For a moment we are as old as the glaciers, as old as the buffalo trails, as old as the spear point I still hold in my hand. It's as if the river is slipping away from us, falling with the tilt of the continent to a distant northern sea.

Once inside, I run to Balmer's study. *The Narrative* is there on the desk where we left it. I unfold the maps until I find the name in Thompson's fine hand, *Clear Water,* beside the river which joins the North Saskatchewan at the foot of the mountains. I repeat the two words as Peggy collects me for bed. The smile on her face tells me we have been somewhere special. The source of the river.

But as she turns out the light, I hear her say to herself: *It's really not down on any map. True places never are.*

NOTES

Author's Note: When I started work on this book ten years ago, I had no idea I would ever have to worry about endnotes. As my inspiration was the work of authors exploring Western history, many books have come and gone in that time. For some of them I made note of publishers and page numbers; for others I just made note of ideas and moved on. As a filmmaker, that seemed enough. Now I am confronted with the need to "source" references in the text. I have done my best but have inevitably come up short where I have the memory of a book or an article but no specifics. In such cases I have listed the book but no page numbers.

Except where noted below, quotations from Peggy are drawn from Gertrude Balmer Watt's personal papers, and quotations from Balmer are drawn from Arthur Balmer Watt's private papers — both in the Radford family collection. Letters from non-family authors quoted in the text, unless noted below, are held in the same collection. Passages quoted from the *Saturday News*, "The Mirror," the *Capitol*, the *Independent Mirror*, and the *Alberta Homestead* are taken from copies of those newspapers held in the collections of the Provincial Archives of Alberta.

PROLOGUE

And then suddenly, all the old anchors of experience were lifted (page 1): Edgar Kemper Broadus, *Saturday Night and Sunday Morning* (Toronto: The Macmillan Company of Canada, 1935), p. 4. Broadus came to Edmonton from Harvard in 1908 to teach English literature at the fledgling University of Alberta. His influence on young writers in the province would be felt for decades to come. From Lovat Dickson to Rudy Wiebe, he endowed Alberta with that sense of place invaluable to the artist.

In fact he had a name in mind (page 6): Edmund Sheppard had been forbidden by the courts to publish a daily as a result of his articles on Canadian army regulars who had sympathized with Louis Riel in the 1885 Resistance. His work as a publisher was an inspiration to Balmer, who yearned for the freedom to speak his mind as a journalist.

CHAPTER 1 — WOLVERINE

Give to me the life I love (page 14): Peggy discovered this poem written on a sheet of paper glued to the inside of a second-hand desk at an Edmonton flea market. She traced its origin to a homesteader who had sold the desk to finance the last stage of his journey to the Peace River country.

The greatest plague the hunter knows (page 20): Ernest Thompson Seton, *The Arctic Prairies* (New York: Harper Colophon Books, 1981), p. 252. Balmer's admiration for Seton's depiction of the north country was the source for Balmer's own travels down the Athabasca, the Peace, and the Mackenzie.

Today Carcajou, once native to most of the continent (page 20): As reported by the Wildlife Conservation Society, headquartered at the Bronx Zoo in New York City; see https://www.wcs.org/our-work/species/wolverines. The wolverine has become a symbol for the threat to wildlife in Alberta, which is also home to the woodland caribou, whose range is fractured by the checkerboard of roads built by the oil and gas industry.

This is the country my journalist uncle, Ted Watt (page 20): Frederick Balmer Watt, 1898–1996, author of *Great Bear: A Journey Remembered*, a harrowing account of a winter prospecting on Great Bear Lake in the 1930s. His book of poetry during the Second World War, *Who Dare to Live,* was praised by John Masefield, then-poet laureate in England, and became the source for a later autobiography, *In All Respects Ready.*

They were young men in a hurry (page 21): Frederick Watt, from an unpublished manuscript, "Pea Green Incorruptible."

For days now there has been nothing (page 23): Gertrude Balmer Watt, notes for *A Woman in the West* (Edmonton: The News Publishing Company, 1907), Radford family collection. Peggy's observations in this book come from a variety of sources — her two books, *A Woman in the West* and *Town and Trail,* as well as her columns in the *Saturday News* and *Alberta Homestead,* weekly newspapers at the time. But maybe most significantly they come from the stories she told me when I was growing up.

How many settlers looking out and seeing (page 25): Gertrude Balmer Watt, *A Woman in the West,* p. 9.

CHAPTER 2 — CANADIAN BORN

It was hard to imagine that this dignified old man (page 40): Peggy kept a diary of the St. Louis trip, which was her first great adventure outside Ontario.

Hard by the Indian lodges, where the bush (page 41): Pauline Johnson, "The Corn Husker," first published in *Harper's Weekly*, 1896.

Women are fonder of me than men are (page 42): Betty Keller, *Pauline: A Biography of Pauline Johnson* (Vancouver: Douglas and McIntyre, 1987), p. 92.

There are those who think they pay me a compliment (page 42): Ernest Thompson Seton quoting Johnson in his "Introduction" to Johnson's volume *The Shagganappi* (Toronto: William Briggs, 1913), pp 5–6.

CHAPTER 3 — STRANGE EMPIRE

Living alongside the tracks, displaced buffalo hunters (page 48): In the 1990s, working with Métis filmmaker Greg Coyes, I filmed *Strange Empire*, Joseph Kinsey Howard's classic account of the last days of the Métis republic. Howard had been able to talk to the last generation of the Resistance, collecting an oral history in the 1940s not unlike Pauline Johnson's Mohawk chronicles fifty years before. Little remained of the Métis Nation his characters had fought for, lost to history, ignored as the world of the dispossessed often is. Joseph Howard asked what would have happened if Sitting Bull and Chief Joseph had brought their armies north to join the ragtag Métis army. Their Sioux and Nez Perce warriors, allied to the Cree and the Blackfoot, could easily have routed the Canadian volunteers, inexperienced at fighting a mounted army on the open prairie. Chiefs like Big Bear and Poundmaker were already part of the Resistance, defeating the Expeditionary Force at Duck Lake, Fish Creek, and Cut Knife. The War Chief Wandering Spirit had struck terror into the hearts of the green recruits from Ontario. A larger confederacy might have changed history, making a Métis and First Nations republic possible. But a key figure, Crowfoot, chief of the Blackfoot Confederacy in southern Alberta and Montana, fell under the influence of a Catholic missionary, Father Albert Lacombe, and decided not to join the alliance. It was a fateful decision for the Indigenous Peoples of the West.

Had I been born on the banks of the Saskatchewan (page 51): Andre Pratt, *Extraordinary Canadians: Wilfrid Laurier* (Toronto: Penguin Canada, 2013).

They saw the steel ribbon of railway tracks (page 53): Hugh Dempsey, *Crowfoot, Chief of the Blackfeet* (Edmonton: Hurtig Publishers, 1972), p. 207.

CHAPTER 4 — NEXT YEAR COUNTRY

Cutting down the slope to the river (page 58): Gertrude Balmer Watt, *A Woman in the West*, p. 22.

Over the brow of the hill in Edmonton (page 61): Gertrude Balmer Watt, *A Woman in the West*, p. 23.

That accomplished, the Liberals handily won Alberta's first election (page 64): Under Frank Oliver's careful watch, Alberta's first election took place on November 4, 1905. The Minister of the Interior's gerrymandering of electoral boundaries was so successful that one constituency Peggy profiled, Clearwater, near Rocky Mountain House, had six voters, five of them Liberals. One thing her article made clear was that the province's government would be in these slippery hands for some time to come. As Haultain had pointed out, that was the problem with the party system. Whether it was the Liberals or the Conservatives, the game was essentially fixed, and the chances of an independent candidate were minimal. Understandably, there were already signs of deep discontent at the election result.

At about twenty-four miles from the Fork are some bituminous fountains (page 65): Barry Gough, *First Across the Continent: Sir Alexander Mackenzie* (Norman, OK: University of Oklahoma Press, 1997). At the heart of *Death of a Delta* was a larger-than-life Métis trapper. I made *Death of a Delta* in 1972 based on the research of biologist Bill Fuller from the University of Alberta. Although hard to track down, the film provides a good overview of the impact of the W.A.C. Bennett Dam.

The morning came with a strong north wind (page 67): Ernest Thompson Seton, *The Arctic Prairies* (New York: Charles Scribner's Sons, 1911), pp. 286–87. When I first revisited Fort Chipewyan in the early 1970s, the sense of Seton's books was everywhere. It was like returning to his books in my grandfather's study in 1953.

Seton was later described by the *Globe and Mail* (page 71): Betty Keller, *Black Wolf: The Life of Ernest Thompson Seton* (Vancouver: Douglas & McIntyre, 1987), back cover.

Something so tender fills the air to-day (page 74): Pauline Johnson, "Benedictus," published in *Canadian Magazine* July 1913. Johnson's sense of the Canadian landscape and the ghosts it was home to was one of the most prophetic qualities of her poetry.

CHAPTER 5 — PEGGY

Market Square was the boiling point of much of Edmonton's life (page 81): Frederick Watt, "Pea Green Incorruptible." My Uncle Ted was the family storyteller in the years after Peggy's and Balmer's deaths in the 1960s.

Smutty is a newsboy (page 82): Gertrude Balmer Watt, *A Woman in the West*, p. 19.

Peggy describes how the air transmits sounds (page 84): Gertrude Balmer Watt, *A Woman in the West*, p. 8.

The sensational feature of today's sitting of the Regina legislature (page 85): Frederick Watt, "Pea Green Incorruptible."

Mr. Scott's admission makes it plain (page 86): Frederick Watt, "Pea Green Incorruptible."

As their son Frederick later remembered (page 87): Frederick Watt, "Pea Green Incorruptible."

CHAPTER 6 — THE FIRST SEPARATIST

Separate geographical units, regarded as colonies (page 91): A. Bramley-Moore, *Canada and Her Colonies; Or Home Rule for Alberta* (London: W. Stewart and Co., 1911), p. 74.

A radical procedure, and rather a practical one (page 92): Bramley-Moore, *Canada and Her Colonies*, p. 150.

CHAPTER 7 — BALMER

April 23, 1775. Salem, Massachusetts (page 103): Samuel Curwen, *The Journal of Samuel Curwen, Loyalist* (Boston: Harvard University Press, 1976), p. 3.

Curwen was a New England District judge (page 104): Curwen, *The Journal of Samuel Curwen*, p. 5.

His father, Captain George Curwen, had led an armed expedition (page 104): Curwen's history in the colony was marked by contradiction. A justice of the peace, he also harboured deep distrust, even hatred of Indigenous Peoples, typical of his time.

Within two blocks lived a number of the most vital and controversial figures (page 107): Frederick Watt, "Pea Green Incorruptible." The relationship between the Watt and Cross families was fraught. Although the parents held deep suspicions about each other, the children became friends for life.

No amount of activity could keep the studio warm (page 108): In Tom Radford, *Ernest Brown, Pioneer Photographer* (Filmwest Associates, 1974). Our interview with Gladys Reeves occurred near the end of her life, but both her perspective on Alberta history and her sense of humour were intact.

CHAPTER 8 — SCANDAL

Too late, Balmer tells his readers (page 118): Frederick Watt, "Pea Green Incorruptible."

In order that there may be no misapprehension about the policy (page 121): Frederick Watt, "Pea Green Incorruptible."

CHAPTER 9 — THE INDEPENDENT MIRROR

The *Bulletin*, Frank Oliver's paper (page 125): Frederick Watt, "Pea Green Incorruptible."

Her performance is hailed as "the great event of the week" (page 133): This praise appears in Balmer Watt's scrapbook of collected theatre reviews, Radford family collection.

That he has a past you know (page 136): Gertrude Balmer Watt, *A Woman in the West*, pp. 18–19.

CHAPTER 10 — PRAIRIE WOMEN

All sorts and conditions of them travelled (page 145): Barbara Villy Cormack, *Perennials and Politics* (Sherwood Park: Professional Printing Ltd, 1968), p. 48.

Is there anything in the world one-half as appealing (page 147): In *A Woman in the West* Peggy often wrote rhapsodically about the prairie. It was as if the open spaces had freed her from the strictures of Ontario society.

The first real achievement of the Countrywomen's Club (page 149): Cormack, *Perennials and Politics*, pp. 57–58. Organizations like this were the origin of the waves of populism that swept across the West in the 1920s and 1930s. A wonderful source on that movement is

Thomas Frank's book *The People, No,* a description of American populism at the turn of the century and its impact on its Canadian counterpart. Men like Henry Wise Wood moved north when the American progressive movement failed to make political headway and were instrumental in forming the United Farmers of Alberta. But it was Social Credit in the 1930s that was able to move populism to the right, where it sits today.

We value our privilege of working on equal terms (page 150): Bradford James Rennie, *The Rise of Agrarian Democracy: The United Farmers and Farm Women of Alberta, 1909—1921* (Toronto: University of Toronto Press, 2000), p. 116. Rennie's book is a valuable compilation of UFA and UFWA history, a much-neglected chapter in Alberta history.

CHAPTER 11 — RIVER OF NO RETURN

My father was waiting for us (page 156): Frederick Watt, "Pea Green Incorruptible."

I wish you could have seen those men (page 157): J. Burgon Bickersteth, *The Land of Open Doors: Being Letters from Western Canada 1911—13.* (Toronto and Buffalo: University of Toronto Press, 1976), p. 194—95.

An end-of-steel town is a wicked place (page 158): Bickersteth, *The Land of Open Doors,* p. 199—200.

She convinces Joel Otto, Schäffer's guide in Fitzhugh (page 159): Otto later guided authors Sir Arthur Conan Doyle and James Oliver Wolcott to the pass. The Canadian Rockies had become a fashionable destination for writers and artists from around the world.

The park is now part of a sacrifice zone (page 161): David Schindler referred to northern Alberta as a sacrifice zone in the film *Tipping Point* (2011).

Nobody understood Russian, and he knew not a single word (page 162): Bickersteth, *The Land of Open Doors,* p. 149—52.

CHAPTER 12 — MAN WHO CHOOSES THE BUSH

With rue my heart is laden (page 170): A.E. Housman, "With rue my heart is laden" in *A Shropshire Lad* (New York: John Lane Company, 1896).

As well as an oil tycoon, Pew was the founder (page 175): *Christianity Today* is an evangelical magazine produced by the followers of Billy Graham.

CHAPTER 13 — A DISTANT WAR

The most interesting expression of the new Western point of view (page 182): Rupert Brooke, *Letters from America* (Toronto: McClelland, Goodchild & Stewart, Ltd., 1916), p. 107.

I travelled from Edmonton to Calgary (page 183): Brooke, *Letters from America,* pp. 128—29.

Pavements are laid down, stores and bigger stores (page 183): Brooke, *Letters from America,* pp. 127, 130—31.

Those who saw the London crowds during the nights (page 184): Bertrand Russell, *Justice in Wartime* (Chicago: Open Court, 1916).

They would have little flags in the window (page 187): Gwynne Dyer, *Canada in the Great Power Game: 1914—2014* (Toronto: Random House Canada, 2014), p. 73. Dyer had come to Edmonton to interview Becky for *War,* his National Film Board series. Her first-hand memories of the home front were an important element of the episode on the First World War.

A mounted policeman once told me (page 187): Dyer, *Canada in the Great Power Game*, pp. 119–20.

My final visit to a most delightful family (page 188): Louise Creighton, ed., *Letters of Oswin Creighton, C.F., 1883–1918* (London: Longmans, Green, and Co., 1920), p. 33. Creighton's mother collected and published her son's letter after his return to England.

The W. Parlbys went down on the same train with me (page 189): Creighton, *Letters of Oswin Creighton*, p. 119.

I went aboard his ship the night before (page 190): Frederick Watt, "Pea Green Incorruptible."

CHAPTER 14 — NORTH STAR

My father, William A. Innis, started out (page 196): William J. Buxton, Michael R. Cheney, and Paul Heyer, eds., *Harold Innis Reflects: Memoir and WWI Writings/Correspondence* (Lanham, MD: Rowman & Littlefield, 2016), p. 15.

All this was a completely new experience (page 197): Buxton et al., eds., *Harold Innis Reflects*, p. 43.

Almost any excuse was used to get up a dance (page 198): Buxton et al., eds., *Harold Innis Reflects*, p. 45.

On July 1st a picnic was held (page 199): Buxton et al., eds., *Harold Innis Reflects*, p. 45.

It is so terrible seeing these young fellows go into action (page 202): Creighton, *Letters of Oswin Creighton*, p. 132.

All the men seemed to have gone (page 203): Dyer, *Canada in the Great Power Game*, p. 83.

The sight of a telegraph boy was a thing of horror (page 204): Dyer, *Canada in the Great Power Game*, p. 83.

Our task, therefore, was that of bringing material (page 205): Alexander John Watson, *Marginal Man: The Dark Vision of Harold Innis* (Toronto: University of Toronto Press, 2006), p. 74.

They had obviously spotted our group (page 206): Watson, p. 75.

More and more the world seems to have lost its charm (page 207): Creighton, *Letters of Oswin Creighton*, p. 196.

Canadians from all areas and all economic classes went off (page 208): George Grant, *Collected Works of George Grant, Volume 3: 1960–1969* (Toronto: University of Toronto Press, 2005), p. 525.

CHAPTER 15 — SACRIFICE ZONE

Ward concluded that "it's happening again, but now it's Volvos…." (page 215): Peter Ward in the film *The End of Evolution* (Radford, dir., 2001).

My greatest fear, for our world (page 215): Peter Ward, *The End of Evolution* (New York: Bantam Books, 1994), p. 276.

Here in the room was a community that had persevered (page 220): David Schindler left a legacy of an Alberta that had the courage to stand up to the huge corporations that now control its fate. He also extended to the world at large knowledge of what was being done to the northern environment. The fact he raised a team of sled dogs like Frank Ladouceur's made him a friend to Alberta's Indigenous Peoples.

CHAPTER 16 — RISE OF THE POPULISTS

A longtime friend of the multinationals (page 228): As early as 1905 Mackenzie King was working for the Rockefellers in New York. The Standard Oil of New Jersey model of resource development would soon be adopted as a prototype for the future of Alberta by both provincial and federal governments.

4th May. Since I last wrote (page 234): Edward Christian, *Unflinching* (London: John Murray, 1937).

Pitchblende, the ore that contained the uranium used to build the first atomic bomb (page 235): Frederick B. Watt, *Great Bear: A Journey Remembered* (Yellowknife: Outcrop Publishers, 1980), p. 6. In a tragic aftermath for the nearby First Nation community of Deline, many of the men who carried sacks of pitchblende ore to Great Bear Lake for shipment later died of cancer.

In a letter to the editor published in *Saturday Night* magazine (page 237): Quoted in Frederick Watt, "Pea Green Incorruptible."

CHAPTER 17 — DUST BOWL

In their days at the University of Toronto (page 242): Both Mackenzie King and Balmer Watt were working as reporters for the campus newspaper in 1895 when a student strike all but shut down the university. Nominated to be a spokesperson for classmates who had boycotted classes in support of a fired professor, Mackenzie King proceeded to make his own deal with the administration, turning his back on the students he was meant to represent. Balmer took the betrayal especially hard when James Tucker, the editor of the *Varsity*, was expelled from campus and the next year died a broken man. It was Balmer's first experience with the power of the establishment to suppress opposition to its interests. If one could take away the freedom of the press within a place of higher learning, then anything was possible. Balmer always maintained that Mackenzie King's role in the affair was a carefully planned deception by a master of appearances.

the newspaper industry ... came together against the would-be dictator Roosevelt (page 246): Thomas Frank, *The People, No: A Brief History of Anti-Populism* (New York: Metropolitan Books, 2020), p. 120. Frank, a former editor of *Harper's*, has written extensively on the rise of populism in the United States. This book exams the relationship between populism and the establishment and provides valuable insights into the challenges Social Credit faced.

I was speaking at a town hall meeting (page 247): Chester Ronning in the film *China Mission* (Radford, dir., 1980). I would often visit Ronning's house in Camrose, the small bungalow he retired to after his career in India and Norway as Canadian High Commissioner. At the head of the street was the wooden building where the Lutheran college had been founded; in its music room, he directed the college choir to the provincial championship in 1933.

As George Orwell wrote in an English newspaper (page 249): George Orwell, *All Art Is Propaganda* (New York: First Mariner Books, 2009).

An unsavoury pack of upwardly mobile scoundrels (page 250): Dating back to her confrontations with Charles Cross in the early days of the *Saturday News*, Peggy never forgave the Liberals.

Charles Clark had written in the *High River Times* (page 252): Charles Clark, the father of Joe Clark, was a good friend of Balmer's.

CHAPTER 18 — MAN FROM MARS

On August 22, 1935, Social Credit relegated both the United Farmers and the Liberals to political oblivion (page 259): No one outside Alberta had given Social Credit a chance in the election. But Chester Ronning warned the UFA cabinet that there was a deep-seated resentment toward the party in power.

Meetings for the coming week would be announced (page 262): John A. Irving, *The Social Credit Movement in Alberta* (Toronto: University of Toronto Press, 1959), p. 110, p. 113.

Populism was one of the first of the great political efforts (page 267): Frank, *The People, No*, p. 11.

On August 17, 1937, the Credit of Alberta Regulation Act (page 270): Bob Hesketh, *Major Douglas and Alberta Social Credit* (Toronto: University of Toronto Press, 1997), p. 165. Hesketh's exploration of Douglas's economic theories provides a valuable background to Balmer's editorials on social credit.

The success of Douglas's strategy depended on an awakened, directed public will (page 270): Hesketh, *Major Douglas*, p. 165.

CHAPTER 19 — THE PULITZER

The overwhelming pressure of mechanization evident in the newspaper and the magazine (page 278): Harold A. Innis, *Changing Concepts of Time* (Lanham, MD: Rowman & Littlefield, Publishers, 2004), pp. 10–11.

[People] tell us that what is put in their papers (page 279): David B. Elliott and Iris Miller, *Bible Bill: A Biography of William Aberhart* (Edmonton: Reidmore Books, 1987), p. 272.

The vituperation of the big papers against the government (page 279): Elliott and Miller, *Bible Bill*, p. 187.

I fear I am going to be forced to come to the conclusion (page 282): Elliott and Miller, *Bible Bill*, p. 187.

If this bill should pass and stand (page 282): Arthur Balmer Watt Fonds, University of Alberta Archives, Edmonton.

In Edmonton, ironically it was Frank Oliver's old paper (page 285): Edmonton *Bulletin*, May 24, 1943.

CHAPTER 20 — FIRESTORM

Balmer worried because between 1941 and 1943 (page 295): For further reading on this point, see Ken Tingley, *For King and Country: Alberta in the Second World War* (Edmonton: Provincial Museum of Alberta and Reidmore Books, 1995).

The Americans had forced Canadian consent (page 296): Donald Creighton, *The Forked Road: Canada 1939–1957* (Toronto: McClelland and Stewart, 1976), 73.

Innis had an undertone, if not of pessimism (page 298): Alexander John Watson, *Marginal Man: The Dark Vision of Harold Innis* (Toronto, University of Toronto Press, 2006), p. 161. Watson's book has little to say about Innis's time in Alberta.

As Peter Lougheed would later recount (page 299): In the documentary *The Life and Times of Peter Lougheed* (Radford, dir., 1994).

The water is wide, I can't cross o'er (page 301): "The Water is Wide," also known as "O Waly, Waly" is a folk song of Scottish origin. A favourite among immigrants at the turn of the twentieth century, it remains popular in folk circles today.

CHAPTER 21 — AN UNQUIET LAND

I was surprised. She was still very much herself (page 315): Frederick Watt, "Pea Green Incorruptible."

A. Balmer Watt, 87, died in an Edmonton hospital (page 317): *Edmonton Journal*, July 13, 1964.

EPILOGUE — SOURCE OF THE RIVER

At last, the Mountains came in sight (page 323): In Jack Nisbet, *Sources of the River: Tracking David Thompson Across Western North America* (Seattle: Sasquatch Books, 1994), p. 19.

While the ship remained at anchor (page 323): In Nisbet, *Sources of the River*, p. 10.

In the years that lay ahead I always admired the tact (page 324): In Nisbet, *Sources of the River*, pp. 37–39.

The Peeagan was an old man (page 324): In Nisbet, *Sources of the River*, p. 20.

My instruments for practical astronomy (page 325): In Nisbet, *Sources of the River*, p. 34. Nisbet describes the rest of Thompson's kit: "In a supply order to London that same year, he requested astronomical almanacs to go along with his instruments, plus two dozen coat buttons, a quire of tracing paper, and ten books, including a spelling dictionary, a pocket-sized New Testament and Milton's *Paradise Lost*" (p. 37).

The Earth is also a divinity, and is alive (page 328): David Thompson, *The Narrative* (New York: William Morrow, 1952), p. 100.

BIBLIOGRAPHY

Berry, Wendell. *Our Only World*. New York: Counterpoint LLC, 1984.

Bickersteth, J. Burgon. *The Land of Open Doors: Being Letters from Western Canada 1911–13*. Toronto and Buffalo: University of Toronto Press, 1976.

Blodgett, E.D. *Poems for a Small Park*. Edmonton: Athabasca University Press, 2008.

Bramley-Moore, A. *Canada and Her Colonies; Or Home Rule for Alberta*. London: W. Stewart and Co., 1911.

Bringhurst, Robert. *A Story as Sharp as a Knife*. Vancouver: Douglas & McIntyre, 1991.

Broadfoot, Barry. *Ten Lost Years 1929–1939*. Toronto: Paperjacks, 1973.

Broadus, Edgar Kemper. *Saturday Night and Sunday Morning*. Toronto: The Macmillan Company of Canada, 1935.

Brooke, Rupert. *Letters from America*. Toronto: McClelland, Goodchild & Stewart, Ltd., 1916.

———. *Rupert Brooke in Canada*. Toronto: RMA Books, 1978.

Butler, William Francis. *The Wild North Land*. Toronto: Musson Book Company, 1924.

Buxton, William J., Michael R. Cheney, and Paul Heyer, eds. *Harold Innis Reflects: Memoir and WWI Writings/Correspondence*. Lanham, MD: Rowman & Littlefield, 2016.

Campbell Marjorie Wilkins. *The Saskatchewan*. New York: Rinehart & Company, 1952.

Cardinal, Harold. The *Unjust Society: The Tragedy of Canada's Indians*. Edmonton: M.G. Hurtig, 1969.

Christian, Edward. *Unflinching*. London: John Murray, 1937.

Colbert, Edwin H. *The Great Dinosaur Hunters and Their Discoveries*. New York: Dover, 1968.

Cormack, Barbara Villy. *Perennials and Politics*. Sherwood Park: Professional Printing Ltd, 1968.

Creighton, Donald. *Harold Adams Innis: Portrait of a Scholar*. Toronto: University of Toronto Press, 1957.

———. *The Forked Road: Canada 1939–1957*. Toronto: McClelland and Stewart, 1976.

Creighton, Louise, ed. *Letters of Oswin Creighton, C.F., 1883–1918*. London: Longmans, Green, and Co., 1920.

Curwen, Samuel. *The Journal of Samuel Curwen, Loyalist*. Boston: Harvard University Press, 1976.

Dempsey, Hugh. *Crowfoot, Chief of the Blackfeet*. Edmonton: Hurtig Publishers, 1972.

Dunae, Patrick A. *Gentlemen Immigrants: From the British Public Schools to the Canadian Frontier*. Vancouver and Toronto: Douglas & McIntyre, 1981.

Dyer, Gwynne. *Canada in the Great Power Game: 1914–2014*. Toronto: Random House Canada, 2014.

Elliott, David R., ed. *Aberhart: Outpourings and Replies*. Calgary: Historical Society of Alberta, 1991.

Elliott, David R., and Iris Miller. *Bible Bill: A Biography of William Aberhart*. Edmonton: Reidmore Books, 1987.

Ferguson, Ted. *Kit Coleman, Queen of Hearts*. Toronto: Doubleday Canada, 1978.

Ferns, H.S., and B. Ostry. *The Age of Mackenzie King: The Rise of the Leader*. London: Heinemann, 1955.

Flannery, Tim. *The Weather Makers: How Man Is Changing the Climate and What It Means for Life on Earth*. New York: Grove/Atlantic, 2006.

Frank, Thomas. *The People, No: A Brief History of Anti-Populism*. New York: Metropolitan Books, 2020.

Gard, Robert E. *Johnny Chinook: Tall Tales and True from the Canadian West*. Edmonton: M.G. Hurtig, 1967.

Gough, Barry. *First Across the Continent: Sir Alexander Mackenzie*. Norman, OK: University of Oklahoma Press, 1997.

Graebner, David, and David Wengrow. *The Dawn of Everything: A New History of Humanity*. Toronto: Signal/McClelland and Stewart, 2023.

Grant, George. *The Empire, Yes or No*. Toronto: Ryerson Press, 1945.

———. *Collected Works of George Grant, Volume 3: 1960–1969*. Toronto: University of Toronto Press, 2005.

Hesketh, Bob. *Major Douglas and Alberta Social Credit*. Toronto: University of Toronto Press, 1997.

Hicks, Kathleen A. *The Life and Times of the Silverthorns of Cherry Hill*. Mississauga, ON: Mississauga Library System, 1999.

Horton, Marc, and Bill Sass. *Voice of a City*: The Edmonton Journal*'s First Century 1903 to 2003*. Edmonton: Edmonton Journal, 2003.

Housman, A.E. *A Shropshire Lad*. New York: John Lane Company, 1896.

Howard, Joseph Kinsey. *Strange Empire: A Narrative of the Northwest*. New York: William Morrow and Company, 1952.

Hughes, Katherine. *Father Lacombe, The Black Robe Voyageur*. New York: Moffat, Yard & Company, 1911.

Hurtig, Mel. *The Betrayal of Canada*. Toronto: Stoddart, 1991.

Innis, Harold A. *The Fur Trade in Canada*. Toronto: University of Toronto Press, 1950.

———. *Changing Concepts of Time*. Lanham, MD: Rowman & Littlefield, Publishers, 2004.

Irving, John A. *The Social Credit Movement in Alberta*. Toronto: University of Toronto Press, 1959.

Johnson, E. Pauline. *The Shagganappi* (Toronto: William Briggs, 1913).

Johnson, E. Pauline, Tekahionwake. *Collected Poems and Selected Prose*. Carole Gerson and Veronica Strong-Boag, eds. Toronto: University of Toronto Press, 2002.

Kay, Linda. *The Sweet Sixteen: The Journey That Inspired the Canadian Women's Press Club*. Montreal: McGill-Queens University Press, 2012.

Keller, Betty. *Black Wolf: The Life of Ernest Thompson Seton*. Vancouver: Douglas & McIntyre, 1987.

———. *Pauline: A Biography of Pauline Johnson*. Vancouver: Douglas & McIntyre, 1987.

Kostash, Myrna. *All of Baba's Children*. Edmonton: Hurtig, 1978.

———. *The Next Canada: In Search of Our Future Nation*. Toronto: McClelland and Stewart, 2000.

——— with Duane Burton. *Reading the River: A Traveller's Companion to the North Saskatchewan River*. Regina: Coteau, 2005.

Kroetsch, Robert. *Alberta*. Toronto: Macmillan of Canada, 1968.

———. *The Words of My Roaring*. Edmonton: University of Alberta Press, 2000.

Lang, Marjory. *Women Who Made the News: Female Journalists in Canada, 1880–1945*. Montreal: McGill-Queens University Press, 1999.

London, Jack. *The Call of the Wild*. New York: Reader's Library Classics, 1903.

Long, Philip S. *Jerry Potts: Scout, Frontiersman and Hero*. Calgary: Bonanza Books, 1974.

MacDonald, George Heath. *Fort Augustus–Edmonton. Northwest Trails and Traffic*. Edmonton: The Douglas Printing Co. Ltd, 1954.

MacEwan, Grant. *Between the Red and the Rockies*, Toronto: McClelland and Stewart, 1952.

———. *Frederick Haultain: Frontier Statesman of the Canadian Northwest*. Saskatoon: Western Producer Prairie Books, 1985.

MacGregor, James G. *Pack Saddles to Tete Jaune Cache*. Toronto: McClelland and Stewart, 1962.

———. *Edmonton Trader: The Story of John A. McDougall*. Toronto: McClelland and Stewart, 1963.

———. *A History of Alberta*. Edmonton: Hurtig Publishers, 1972.

Macpherson, C.B. *Democracy in Alberta: Social Credit and the Party System*. Toronto: University of Toronto Press, 1953.

Marsh, James H. *Know It All: Finding the Impossible Country*. Durvile, 2022.

Martin, Sandra, and Roger Hall. *Rupert Brooke in Canada*. Toronto: PMA Books, 1978.

Marty, Sid. *Oldman's River: New and Collected Poems*. Edmonton: Newest Press, 2023.

McDougall, John. *In the Days of the Red River Rebellion: Life and Adventure in the Far West of Canada (1868–1872)*. Toronto: Briggs, 1903.

McKibben, Bill. *The End of Nature*. New York: Random House, 1989.

McNaught, Kenneth. *A Prophet in Politics: A Biography of J.S. Woodsworth*. Toronto: University of Toronto Press, 1959.

Monbiot, George. *Heat: How to Stop the Planet from Burning*. Toronto: Anchor Canada, 2007.

Mowat, Farley. *The Desperate People*. Toronto: Seal Books, 1959.

Nevitt, R.B. *A Winter at Fort Macleod*. Calgary: Glenbow, 1974.

Nikiforuk, Andrew. *Tar Sands: Dirty Oil and the Future of a Continent*. Vancouver: Greystone, 2008.

Nisbet, Jack. *Sources of the River: Tracking David Thompson Across Western North America*. Seattle: Sasquatch Books, 1994.

Orwell, George. *All Art Is Propaganda*. New York: First Mariner Books, 2009.

Pratt, Andre. *Extraordinary Canadians: Wilfrid Laurier*. Toronto: Penguin Canada, 2013.

Pratt, Larry, and Ian Urquhart. *The Last Great Forest*. Edmonton: Newest Press, 1994.

Radford, Tom. "Death of a Delta." In *Bucking Conservatism: Alternative Stories of Alberta from the 1960s and 1970s*. Leon Crane Bear, Larry Hannant, and Karissa Robyn Patton, eds. Edmonton: Athabasca University Press, 2021.

Radford, Tom, dir. *Death of a Delta*. Filmwest Associates, 1972.

———, dir. *Ernest Brown, Pioneer Photographer*. Filmwest Associates, 1974.

———, dir. *Man Who Chooses the Bush*. National Film Board of Canada, 1975.

———, dir. *China Mission*. National Film Board of Canada, 1980.

———, dir. *The Life and Times of Peter Lougheed*. Clearwater Documentary, 1994.

———, dir. *The End of Evolution*. National Film Board of Canada, 2001.

———, dir. *Tipping Point*. Clearwater Documentary, 2009.

Rennie, Bradford James. *The Rise of Agrarian Democracy: The United Farmers and Farm Women of Alberta, 1909–1921*. (Toronto: University of Toronto Press, 2000).

Russell, Bertrand. *Justice in Wartime*. Chicago: Open Court, 1916.

Seton, Ernest Thompson. "Introduction". In Pauline Johnson, *The Shagganappi*. Toronto: William Briggs, 1913.

———. *The Arctic Prairies: A Canoe-Journey of 2,000 Miles in Search of the Caribou*. New York: Charles Scribner's Sons, 1911.

Sommervill, Barbara A. *Ida Tarbell, Pioneer Investigative Reporter*. Greensboro, NC: M. Reynolds, 2002.

Stegner, Wallace. *Wolf Willow*. New York: Viking, 1955.

Stenson, Fred. *The Trade*. Vancouver: Douglas & McIntyre, 2000.

Talman, James J. *Loyalist Narratives from Upper Canada*. Toronto: Champlain Society, 1946.

Thomas, L.G. *The Liberal Party in Alberta: A History of Politics in the Province of Alberta 1905–1921*. Toronto: University of Toronto Press, 1959.

Thompson, David. *The Narrative*. New York: William Morrow, 1952.

Thorsell, William. *Crest to Crest: Riding the Boomer Wave*. NP: Amazon, 2022.

Tingley, Ken. *For King and Country: Alberta in the Second World War*. Edmonton: Provincial Museum of Alberta and Reidmore Books, 1995.

Vaillant, John. *Fire Weather*. Toronto: Knopf Canada, 2023.

Wallace, W. Stewart. *The United Empire Loyalists: A Chronicle of the Great Migration*. Toronto: Glasgow, Brook & Co., 1914.

Walley, George. *The Legend of John Hornby*. Toronto: Macmillan of Canada, 1962.

Walters, Marylu. *CKUA: Radio Worth Fighting For*. Edmonton: University of Alberta Press, 2002.

Ward, Peter. *The End of Evolution*. New York: Bantam Books, 1994.

Watson, Alexander John. *Marginal Man: The Dark Vision of Harold Innis*. Toronto, University of Toronto Press, 2006.

Watt, Arthur Balmer. Arthur Balmer Watt Fonds. University of Alberta Archives, Edmonton.

Watt, Frederick B. *Great Bear: A Journey Remembered*. Yellowknife: Outcrop Publishers, 1980.

———. *In All Respects Ready*. Toronto: Prentice Hall of Canada, 1985.

Watt, Gertrude Balmer. *A Woman in the West*. Edmonton: The News Publishing Company, 1907.

———. *Town and Trail*. Edmonton: The News Publishing Company, 1908.

———. Gertrude Balmer Watt Fonds. University of Alberta Archives, Edmonton.

Wiebe, Rudy. *The Temptations of Big Bear*, New Canadian Library, 1995.

Wilson, E.O. *Consilience: The Unity of Knowledge*. New York: Vintage, 1999.

Wood, David G. *The Lougheed Legacy*. Key Porter Books, 1985.

Woodcock, George. *Gabriel Dumont: The Metis Chief and His Lost World*. Edmonton: Hurtig, 1975.

Wooley, Clive Phillips. *Songs from a Young Man's Land*. Toronto: Thomas Allen, 1917.

Wright, Ronald. *What Is America? A Short History of the New World Order*. New York: Knopf, 2008.

PERMISSIONS

Unless noted below, images in this book are drawn from the Radford Family Collection.

page xiv: Provincial Archives of Alberta, PA B6210.. Used with permission.

page 88: Courtesy of Glenbow Library and Archives Collection, Libraries and Cultural Resources Digital Collections, University of Calgary.

page 164: Provincial Archives of Alberta, PAA B2980. Used with permission.

page 178: Reproduced from The Land of Open Doors: Being Letters from Western Canada 1911–1913 by J. Burgon Bickersteth (Toronto: The Musson Book Company, 1914), between page 48 and page 49.

page 192: Courtesy of Glenbow Library and Archives Collection, Libraries and Cultural Resources Digital Collections, University of Calgary.

page 210: Courtesy of Glenbow Library and Archives Collection, Libraries and Cultural Resources Digital Collections, University of Calgary.

page 224: Courtesy of Glenbow Library and Archives Collection, Libraries and Cultural Resources Digital Collections, University of Calgary.

page 256: Courtesy of Glenbow Library and Archives Collection, Libraries and Cultural Resources Digital Collections, University of Calgary.

Portions of this text appeared previously, in somewhat different form, in the essay "Death of a Delta," published in Bucking Conservatism: Alternative Stories of Alberta from the 1960s and 1970s, Leon Crane Bear, Larry Hannant, and Karissa Robyn Patton, eds. (Edmonton: Athabasca University Press, 2021), pages 303–314.

Lines from Poems for a Small Park by E.D. Blodgett (2008) are used by permission of Athabasca University Press.

ABOUT THE AUTHOR

Tom Radford is a writer and documentary filmmaker working in Edmonton. Born to a newspaper family, he has explored both the character of western Canada and the issues that have plagued "next year country" in confederation. Over a fifty-year career he has worked extensively with First Nations, environmentalists, and historians to portray the unique culture of Alberta under stress. Five films on Fort Chipewyan and the impact of the oil sands have recorded the challenges faced by resource development in the North.